# DUKE ELLINGTON

The Notes the World Was Not Ready to Hear

Library of Congress Control Number: 2021947852

ISBN (hardcover): 978-1-956450-04-0
(paperback):978-1-956450-05-7
(eBook): 978-1-956450-06-4
Published in cooperation with Rakeiho Publishing Company

Armin Lear Press Inc
215 W Riverside Drive, #4362
Estes Park, CO 80517

# DUKE ELLINGTON

## The Notes the World Was Not Ready to Hear

*Karen S. Barbera*
*with Randall Keith Horton*

*This book is dedicated to those who dare to dream.*
*Who selflessly embark upon paths of bold and often thankless action.*
*For they are the leaders who have... and will continue to... quietly*
*and honorably inch our world forward.*

- Karen S. Barbera

_____

*To my parents, Lloyd Trevor Horton and Helen Taylor Horton*

- Randall Keith Horton

*MUSIC is like water.*
*It seeks the path of greatest freedom…to simply "Be."*

*It springs forth from the deepest recesses,*
*with the innate ability to sculpt, nourish and soothe.*

*It envelopes, whisks, challenges, entertains and astounds.*

*It assumes a myriad of arrangements…*
*a still pond, a burbling creek, a crashing waterfall.*

*It absorbs the elemental ingredients through which it percolates,*
*reflecting the essence of its surroundings.*

*It can be restrained with great effort,*
*but roils against artificial barriers.*

*It is treasured by those long nourished by it,*
*and frequently misunderstood by those who have not.*

*It is buoyant, oppressive and sustaining.*

*Without water, we cease to exist.*
*Without music? I fear the same result.*

*Karen S. Barbera*

# CONTENTS

# SETTING THE STAGE

This 1989 *The Washington Post* article captured what Duke Ellington and his orchestra intrinsically and consistently represented throughout their 50-year history.[1]

## Union Station
### *New York City - 1930*

"Fourteen-year-old Stanley Nelson witnessed a group of black men stepping off the train at Union Station in the 1930's, elegantly dressed and commanding attention with their strides. 'I had never seen a group of black men so proud and magnificent in their presentation,' recalled Nelson, later a dentist in New York. It 'wasn't just the clothes, it was the way they wore them.' The men were Duke Ellington and his orchestra. At a time when stereotypes reigned as truths, when whites perpetuated the image of black men as shuffling, singing, back-bent men, there was

1    Patrice Gaines-Carter, "Ellington The Duke Of Musical Royalty." *The Washington Post*, April, 28, 1989, https://www.washingtonpost.com/archive/local/1989/04/29/ellington-the-duke-ofmusicalroyalty7eee8a04-9d1d-4375-a0af-5e822b8b4e38/.

Ellington. He shattered stereotypes, wore none of their myths, composed music that defied definition in its range: Jazz, sacred music, symphonic scores. 'I was young and impressionable, and I never forgot that moment. It was in my bone marrow after that, that a black man could have that kind of respect and be that magnificent.'"

# AUTHOR'S NOTE

Acts that move the world forward begin as simple intentions that spring from the minds of pioneering thinkers who dare to challenge the status quo. Their efforts are often greeted with criticism and resistance. It requires tenacity to stay the course in the face of withering opposition.

I believe in the power of setting intentions, of committing oneself to tasks and silently asking the powers that be for help in achieving them. The simple act seems to create a personal sonar that pings one's dreams outward, illuminating pathways and attracting like-minded individuals. And when intentions align with natural gifts, startling things happen: The beauty being, that even if one's ultimate goal is never achieved, the journey is enjoyed, and the world is inched forward.

I find it fascinating to delve into people's backgrounds, particularly their early childhood, for so often in these formative years, seeds are sown that ignite interests and influence ambitions that ultimately determine the course of their adult lives. There is a purity to each of us in our youth. We naturally gravitate toward interests and activities that play to our greatest strengths. By adulthood, this intuitive self-knowledge becomes obscured. We grow adept at donning and doffing phantom personas and second guessing ourselves and others.

My early interest in stories led me to a career in writing and placing newsworthy stories in the public relations field. This led to writing magazine articles, investigative news pieces and biographical books, which might also explain why I was so captivated by the following story of a complete stranger whom I randomly met on an Amtrak train.

# TAKE THE 'A'(AMTRAK) TRAIN

*"There is no art without intention."*

- Duke Ellington

In 2013, our 20-year-old daughter, Cameron, and I set off on a three-day train trip from our home in Southern California to Ottumwa, Iowa, where she planned to attend college on a soccer scholarship. It was her idea to embark on this train trip together instead of flying, possibly, as I would have liked to believe, to bond and mend fences after her head-strong high school years, but more likely, because there were no baggage limits on Amtrak. Whatever the reason, I was a willing partner, happy to have the one-on-one time with her and check off "overnight train trip" from my bucket list. *Maybe I'll meet someone interesting on this train*, I mused prophetically.

The first two days of our trip went surprisingly well, but events took a nosedive in the early morning hours of our third and final day when I learned my daughter wasn't attending college in Iowa because a soccer coach randomly recruited her. Her scholarship was real, thank goodness, but she was primarily following a boyfriend with a dubious track record; a young man whom she assured us was in her rear-view mirror. The discovery was a blow. It demolished the foundation of our recent, hard-won détente. We stared silently at one another across the frigid rift that now divided us, but managed a united, albeit fragile, front as we headed to the dining car for our final onboard breakfast. Neither of us was in any mood to converse with each other, let alone the stranger in the booth across from whom we were randomly seated.

Our meeting began with a courteous, "Hello."

* * *

Cameron and I slide across the leather banquet. The waiter saves us from further conversation with a flurry of menu proffering and order-taking.

"Good morning," our new breakfast companion says cheerfully in a soothing, upbeat voice after the waiter departs. "Where is your journey taking you to or from?"

I surface from my roiling emotions to process what the professorial-looking African American gentleman in his early 70s has just asked. He wears the uniform of an Ivy League academic: wire-rimmed glasses, close-cropped salt and pepper hair, the ubiquitous tweed sport coat with suede elbow patches and a white, open-collared dress shirt.

"We are heading to Iowa," I manage in an attempt to be polite. "We started out in Southern California." I nod to my right. "I'm taking my daughter Cameron to college in Ottumwa."

Cameron remains defiantly engrossed in her cell phone, which forces me to continue the conversation against my will.

"I'm Karen Barbera," I say as I extend my hand directly across the table.

"Randall Keith Horton. Pleased to meet you!" Our breakfast companion says in return, shaking my hand.

"…and this is my daughter, Cameron," I add.

Horton perceptively sizes up my daughter's closed-off body language. It is a longer, diagonal reach across the table for a handshake with her, but not impossible. "Nice to meet you too, Cameron," he says with a nod and a welcoming smile.

Cameron glances up and offers a weak acknowledgement and a barely audible "hi" before replacing her ear buds and diving back into the Rap music on her phone. These are pet peeves of mine and she knows it: rudeness, offensive lyrics and cell phones at the table. I am embarrassed by her behavior and the conclusions this genial stranger must be drawing about her… and my seeming lack of parenting skills. I make a passing, self-conscious comment about not being a fan of today's often violent and degrading lyrics. Cameron pretends not to hear.

Then Horton delivers a string of softly phrased words, a totally non-judgmental bridge of understanding and common ground, at least with me. He kindly says, "Yes, we have to be vigilant about what we *do* and *do not* allow into our minds. What we allow in is powerful. It leaves a lasting impression; good music, good ideas, good images, good deeds move us forward; the negative stuff, unfortunately, not so much."

The comments of this stranger command my rapt attention. His message is one I desperately want Cameron to absorb; better odds, I figure, coming from an unbiased third party. I glance hopefully in her direction. Nothing. But the insight and power of his words shift my mood. I am intrigued by our new acquaintance. He is intelligent, elegant in manner and states informed opinions. He is thoughtful in the selection, precision and delivery of his words, so as to be exact and not offend. I continue to mine the musical topic we have just embarked upon. I learn that he plays the piano, composes, and conducts. He is returning to his home in Queens, New York, from a music project in the San Francisco area and prefers train travel whenever his schedule permits for the sheer beauty, languorous pace and abundant time for rejuvenation and creativity.

"I find it very relaxing," he says. "It's a luxury, really. Well, maybe not to everyone," he corrects himself, chuckling, "but for me, it most definitely is." Then, as if reminiscing, "Takes me back to an earlier, slower time."

Miraculously, he returns my opening volleys with questions of his own. This is refreshing and rare. I tell him about my public relations background. He asks follow-up questions, and we bob along on an enjoyable, intelligent stream of conversation. Then our dialogue switches tracks from interesting to fascinating. Randall Keith Horton explains that he is particularly interested in my public relations experience because he has been trying to champion a very personal music project for the last thirty years.

"Hmmm... What have you been trying to promote?" I ask.

"Well, it's a rather long story," he hedges.

I shrug as if to say, *I'm all ears.* Ottumwa, Iowa is still several hours down the tracks.

"I was Duke Ellington's former assistant composer, conductor and pianist for a brief time in the early '70s," he continues somewhat reluctantly. "After his death, I was commissioned by his sister Ruth Ellington-Boatwright to concertize her brother's three *Sacred Concerts*, and by his son Mercer Ellington and G. Schirmer Publishing to write a full-length *concerto grosso* orchestration of his father's magnum opus, the big band piece *Black, Brown and Beige*. They were extended-length works that Ellington considered 'the most important music he ever wrote,' but which remain largely unknown, and certainly under-appreciated to this day."[2]

---

2    Duke Ellington was quoted as saying this about his first *Sacred Concert* in 1965; however, several songs from the composer's 1943 *Black, Brown and Beige* wiggled their way into each of his three *Sacred Concerts*. It is for this reason that this quote is extended to all four compositions (three *Sacred Concerts* and *Black, Brown and Beige*).

There is an audible *click!* in the contextual layer of my brain. *Be careful what you ask for,* I think as I realize I am not only in the presence of an interesting person but also a historically significant individual. I have never heard of the specific compositions to which Horton alludes, but I do know Duke Ellington. Doesn't everyone?

"What? No kidding!" I exclaim with surprise and enthusiasm.

And with that, it is abruptly time to say goodbye. We have lingered over the crumbs of our breakfast in the now empty dining car. Our waiter is hovering to refresh the linens for the next seating. There are so many questions I still want to ask, so much more I want to know. Horton and I share quick pleasantries and exchange names and phone numbers on scraps of newsprint torn from his morning paper.

I rub my thumb over the soft fibers of the newsprint in my pocket and marvel at my good fortune as Cameron and I make our way back to our sleeping car. *I just met Duke Ellington's former assistant composer, conductor, and pianist!* I think in disbelief. My casual intention is certainly fulfilled. Yet, in the back of my mind, I am greedily hoping for more. I find myself setting a new and highly improbable intention. I now fervently hope that my dialogue with this stranger continues.

Two weeks after my daughter's and my transcontinental train trip, I receive a call and speak at length with the stranger on the train, Randall Keith Horton. Over the next several years, we enjoy many more telephone conversations at scattered intervals as this kindly gentleman shares his life story. He is a natural educator with the patience of a saint and the detail and precision of an atomic clock. I find myself trying to take sips from the fire hose of information he provides. He has an encyclopedic mind for names, dates, places, details and all things *Ellingtonian*, especially the composer's mysterious extended-length compositions. And the only way to capture his explosion of information is to take copious, furiously written notes. I exhaust the ink in several pens compiling his life's facts in stacks of notebooks. And all the while I am silently asking myself, *Can this humble, unassuming 71-year-old gentleman really be who he says he is?* And if he is, if everything he is telling me is true, and this man altruistically championed Ellington's *Sacred Concerts* and *Black, Brown and Beige* for decades, *Why is he virtually unknown for his expertise and tireless efforts to elevate the music?* And, if this music of Duke Ellington is as pioneering and important as he asserts, *Why is it so little-known?*

There are secondary riddles as well, like why did Horton walk away from a promising musical career with Motown greats Marvin Gaye, Martha Reeves (of the *Vandellas*), Mary Wilson (of the *Supremes*) and the *Jackson Five*? It doesn't seem to make sense until I tumble down the rabbit hole of his childhood experiences.

His stories fascinate. I force myself to slow down, to absorb and process the facts before moving in to investigate more thoroughly. I research the proffered names, dates, facts, references, and timelines and am strangely exhilarated as each falls neatly into place. Horton's intimate knowledge of Duke Ellington's obscure compositions, the insights and endorsements he received from the Ellington family, his extensive experience consulting, concertizing, orchestrating, conducting and performing the music, his twenty-year study of classical conducting and composing under elite professionals and his forty-year career in musical directorships for churches and synagogues unmistakably qualify him as the leading expert on these four[3] distinct compositions. Yet, Horton is reluctant to claim the title for himself. In fact, he repeatedly cautions me at every turn.

"There are people who will vehemently challenge any such claim," Horton insists. "It's very important that you *hear* this! It's not just talk! I have experienced it first hand for the last three decades. I've been called a liar and an imposter. I've been told to cease and desist performing or

---

3     Ellington's *Black, Brown and Beige* and three *Sacred Concerts*.

attaching my name in any way to Ellington and his music. Individuals have tried, and in some cases succeeded, in blocking my efforts to publish, perform and professionally record the music. "And as an African American, I don't mind telling you that I take these threats and warnings very seriously. And of course, there were also my own personal failings along the way."

Why then, I wonder, is he so dedicated to his quest? There is little money or glory in it; in fact, it's quite the opposite. To concertize, orchestrate and perform Ellington's compositions, Horton has had to scrounge for funding, beg for services, work at-or-below minimum wage and assume personal debt.

"It has been overwhelming at times," Horton acknowledges. "I have wanted to lay down the burden and walk away on more than one occasion, and I don't think anyone would fault me if I did. But this," he says, grasping at something intangible, "this is what I feel I was put on this earth to do. I may never achieve my goal of publishing, performing, professionally recording and re-introducing the music to younger generations, so its notes and important messages can be heard and accorded the recognition and appreciation they deserve, but I can certainly remain faithful to my *calling*."

## BOSTON WNTN-AM RADIO

*(2017 radio interview between Randall Keith Horton and Paul Roberts, host of 1550 TODAY)*

**Paul:** *How old are you now, Randall, if you don't mind me asking?*

**Randall:** *I'm seventy-four.*

**Paul:** *How old were you when this happened?*

**Randall:** *Twenty-two.*

**Paul:** *So fifty-two years ago!*

**Randall:** *[Laughing]* *"Yes!"*

**Paul:** *What kind of light was it?*

**Randall:** *[Pausing for a moment of reflection] I don't know how else to explain it other than to say that it was like a laser beam of light.*

**Paul:** *White or blue?*

**Randall:** *Pardon me?*

**Paul:** *Was the light white or blue in color?*

**Randall:** *It was white.*

**Paul:** *How wide? An inch… several inches?*

**Randall:** *About a quarter of an inch wide. It came down from above, entered through the top of my head and filled my entire body… and then the room… with a brightness… and a warmth."*

**Randall:** *[Pausing, a moment of apparent disquietude] I don't share that with many people, because they might think I'm crazy! [With humor, authority and a touch of defiance] But that is precisely what happened. A white, laser beam-like light manifested itself in me and changed the course of my entire life in a single moment. There was no question…not a doubt…that I would, or could, do anything other than precisely what it commanded me to do.*

**Paul:** *What did it command you to do?*

**Randall:** *Go to San Francisco and Study Music!*

* * *

The more Randall Keith Horton and I talk, the more the importance of his story resonates with me. His experiences and the knowledge he possesses about this little-known aspect of Ellington's legacy are not only valuable pieces of American and Jazz history, but also of America's cultural struggle toward racial equality. Ellington's pioneering *Black, Brown and Beige* was Ellington's (and some believe, Jazz's) first musical composition of symphonic dimension. It celebrated African American history in three descriptive movements and was the composer's call for parity... between blacks and whites and between American Jazz and classical European music.

Ellington's three subsequent *Sacred Concerts* evolved from *Black, Brown and Beige*. These were inspired by his familiarity with Old and New Testament Biblical texts and created a daring new form of meditative, worshipful Jazz. The concerts became a medium through which the enigmatic composer shared his own personal faith, his profound belief in the common ground between people of all races, religions, cultures and socio-economic backgrounds, as well as the righteousness of Jazz to praise a universal God. Together, these four compositions represent the apogee of Ellington's sub-musical, human rights statements. *Come Sunday*, the featured melody in the original (1943) *Black, Brown and Beige* Carnegie Hall recording, was expanded with lyrics in Ellington's 1958 album (also titled *Black, Brown and Beige*) and later included in Ellington's *Sacred Concerts*. *Come Sunday* created a common thread that linked all four compositions, eventually evolving into an anthem of hope during America's Civil Rights Movement.

Horton's noteworthy contributions to this important part of Ellington's musical legacy beg at least to be documented; and at best, to be the topic of a book, a documentary, a film. His orchestration of Ellington's *Black, Brown and Beige* and his concertizing and leadership of his three *Sacred Concerts* cry out to be performed and properly recorded and reintroduced to the ears, minds and hearts of new generations of listeners who, almost 100 years later, may finally be ready to hear and appreciate the composer's pioneering notes and messages.

Perhaps my chance meeting of Horton is fate; the world moving in mysterious ways to bring Ellington's forgotten compositions back to the forefront of an increasingly fractured world in need of the music's rallying cries for unity. Any failure that occurred in presenting the music in 1943, 1958, 1965, 1968 or 1973[4] was not in Ellington's choice of notes, themes, or venues. The failure was in the public's ability to accept an African American composer and his African American musicians who dared to step outside their prescribed boundaries to present music and messages that celebrated the history, experiences and contributions of their own culture and espoused (gasp!) a shared desire for faith, love, tolerance, acceptance, forgiveness, and inclusion of all people the world over.

My partnership with Horton – for that is certainly what it becomes over the next eight years – morphs into a rather unimpressive sculling team of two, pulling feverishly upstream to elevate, record and perform the "rejected" music and messages of the most significant and prolific composer in Jazz history and one of the most famous American (world) composers of any genre, Edward Kennedy "Duke" Ellington.

* * *

History is the record of human events, but music and art are the enduring records of our emotional response to them. Popular music, therefore, cannot help but reflect the thoughts, challenges, culture and identities of each new generation. But before a single note can be written by composers of any era, they must first ask, *What is going on around me? What am I feeling? How do I want my listeners to feel when they hear my music?* And in turn, their intellectual and emotional interpretations of events educate and influence how we, as listeners, feel. The tempo, mode, loudness, melody and rhythm of their music set moods, create atmospheres and affect behaviors. Musical styles and lyrics play a role in determining what people perceive as *right* or *wrong, okay* or *not okay, good* or *bad*. And the more familiar a song becomes, the more intensely we absorb its messages and emotional impact. Randall Keith Horton's

---

4    1943: *Black, Brown and Beige*; 1958: *Black, Brown and Beige* (album); 1965: *First Sacred Concert*; 1968: *Second Sacred Concert*; and 1973: *Third Sacred Concert*.

statement on the Amtrak train was prophetic, "We [*do*] have to be vigilant about what we *do* and *do not* allow into our minds these days. What we allow in *is* powerful." Considering that the average American listens to four hours of music every day, it is also a profound observation. The music continually swirling around us today, and throughout history, can be positively, or negatively, influential.[5]

When Duke Ellington's music expressed the emotional reality of African Americans' struggles, it was unsettling to his predominantly white critics and audiences who found it easier to reject outright his extended-length compositions than to acknowledge their painful cultural truths; less so for his European counterparts who demonstrated a greater understanding and appreciation for Ellington's pioneering efforts. Alas, never a prophet in your own land. But before meaningful change of any kind can take place, people must first acknowledge the existence of a problem, and that was something Americans were incapable of doing in Ellington's era. The emotional music and messages of *Black, Brown and Beige* and Ellington's *Sacred Concerts* were decades ahead of their time and viewed as dangerously unsettling.

Stumbling upon Randall Keith Horton in the dining car of the eastbound Amtrak California Zephyr is the equivalent of finding the mythical gatekeeper to a hidden chamber of King Tut's tomb. He proves to be an untapped treasure trove of information on an equally royal figure, "The Duke" of American music and cultural advancement—and who knew?—impassioned human rights advocate, Edward Kennedy "Duke" Ellington.

---

5    Alf Gabrielsson, et al. "The Influence of Music on Structure on Emotional Expression." *Handbook of Music and Emotion: Theory, Research, Applications*, USA: Oxford University Press, 2001, pp. 223–243.

# HISTORICAL CONTEXT
## 1915 - 1949

Between 1916 and 1970, over six million African Americans flee the South with its harsh Jim Crow laws and lynchings and seek well-paying industrial jobs in several northern cities in what comes to be known as The Great Migration[6]. Many settle in Harlem, the epicenter of an overlapping movement called *The Harlem Renaissance* (1918-1930) which attempts to change the pervasiveness of racism and negative African American stereotypes by creating a "New Negro" identity. This literary and artistic movement encourages education and the intellectual production and expression of African American poetry, literature, art, fashion, music and thought. It is a time of tremendous geographical and cultural movement where regional Jazz styles coalesce in various new locations with one important constant: The music remains a *safe* medium through which the "Old" and "New" Negro can freely express his/her true thoughts, experiences and emotions.

Stride piano playing (1920's-1930's), of which Duke Ellington is a fan and practitioner, evolves on the northeast coast, mainly New York City, during this period.[7] It is an early style of Jazz that features highly creative musical techniques, tackling a wider range of tempos, with an emphasis on improvisation and a leaping left hand. In the mid 1920's, Sidney Bechet, the King of the Soprano Sax, is one of the first to introduce Jazz to European audiences when he travels to France (1924) along with other members of the *Revue Nègre*. He tours Europe again in 1926

---

6    "The Great Migration was one of the largest and most rapid mass internal movements in history—perhaps the greatest not caused by the immediate threat of execution or starvation. In sheer numbers it outranks the migration of any other ethnic group—Italians or Irish or Jews or Poles—to [the United States]. For blacks, the migration meant leaving what had always been their economic and social base in America, and finding a new one." From Nicholas Lemann, *The Promised Land: The Great Black Migration and How It Changed America* (New York: Alfred A. Knopf, 1991), p. 6.

7    James P. Johnson (1894-1955) is credited as the "Father of Stride." Other notables include Willie "The Lion" Smith (1893-1973), Thomas "Fats" Waller (1904-1943) and Luckey Roberts (1893-1968).

and 1928 with various bands, entertaining listeners as far away as Russia. This lays the groundwork and demand for The Ellington Orchestra to make its first tour of Europe in 1933, the same year Hitler becomes Germany's new chancellor and promptly bans the "inferiority" of Jazz music from German airwaves. But several high profile African American achievements soon contradict Hitler's racist Aryan ideology on the world stage: Track star Jesse Owens wins four gold medals at the 1936 Summer Olympics in Munich and Joe Louis reigns as the World's Heavyweight Boxing Champion for twelve consecutive years beginning in 1937.

According to Larry Schwartz's 2000 ESPN program *Owens Pierced a Myth*, Jesse Owens was the most successful athlete at the [Munich Olympics] and, as a black man, was credited with "single-handedly crushing Hitler's myth of Aryan supremacy," although he "wasn't invited to the White House to shake hands with the President, [upon his return] either."

The live, swinging music of big bands becomes the rage for dancing in the late 1920's, 1930's and 1940's as Jazz enjoys its golden years. During this time, Crooners (male and female soloists backed up by orchestras and big bands) begin to gain popularity.[8] Live radio broadcasts follow, expanding the reach of both and delivering their respective sounds right into Americans' (and Europeans') living rooms – none better than Duke Ellington who writes some of his most enduring music during this period.

---

8    Crooners included Billie Holiday, Frank Sinatra, Sarah Vaughan, Louis Armstrong, Nat King Cole, Billy Eckstine, Bing Crosby, Ella Fitzgerald, Vaughn De Leath, Annette Hanshaw, Mildred Bailey (at the beginning of her career), Helen Rowland and others.

## CHAPTER 1

# IT AIN'T WHAT YOU DO
# (IT'S THE WAY THAT YOU DO IT)

*"It's like murder.*
*You play with the intent to commit something."*
- Duke Ellington

Certain things in life are impossible to comprehend fully unless one experiences them firsthand: war, childbirth, rape, physical or emotional abuse, and discrimination, to name a few. As I talk with Randall Keith Horton and conduct my research, I am astonished by the relentless, soul-crushing reality of racism and discrimination, which can only be explained as the byproducts of ignorance and absurd reasoning; like hosting a race between identical boats, feeling the need to arbitrarily strip the rudders from those painted a different color, continuing the competition, imagining it to be fair, and even celebrating the "superiority" of the inevitable winner.

When Ellington arrives on the American Jazz scene in the mid-1920's, he is nothing short of an anachronism -- a talented captain armed with his own rudder, a never-before-experienced outboard motor (in the form of his band) and the musical and moral audacity to celebrate African American history, culture, and contributions.

But who exactly is Duke Ellington? Most people have a cursory understanding of him as an iconic, tuxedoed Jazz musician, but may be hard pressed to name the title of even one of his musical blockbusters. Yet his melodies, when heard, are instantly recognizable. In fact, so profound are his pioneering influences that his music still swirls around us every minute of every day nearly a half-century after his death (at this writing). We hear it in the soundtracks of movies, cartoons, TV shows, commercials, Broadway plays, coffee shop playlists, physical/cyber/cellular waiting rooms, ring tones, bars, nightclubs, restaurants, radio stations, streaming services, and more. It also lives in the Ellington-inspired thoughts and notes of almost four generations of modern-day musicians of varying genres.

In fact, Duke Ellington does more than any other Jazz musician of his time to elevate Jazz from the so-called "Nigger music" relegated to funeral processions, brothels and bars, to an art form worthy of radio, television, cinema, churches and concert halls. During his career, the Ellington Orchestra performs at the Cotton Club in Harlem, plays music on some of the first national radio broadcasts, tours internationally, appears in movies and pioneers and performs musical soundtracks for Hollywood films. He receives twenty-two Grammy nominations with eleven Grammy wins. He is inducted into the Grammy Hall of Fame, becomes a Grammy Trustee and receives the Lifetime Achievement Award. His accomplishments continue even after his death when nine of his previously recorded hits are inducted into the Grammy Hall of Fame. He travels the world as an ambassador of American excellence and freedom for the US State Department, and in 1970, President

Nixon presents him with the Presidential Medal of Freedom, the highest honor presented to American citizens. He shatters racial, cultural and musical barriers and in the process, becomes one of America's biggest celebrities as well as a global musical and cultural force. Ellington uses his music, his eloquence, his personal elegance, and his band's impeccable appearance to shine a positive light on African Americans, and that in turn helps create a paradigm shift in America.

* * *

Edward Kennedy Ellington is born in 1899 and raised in a middle-class family in Washington, D.C. His Methodist father works as a blueprint maker for the US Navy, a butler for a prominent doctor, and a server in a catering business for stylish soirees, including many at the White House. He plays operatic music on the piano and is known to be quite charming.

His mother, a Southern Baptist with an Irish bloodline from her father,[9] encourages fine manners and elegant living and prefers playing popular parlor tunes on the family piano. She pampers and spoils their only son and constantly reminds him from an early age how blessed he is.

"My mother told me I was *blessed*," said Ellington, "and I have always taken her word for it. Being born of — or reincarnated from — royalty is nothing like being *blessed*. Royalty is inherited from another human being; *blessedness* comes from God."[10]

In his early teens, Ellington's good looks, stylish dress and eloquent, charismatic demeanor earn him his nickname "Duke," which he parlays into a job as a soda fountain jerk at his hometown Poodle Dog Café. Although he takes intermittent piano lessons beginning at age seven,

---

9    His mother's Irish lineage perhaps explains the selection of Edward *Kennedy* (Duke) Ellington's middle name.

10    Quotetab, "Duke Ellington: My mother told me I was blessed, and I have always taken her...," 2019; www.quotetab.com/quote/by-duke-ellington/my-mother-told-me-i-was-blessed-and-i-have-always-taken-her-word-for-it-being-b.

he struggles to read or write music, preferring to spend most of his time on baseball fields. Nonetheless, in 1914 he composes his first song *Soda Fountain Rag* to simulate the rhythms and sounds of his soda jerk job and performs it from memory on numerous occasions.

"I never had much interest in the piano," recounted Ellington, "until I realized that every time I played, a girl would appear on the piano bench to my left and another to my right."

By age fourteen, the budding musician begins sneaking into the local pool halls to listen to the resident piano players and is particularly fascinated with the sound and showmanship of the stride piano[11] players he witnesses during summer vacations with his mother in Philadelphia and New Jersey. The exposure solidifies his interest in the piano, and he dedicates his senior year of high school to learning how to read music, figuring out harmonies, refining his techniques and perfecting his showmanship.

Although he excels in commercial art and is offered an art scholarship to the Pratt Institute in Brooklyn, Ellington drops out of high school three months shy of graduation. He starts a sign painting business and works briefly as a messenger for the US Navy where he makes valuable contacts. When customers hire him to paint signs for their parties, he inquires if they need a band, and soon becomes a booking agent and eventually, the leader of his own bands: *The Serenaders* and *The Washingtonians*. He earns quite a reputation playing society balls and embassy parties for mixed audiences, a rarity for the time.

By 1926, at the age of 27, Ellington's experiences playing in bands[12] in Harlem, Atlantic City and New Jersey brings him to the attention of

---

11    An upbeat Jazz piano style with a wide range of tempos and emphasis on improvisation, popular in the large cities of the East Coast during the 1920's and 1930's. It is very physical, with hands jumping up and down the keyboard.

12    Wilbur Sweatman Orchestra; Elmer Snowden and his Black Sox Orchestra, later renamed the Washingtonians; Duke Ellington and his Kentucky Club Orchestra.

music publisher and agent Irving Mills who quickly signs him as a client and to nearly every record label spinning at the time.[13] Mills also helps build a gold-plated image for Ellington, something unprecedented for an African American. One year later, Ellington earns a career-altering break. When King Oliver[14] turns down his regular gig as the Cotton Club's house band, Mills set up an audition for Ellington. Ellington shows up late for the audition. Fortunately, so does the *Cotton Club* owner and organized crime figure Owney "The Killer" Madden.

> "Mr. Ellington got the booking, but first he had to be released from a theater engagement in Philadelphia. This was easily arranged when the 'The Killer' asked some of his *associates* in Philadelphia to call on the theater manager with the following proposition: 'Be big or you'll be dead.'"[15]

The manager chooses to be *big*, and Duke Ellington begins his five-year association with the *Cotton Club* along with a baptism by fire into the frenetic pace of the entertainment industry, writing music on short deadlines for the *Cotton Club's* extravagant musical and dance productions which change every six months. As Ellington's star begins to rise, big band leader Paul Whiteman[16] and his arranger Ferde Grofé would attend Duke's *Cotton Club* performances night after night, trying to notate and duplicate what his musicians are playing. They eventually give up.[17]

---

13    During the 1920's and 1930's, Ellington recorded with almost every record label: BluDisc, Pathé, Perfect, Victor, Brunswick, Columbia Records, Okeh, Vocalion, Cameo, Romeo, Lincoln, Banner, Domino, Jewel and Hit of the Week.

14    King Oliver (1881-1938) was a Jazz musician and cornet player who pioneered the use of mutes for trumpets and cornets and was a mentor to Armstrong.

15    Owen Vincent Madden (1891-1965), known as Owney Madden and nicknamed "The Killer," was a notorious Manhattan underworld figure. While he was most notable for involvement in Prohibition-era organized crime, he also ran the famous Cotton Club and was a leading boxing promoter in the 1930's.

16    Paul Whiteman (1890 – 1967) was an American big band leader, composer, orchestral director, and violist billed as the "King of Jazz" in the 1920's and 1930's.

17    John S. Wilson, "Duke Ellington A Master Of Music Dies At 75", *New York Times* (New York), May 25, 1974, Front Page.

In later years, Andre Previn (who arranged and composed music for more than 50 Hollywood film scores and understood both classical and Jazz music) reportedly shook his head in amazement as he noted, "Stan Kenton can stand in front of a thousand fiddles and a thousand brass and make a dramatic gesture and every audio arranger can nod his head and say, 'Oh, yes, that's done like this.' But Duke merely lifts his finger, three horns make a sound, and I don't know what it is!"[18]

"You can do everything right and be of no interest at all," said James Conlon, the music director of the *Los Angeles Opera*. "… you can be baffling and effective," he concludes, summing up the art of conducting, "… ultimately some intangible, charismatic element trumps it all. Nobody has ever bottled it. To which I say, 'Thank God.'"[19] [20] Oh, the magical Ellington effect!

Ellington, "the consummate autodidact," quickly learns to write and perform complete soundtracks for a variety of themes and performers; a perfect fit for Ellington with his uncanny ability to read and control the energy of an entire room — band members, performers and patrons — heating them up, cooling them down and conjuring a smorgasbord of emotions and moods.[21] His ear is innately drawn to the *shininess* of uncommon sounds and talents which he collects unabashedly like a magpie. He views his entire band as an instrument and writes to showcase the unique talents of each musician.

---

18  *Ibid.*

19  Daniel J. Wakin, "The Maestro's Mojo," *New York Times* (New York), April 8, 2012, Section AR, www.nytimes.com/2012/04/08/arts/music/breaking-conductors-down-by-gesture-and-body-part.html.

20  *Ibid.*

21  Ellington received "valuable lessons in orchestration" from Will Vodery (1885 – 1951), an African American composer, conductor, orchestrator, and arranger, most famous for his vocal and choral arrangements for the Broadway musical *Show Boat* (1927) and composing for Florenz Ziegfeld. According to author Barry Ulanov, "From Vodery, as he (Ellington) says himself, he drew his chromatic convictions, his uses of the tones ordinarily extraneous to the diatonic scale, with the consequent alteration of the harmonic character of his music, its broadening, the deepening of his resources. It has become customary to ascribe the classical influences upon Duke – Delius, Debussy and Ravel – to direct contact with their music. Actually his serious appreciation of those and other modern composers, came after his meeting with Vodery." Barry Ulanov, (1946) *Duke Ellington, Creative Age Press.*

"My aim is and always has been to mold the music around the man," stated Ellington. "I study each man in the orchestra and find out what he can do best, and what he would like to do."[22]

His future composer and pianist Billy Strayhorn would later sum it up, saying, "Ellington plays the piano, but his real instrument is his band."

Ellington's high-brow-style of composing makes the musicians and the Ellington Orchestra sound their best, something that other bands playing the exact same music simply cannot reproduce. This engenders a loyalty among band members, some of whom stay with the orchestra for decades. Ellington's commitment to each of his musicians is unwavering. Everything else, however, is open to interpretation based upon the environment, energy and emotion surrounding each performance. Jazz provides Ellington with the freedom to convey uniquely (black) American experiences with the immediacy and excitement of improvisation and the authenticity of the real-time sentiments and skills. His composing develops through the musical-coloristic individuality of each of his band's soloists, and through their inimitable collective, improvisational ensemble abilities. In this sense, the *Ellington Orchestra* is unique in the entire field of music, especially in live-concert performances.

Over time, Ellington transforms into a master painter who manipulates and blends the coveted "pigments" of his carefully selected band members to create instrumental portraits that inspire, challenge and entertain the world. His elegantly attired, eleven-piece big band[23], which plays to the *Cotton Club's* well-heeled, exclusively-white patrons, transforms prevailing stereotypes from shuffling Jazz entertainers in bordellos and lowly bars to skilled musicians of the highest order. He charms. He

---

22    Howard Reich, "The Story Behind the First Pulitzer for Jazz," NiemanReports, June 20, 2016, niemanreports.org/articles/the-story-behind-the-first-pulitzer-for-Jazz/.

23    Ellington's band gradually grew to 15-16 members.

entertains. He astounds. And beneath it all, he educates and demands more of white America.

Although it is inconceivable by today's standards, the theme of the *Cotton Club*, the most iconic nightclub in New York City in the late 1920's and 1930's, is a *faux* plantation complete with a white-columned bandstand dressed up like a southern mansion in front of a backdrop of cotton fields and slave quarters. Allusions to the idyllic life of Southern whites extends to the audience as well. Performers are predominantly black, or in the case of the chorus girls, light-skinned, but prospective black patrons are turned away at the front door by either force of law or muscle. Even Ellington himself is made to ask permission for his friends to enter the club to see his shows. Nonetheless, his genius blossoms during his tenure at the *Cotton Club*, and he becomes adept at making the best of difficult situations.

> For the [*Cotton Club's*] big revues, with their plots about black savages and threatened maidens, he devised music of sophistication and cheekily exotic allure, under such titles as *Jungle Blues*, *Jungle Night in Harlem* and the sinister *The Mooche*. But even before the band sounded a note it delivered a statement: impeccably dressed in matching tuxedos and bou-tonnières, its members were of a class with the biggest swells in the room. And Ellington was the swellest of all: unfailingly *soigné*, magisterially presiding over the urban jungle, he stood untouched and never lost his smile.[24]

Live national radio broadcasts from the club (1927-1933) earn the band an even larger following and extend the reach of Ellington's swinging music into Americans' homes. Before long (1941), the maestro

---

24   Claudia Roth Pierpoint, "Black, Brown, And Beige: Duke Ellington's music and race in America," *New Yorker*, May 10, 2010, www.newyorker.com/magazine/2010/05/17/black-brown-and-beige.

and his orchestra jump another hurdle, serenading moviegoers from the silver screen, cast respectfully as themselves at Ellington's insistence.

Ellington rarely thinks, sees or hears things as strictly "black" or "white." He leads his life and chooses his ambitions not only as a talented musician driven to create but also as a respected "race man."[25] He is a shining example to his race, exemplifying throughout his career the truth of what could, and should, be. In comments from the stage of Carnegie Hall (*Black, Brown and Beige*, 1943) he speaks of the "Negro" in what can be interpreted as thinking in "black" sensibilities. His composition, *Black Beauty* is only one of a few with titles that honor black heroes (for example, Florence Mills, Bill "Bojangles" Robinson, and others). His musical reviews are all about race: *Jump for Joy; Good Riddance, Jim Crow!; My People* and the list continues.

Duke Ellington shatters racial barriers in part because he effectively charms his way past the limitations foisted upon African Americans of his era. He is a magician with the ability to make racial prejudices temporarily disappear in his presence with one fell swoop of his masterful hand. This would be an astounding feat for an established white musician of the period, let alone an African American conductor of predominantly African American Jazz musicians. The churning power of Duke Ellington and his orchestra is changing America and her music. Yet, because of nothing more than the tone of his skin, even the iconic Ellington experiences his share of discrimination.

According to music scholar Mark Tucker,[26] "Ellington gave the impression of being unscathed by racism though it defined almost

---

25    Race man: "Since emancipation, Drake and Cayton argue, black people have had to prove, actively and consistently, that they were not the inferior beings that their status as second-class citizens declared them to be: hence an aggressive demonstration of their superiority in some field of achievement, either individually or collectively, was what established race pride: 'the success of one Negro' was interpreted as 'the success of all.' The result of the pursuit of "race consciousness, race pride, and race solidarity' was the emergence of particular social types, among which was the Race Man." Excerpt from Hazel V. Carby, "Race Men," Introduction, accessed via *New York Times Books*, https://archive.nytimes.com/www.nytimes.com/books/first/c/carby-race.html.

26    Mark Tucker, PhD (1954-2000) was a professor, musician and scholar who wrote *Ellington: The Early Years* (1991) and *The Duke Ellington Reader* (1993).

every move he made: where he could play his music, who could come to listen, whether he could attend another musician's show and where (or whether) he and his musicians could find lodging or something to eat when their shows were over. During the band's many international tours he was recognized as a great artist only to return to his own country and have to fight for the recognition and opportunities his music and musicians deserved."

In *Art or Debauchery?: The Reception of Ellington in the UK*, Catherine Tackleyn states, "There is not a note which comes from the remarkable brass section, or from that rich tones of the saxes, that is not directly an expression of Duke's genius."[27]

Jazz is, in fact, one of the few acceptable mediums through which African Americans are allowed to express themselves freely in America. Ellington is quoted as saying, "What we could not say openly, we expressed in music. The characteristic, melancholic music of my race has been forged from the very white heat of our sorrow…"[28]

And while nightclubs, Hollywood and record labels roll out the welcome mat for the iconic band, the elegant doors to respected concert halls remain securely barred. Their symbolic dismissal of Jazz chafes and eventually fuels yet another audacious Ellington aspiration: to elevate Jazz, the uniquely American art form, on par with classical European music. In the late 1920's, he contemplates writing a symphonic suite and opera entitled *Boola* that will tell the history of American Negroes for the first time from the perspective of an American Negro, using his own musical (Jazz) vernacular.[29] It is a long and arduous history that requires more time to tell than the standard two to three minute

---

27    Catherine Tackleyn, "'Art or Debauchery?': The Reception of Ellington in the UK," *Duke Ellington Studies*, edited by John Howland, Cambridge University Press, 2017, 76-107.

28    Duke Ellington, "The Duke Steps Out," *Rhythm* (March 1931): 20–22, collected in *The Duke Ellington Reader*, ed. Mark Tucker (New York, 1993), p. 49.

29    Another example of Duke Ellington the "race man."

recording lengths of his popular Jazz hits[30], so Ellington begins writing, experimenting and recording his six-minute *Tiger Rag* (1929) followed by even longer compositions: the nine-minute *Creole Rhapsody* (1931), twelve-minute *Reminiscing in Tempo* (1935) and the fourteen-minute, conjoined *Diminuendo and Crescendo in Blue* (1937), all of which take up two or more sides of a 78 RPM record, something completely new for a Jazz band and more in line with what classical orchestras do.[31]

In the midst of this experimentation, Duke Ellington and his musicians embark on their first international tour through England, Belgium and France (1933). They discover European audiences who are not only familiar with their songs but also extremely knowledgeable about them. The band appears at the countries' largest venues and concert halls and are met with a respect that, for all the band's popularity, it has never known in the United States. According to trombonist Juan Tizol, the band is shocked by English audiences bestowing upon them the kind of reception usually accorded to classical artists, including ovations of five to ten minutes before the band plays a note.[32] They have never experienced anything like this in America. In fact, in Europe, members of the Ellington Orchestra are even discussed in the same breath as the titans of classical music.

In London alone, the Ellington Orchestra performs for two sold out weeks at the 2,286 seat Palladium, the country's most esteemed theater, which prompts British music critic Constant Lambert to proclaim that "Ellington is 'skillful as compared with other Jazz composers,' but that his music could stand alongside the European masters: 'I know of

---

30    The relatively crude disc-cutting techniques of the time and the thickness of the needles used on record players limited the number of grooves per inch that could be inscribed on the disc surface, and a high rotation speed was necessary to achieve acceptable recording and playback fidelity. 78 rpm was chosen as the standard because of the introduction of the electrically-powered synchronous turntable motor in 1925, resulted in a rotation speed of 78.26 rpm. Songwriters and performers increasingly tailored their output to fit on a single side of the new medium with three-minute singles remaining the standard into the 1960's.

31    A single side of a 78 RPM record provided between two and three minutes of audio play time.

32    Harvey G. Cohen, *Duke Ellington's America* (University of Chicago Press, 2011), p. 114.

nothing in Ravel so dexterous, nothing in Stravinsky more dynamic.'The names of Ralph Vaughan Williams, Paul Hindemith, and César Franck are dropped in as well."[33] European critics also begin to draw parallels between Ellington and Bach, composers both known to write music with the skills of individual musicians in mind. And what is Ellington's response to being ranked with Bach? A simple "Hot damn!" While he appreciates the compliment, he does not aspire to copy other composers or musical styles. He adheres to his own principles and style and sums it up later in his career, advising others to "Be the number one you and not a number two somebody else."

The virtual lack of discrimination they experience in Europe is painted in even sharper relief during the band's first tour of the American South one short month after their return (1933). They travel out of necessity and safety in a supremely insulated style: two private Pullman railroad cars for sleeping and dining, with a third baggage car for the elaborate wardrobe, scenery, and lights needed to present shows that dazzled the residents in each sleepy little town. Ellington also makes special efforts to perform for black audiences even though it often means adding midnight shows after earlier performances for exclusively white audiences.[34] The musicians outdo themselves for both. In signature fashion, Ellington spins the otherwise negative necessity with a sophisticated parallel, saying "We travel the way the Presidents travel." Unfortunately, the discrimination and segregation extend beyond the Deep South.

Through most of Ellington's career, Jazz is surrounded by economic and social barriers. He even fights the word Jazz, preferring "Negro Music" instead, because Jazz "comes to represent an economic ghetto for musical minorities"[35] and the continuation of social inequality. Jazz

---

33    John Wriggle, "Ellington as Composer: Beyond Category?," *L.A. Review of Books*, September 6, 2012: lareviewofbooks.org/article/ellington-as-composer-beyond-category/.

34    Another example of Duke Ellington the "race man."

35    Irving Townsend, "Ellington in Private," *The Atlantic Monthly* 235, no. 5 (1975), www.theatlantic.com/past/docs/unbound/Jazz/townsend.htm.

musicians cannot freely enter through the front of the buildings whose stages they play upon. They cannot stay in the hotels that hire them. And many restaurants refuse them service.

One such incident in St. Louis is witnessed by writer Richard O. Boyer from *The New Yorker* as he travels with Ellington's orchestra who describes the scene as follows:

> Ellington's two "white employees" were able to quickly hail a taxi to one of the town's good hotels while the African American members of the band — after considerable begging — were taken to a rickety hotel in the African American part of the city. The next day, the group was unable to purchase food before the concert and performed hungry. These difficulties encountered by the band members in obtaining food, housing, and transportation were often accompanied by vicious racial insults.[36]

Perhaps buoyed by the glimpse of what equality "could be" from the band's warm European reception, Ellington doubles down on his commitment to celebrate and elevate all that racism in America hopes to obscure: the beauty, history, talents, contributions, and value of his race. He writes and appears in a nine-minute, orchestrated, programmatic film called *Symphony in Black* (1935) which features alternating glimpses of him composing "a 'new symphony of Negro moods'" in his studio while his orchestra performs the music against a motif of scenes depicted in the score: groups of men at work (*The Laborers*); a lover spurned (*A Triangle* in three parts: *Dance, Jealousy, and Blues*, the last of these featuring a young Billie Holiday); a child's funeral (*A Hymn of Sorrow*);

---

36    Richard O. Boyer, "The Hot Bach - II," *New Yorker*, July 1, 1944, www.newyorker.com/magazine/1944/07/01/the-hot-bach-ii.

and an exuberant nightclub dance (*Harlem Rhythm*).[37] [38] He records his orchestra's performance directly onto the film's audio track, pioneering the underutilized technique that provides unlimited recording time with the highest available sound quality.[39] As the quality of audio recordings continues to evolve, the Ellington Orchestra's visual image is already undeniably powerful and impactful.

Three years later in 1938, as the European continent teeters on the brink of World War II, the 39-year-old Ellington meets a 23-year-old lyricist, composer, pianist and arranger named Billy Strayhorn, whose earliest hopes of becoming a classical composer are considered beyond the scope of an African American and redirected to the more "appropriate" genre of Jazz. Strayhorn attends one of the Ellington Orchestra performances at the Crawford Grill in downtown Pittsburgh. Learning of the young man's prodigious skills, Ellington invites him backstage after the performance. The two discuss lyrics and arrangements, two of Strayhorn's greatest strengths. To better illustrate some of his arranging thoughts, Strayhorn sits down at an upright and demonstrates *exactly* how Ellington played *Sophisticated Lady*. Then he says, "Now, this is the way I would play it," changing the key and upping the tempo slightly. He does the same thing with *Solitude*. Ellington is not offended. He is intrigued and asks long-term band member Harry Carney to listen to Strayhorn play. Before long, Carney hustles out and brings back Johnny Hodges and Ivie Anderson.[40]

Ever the great observer of human nature, Ellington maintains a simple paradigm: If an individual elevates his musical expression and is in step with him, he becomes a valued member of his team. He is, after all, an innovator and like most innovators, has little interest in bobbing along

---

37    Mike Tucker, "The Genesis of *Black, Brown and Beige*," *Black Music Research Journal* 13, no. 2 (Autumn 1993): 73, doi.org/10.2307/779513.

38    Another example of Duke Ellington the "race man."

39    Andrew Homzy, "'Black, Brown and Beige' in Duke Ellington's Repertoire, 1943-1973," *Black Music Research Journal*, 13, No. 2 (Autumn 1993): 91, doi.org/10.2307/779514.

40    David Hajdu, *Lush Life: A Biography of Billy Strayhorn* (New York: North Point Press, 1997), p. 50.

with the masses and even less patience for anyone sapping or slowing his forward progress. His modus operandi at all times is full speed ahead.

A short time later, Strayhorn shows up again at one of Ellington's New York appearances. This time he has written an original song to impress Ellington, inspired by the directions Ellington gave him to his home in Harlem. Ralph Koger, a reporter for the *Pittsburgh Courier* is sitting with Strayhorn when he plays it, "and, sure enough," Courier says, "it [tells] you how to get to Harlem: *Take the 'A' Train*.[41] That will bring you right into Harlem."[42] Ellington must have been impressed because Strayhorn is immediately snapped up into the band's rip current.

Over the next three decades, Ellington and Strayhorn become a partnership of virtuosic equals with Ellington as the front man and Strayhorn diligently composing and arranging behind the scenes. It is a liberating alliance for Strayhorn that allows him to live as an openly gay musician, a rarity for the time, and to infuse his classically based harmonic clarity, taste and polish into many of Ellington's compositions. Strayhorn writes prolifically for Ellington during the 1941 ASCAP strike (American Society of Composers, Authors and Publishers) that prevents Ellington and all ASCAP members from broadcasting their published songs over the radio due to royalty disputes. The strike restricts Ellington from the air waves, but Strayhorn, who is not a union member, is free to compose and keep the Ellington Orchestra on the radio for several months with his own rapidly written songs. He bangs-out the blockbuster *Take The 'A' Train*, (1941) which eventually becomes the band's signature song, and continues writing additional hits like *Chelsea Bridge, Something to Live For, Day Dream, My Little Brown Book* and *Lotus Blossom* under Ellington's guidance.

In describing his relationship with the world, Ellington often uses the word "parallel," moving in sync with his musicians, friends, and

---

41    "Take The "A" Train" was also used as the opening song/theme for Voice of America's international radio broadcasts of "The Jazz Hour" (1955 - 2003).

42    David Hajdu, *Lush Life: A Biography of Billy Strayhorn* (New York: North Point Press, 1997), p. 55.

acquaintances; "never quite touching, yet never far apart."[43] His relationship with Strayhorn is no different. They are of one mind creatively, yet their antithetical personalities offer insight into the enigmatic Ellington. Strayhorn's broad awareness of those around him allows him to effortlessly inhabit their emotional worlds with complete empathy. He welcomes people into his life and excels at deep friendships, offering meaningful support. Ellington, by contrast, has an extremely vertical depth of focus, detachedly observing and interpreting people's emotions and experiences as inspiration for his music. He sweeps into his orchestra those who can help elevate his notes and skills, but remains emotionally aloof.

Strayhorn lives his life consistently both on and off the stage. Ellington seems to don and doff markedly different personas. In front of the velvet curtain, he is sophisticated, charismatic, and engaging, the supreme showman and host. But behind the velvet curtain, he can be introspective and reclusive, consumed with capturing and expressing in musical rhythms all that he sees, feels, and experiences around him on a daily basis. He lives to compose, create and entertain and comes to life with the opening notes of each new composition or the improvised restructuring of existing standards.

"Music, of course, is what I hear and something that I more or less live by," Ellington says self-knowingly. "It's not an occupation or profession, it's a compulsion."

As a result, people love Ellington, but few really know him. His true essence and thoughts are most eloquently expressed in the notes and themes of his music: his hopes, his dreams, his intellect and his visceral rejection of categories of all kinds whose only purpose, he purports, is to damage and divide.

As the composing power of the Ellington-Strayhorn partnership flourishes, Ellington grows emboldened in his intention to elevate Jazz on par with classical music's lofty status. It isn't long before the perfect opportunity manifests itself.

---

43    Irving Townsend, "Ellington in Private", *The Atlantic Monthly*, May 1975.

## HISTORICAL CONTEXT
### 1941-1944

The Ellington Orchestra is at the height of its popularity in the 1940's. NBC launches its first commercial television broadcast in 1941 on which Ellington and his elegantly-attired musicians appear and further transform the visual image of African Americans. That same year, the Japanese bomb Pearl Harbor. The United States enters World War II, and Jazz bands lose skilled musicians to the war effort. Gas and rubber rationing create a shortage of tires for civilian use which curtails big bands' touring schedules. And a shortage of shellac makes it difficult for bands to press new records.

Another blow to Big Bands comes in 1941, when the American Federation of Musicians bans its members from making recordings for commercial record companies over royalty disputes. The strike lasts two years (1942-1944) and remains the longest strike in entertainment history. It keeps the big bands off the air and their records off store shelves. This allows vocalists and crooners, who are still allowed to record during the strike, to gain greater prominence. Demand for bands decreases even further with the advent of the electrified microphone which enables singers to be backed up with smaller vocal and/or instrumental ensembles.

With male dance partners in short supply, Bebop begins to emerge with smaller groups of Jazz musicians exploring faster tempos and more complex music geared more toward listening. African American soldiers who serve in World War II do so in segregated units. After fighting for freedom abroad, these soldiers return home to the same pervasive discriminatory practices in private employment, housing, and city services. The resulting tensions and frustrations are exacerbated by war-time shortages. After Ellington's barrier shattering performance at Carnegie Hall, riots break out in Harlem when a returning black soldier is shot while trying to intervene in the arrest of a black woman by a white police officer for disorderly conduct. Six people are killed, hundreds injured and 600 arrested by 7,500 white officers. Volunteers are called in to restore order with 8,000 additional guardsmen ordered on standby.[44]

---

44    "1943 HARLEM RIOT KILLED 5, HURT 500; It Began When a Policeman Shot a Negro Soldier," *The New York Times,* July 19, 1964, p. 54.

## CHAPTER 2
# BLACK, BROWN & BEIGE

---

*"Art is dangerous. It is one of the attractions:*
*when it ceases to be dangerous, you don't want it."*[45]
- Duke Ellington

We seem to be fascinated with enigmas, perhaps because they require greater energy to figure out. We are innately wired to quickly categorize people and things as either "safe" or "dangerous." We swiftly turn our attention away from those we deem familiar or "safe." But those who defy immediate categorization demand our continued attention and vigilant study.

This may explain why Duke Ellington and his composing partner Billy Strayhorn, two men of complementary and some may say comparable composing genius, receive such divergent receptions. Strayhorn, is focused, sensitive, supportive, nurturing, emotive and safe; in contrast,

---

45    Victor Cooper and Rodney Franks. "Stories of Standards: 'Rain Check' by Billy Strayhorn." *Jazz With Victor Cooper*, episode Stories of Standards: "Rain Check" by Billy Strayhorn, Public Radio, 2019, https://www.kuvo.org/stories-of-standards-rain-check-by-billy-strayhorn/.

Duke presents as inwardly focused, mysterious, elusive, unpredictable, challenging the status quo, beyond easy categorization, fascinating and just possibly dangerous. Someone upon whom to keep a watchful eye.

Until the mid-1930's, American concert halls are almost the exclusive domain of classical European music written by classically trained, (white) European composers for the enjoyment of predominantly white audiences. And in the few instances where the notes of Jazz infiltrate the rarified air of concert halls, the music, composed about African American experiences by black composers, is almost exclusively performed by white conductors and musicians.[46] The lacking magical ingredient that daring white patrons enthusiastically seek at Jazz venues like the *Cotton Club* is African American musicians being "allowed" to write and perform their own *audio*-biographical music. Authenticity! Something each of us is subliminally aware of, attracted to and soothed by; anything less creating an unsettling sense of dissonance.

Although Ellington has a long-standing interest in writing and presenting extended-length Jazz compositions, the doors to Carnegie Hall swing open to him in large part due to the tireless efforts of American bandleader and composer Paul Whiteman, who is an ardent advocate of symphonic-length Jazz compositions.[47]

"Don't let them kid you about Whiteman," Ellington is quoted as saying in 1943. "He has been a big man in our music. He's done a lot for it, especially with his concerts where he gave composers a chance to write new, extended works."[48]

---

46    Early Jazz was first heard at Carnegie Hall in 1912 as part of an exhibition of African American music performed by James Reese Europe's (all black) Clef Club Orchestra. 26 more years ticked by before the Benny Goodman Orchestra, the first integrated Jazz band led by a white conductor, headlined a concert at Carnegie Hall in 1938. It was considered "Jazz's coming out party to the world of "respectable" music" by critic Bruce Eder. In 1939, Louis Armstrong became the first featured black Jazz musician to grace the Carnegie stage, but four more years would pass before Duke Ellington and his orchestra were invited to perform.

47    He helped create a favorable climate for pieces like "Black, Brown and Beige" to emerge. This experimentation with Jazz and symphony, however, earned him criticism from Eddie Condon, leading figure and musician of the Chicago and New York Jazz scenes, for attempting to "make a lady" out of Jazz.

48    Mark Tucker, "The Genesis of Black, Brown and Beige," *Black Music Research Journal* 22, supplement: Best of BMRJ (2002): 84, https://doi.org/10.2307/1519946.

And yet, in 1943, at the height of Ellington's career, it is still a shock when the bastions of classical music open their doors and allow him to conduct his own musicians in an original composition; not for the night-clubs this time, but for the concert hall. And not just any hall, but Carnegie, the pinnacle of American concert halls in the heart of New York City. It is uncharted territory. But instead of treading carefully, Ellington takes a calculated risk. He commits himself to write a 47-minute, extended-length Jazz composition, a remarkable departure from his familiar and highly successful two or three-minute Jazz recordings. He tempts fate even further with the subject matter for his magnum opus: the history, struggles and acculturation of African Americans.

In writing *Black, Brown and Beige*, Ellington endeavors to create a Jazz composition as sweeping as any classical work, with the following bold statement: "unhampered by any musical form, in which I intend to portray the experiences of the colored races in America in the syncopated idiom... I am putting all I have learned into it in the hope that I shall have achieved something really worthwhile in the literature of music, and that an authentic record of my race written by a member of it shall be placed on record."[49]

The concert is set for January 23, 1943. But in true Ellington fashion, he does not begin composing in earnest until just six weeks prior to the performance. "Without a deadline, baby," Ellington is known to have said, "I wouldn't get nothing done!" Although Ellington writes the bulk of his composition in less than two months, his conceptual exploration stretches back to the early 1930's from *Boola*, the opera he worked on, but never realized. In it, Ellington endeavored to tell "the story of the Negro people, [tracing] the history of this great nation from its beginning here through chattel slavery, reconstruction to the present."[50]

49    Duke Ellington, "The Duke Steps Out," *Rhythm*, Britain, March 20-22, 1931, collected in *The Duke Ellington Reader*, ed. Mark Tucker (New York, 1993), pp. 72-73.

50    Mark Tucker, "The Genesis of "Black, Brown and Beige". Black Music Research Journal (2002): Accessed September 6, 2021. doi:10.2307/1519946.

The thirty-nine-page typescript for the opera entitled *Boola*, (written in verse-narrative form and currently residing in the Ellington collection at the Smithsonian Institution in Washington, DC), tells the story of an African named *Boola*: his arrival in the New World on a slave ship, his servitude, his search for solace in the Bible, his emancipation and his contributions to Black-American history. The spirit of Boola, the symbolic representation of Ellington's own race, "… is the name Negro historians use to symbolize their race," explains Ellington. "If they want to tell you that Negroes took part in this or that event, they say 'Boola' was there."

A decade later in 1943, this operatic narrative evolves into the thematic genesis for Ellington's magnum opus *Black, Brown and Beige*. He utilizes and expands on *Boola's* inspiring theme to compose a deeply felt tone poem entitled *Black, Brown and Beige*, through which he endeavors to tell the history of African Americans in three distinct phases:

**BLACK** - The arrival of slaves to the New World and the plantation experience (Negro Work Songs & Spirituals)

**BROWN** - The American/Caribbean slave experience, the Emancipation Proclamation and the Great Depression (Blues/Downheartedness/Lost Romantic Love)

**BEIGE** -The Harlem Renaissance in the 1920's - a time of great optimism (Swing/Big Band)

Even the ideas for several of its song titles such as *Come Sunday, The West Indian Dance, The Emancipation Celebration* and *The Blues* wiggle their way out of *Boola's* narrative and into *Black, Brown and Beige*. The composition adds contextual dimension and Ellington's own musical voice to the themes of racial pride and the dreams of equality similarly being explored by singers (Marian Anderson, Louis Armstrong, Billie

Holiday, Fats Waller, J. Rosamond Johnson); artists (Aaron Douglas, Lois Mailou Jones); poets (Georgia Douglas Johnson, Langston Hughes, Alice Dunbar, Countee Cullen); writers (Zora Neale Hurtson, Claude McKay, Hallie Quinn, James Weldon Johnson) and journalists (Alice Dunbar-Nelson, W.E.B. Dubois, Augusta Savage). These individuals are the pioneering vanguard of the literary Harlem Renaissance, and Ellington becomes its musical exponent.

Ellington completes the first draft of *Black, Brown* and *Beige* on January 16, 1943, just in time for a week of concentrated rehearsals at New York's Nola Studios on Broadway between 51st and 52nd streets. On Friday, January 22, the night before the Carnegie appearance, the Ellington Orchestra puts on a dress rehearsal/concert in the nearby Rye High School auditorium. It is the first time band members are able to perform the score uninterrupted from beginning to end , and the first time for Ellington to hear it in its entirety. Corrections are made, parts are massaged or eliminated entirely, and it is likely that none of the participants in this high stakes drama sleep in the twenty-four hours preceding its New York premiere.

*Duke Ellington and the Ellington Orchestra at Carnegie Hall for the premiere of "Black, Brown and Beige" (1943)*

The following night Carnegie Hall brims to capacity, drawn by the caché of the Ellington Orchestra and its reputation for swinging entertainment. "The audience itself, described in the press as 'black, brown, and beige'—hardly the usual Carnegie crowd—included Eleanor Roosevelt, Leopold Stokowski,[51] Count Basie, and Frank Sinatra, all waiting for the revelation of a truly uniting, truly

51   A leading conductor from the early and mid-20th century, Stokowski was best known for his association with the Philadelphia Orchestra and an appearance in Disney's *Fantasia*. He conducted free hand instead of utilizing the traditional baton, and obtained what became a characteristically opulent sound from his orchestras.

American music."[52] Overflow audience members are seated on stage on both sides of the band.

When the curtain goes up at 8:45 p.m., the tuxedoed Ellington Orchestra, adhering to classical protocol, sits uncharacteristically silent on stage anticipating their Maestro's entrance. The applause is uproarious as the charismatic and impeccably-attired Ellington strides to center stage, forgetting his music in the process, to nervously address his audience.

> "And now, friends," begins the maestro, "uh, our latest a-attempt… probably our most serious attempt, and definitely our longest compo… composition. However, in mentioning the length of *Black, Brown and Beige*, we would like to say that this is a parallel to the history of the American Negro, and of course it, it… tells a long story. And I hope you will take into consideration the fact that in telling the… the… story of the *Work Song* for instance, which is the first theme, we use it in its many forms. For instance, you know… uh… the *Work Song* is sung while you *work*. Of course there is a place for the song, and there's a place for *grunting*… you know, and… uh… the impact of your work. And of course, after that comes the… the *Spiritual Theme* which is the second theme of the first movement."[53]

With the uncharacteristically scattered formalities concluded, Ellington takes a deep breath and steps into his familiar conducting role. For every musician on stage, including Ellington, it is a barrier-busting test of nerves, music, social acceptance, and human worth. It is, in fact,

---

52    Claudia R. Pierpont, "Black, Brown, And Beige Duke Ellington's Music and Race in America." *The New Yorker*, 17 May 2010.

53    *Duke Ellington & His Orchestra- Live At Carnegie Hall - January 23, 1943 (Full Concert)*, Youtube video, 2:14:28, posted by "Jazz Time with Jarvis X," November 18, 2017, https://www.youtube.com/watch?v=WxqZNeMGUxg.

uncharted territory for every person in the hall, performers and audience alike, and there is a frisson of nervous energy in the air.

And so, on the evening of January 23, 1943, and perhaps without full comprehension of the significance of the moment, the audience at Carnegie Hall witnesses standing before them a 43-year-old African American composer and conductor whose ancestors struggled under slavery, whose grandparents lived under the Jim Crow laws of the rural South and whose parents worked in service positions. They hear an extended composition about the history of African Americans written for the first time from an American Negro's perspective and told in the musical vernacular uniquely created by them. It is "unlikely that any other musical début carried such hope of repairing divisions: between Jazz and classical, between black and white."[54]

"I wrote it [*Black, Brown and Beige*]," explains Ellington, "because I want to rescue Negro music from its well-meaning friends... All arrangements of historic American Negro music have been made by conservatory-trained musicians who inevitably handle it with a European technique. It's time a big piece of music was written from the inside by a Negro."[55]

Once again, Ellington lets his music speak his deepest thoughts, believing he will achieve greater effect through the beauty of music than harsh rhetoric.

"Music is a piece of art that goes into the ears and straight to the heart," Ellington once says, summing up his approach.

As the Ellington Orchestra performs the physical and emotional history of African Americans, the composer himself offers a corporeal example of his people's progress: elegant, accomplished and successful. "By using his Carnegie debut to celebrate African-American

54    Claudia R. Pierpont, "Black, Brown, And Beige: Duke Ellington's Music and Race in America." *The New Yorker*, 17 May 2010.

55    Mark Tucker, "The Genesis of "Black, Brown and Beige"." *Black Music Research Journal* 22 (2002): 131-50. Accessed September 6, 2021. doi:10.2307/1519946, pp. 75-76.

achievement with a work of heroic proportions and bold ambition, Ellington wrote himself into the script, assuming the lead role of *Boola* in the grand historical pageant *Black, Brown and Beige.*"[56]

The performance creates a paradigm shift that catches its audience, and America, unaware. Patrons are confused by the juxtaposition of Ellington and a Jazz concerto being performed in a concert hall. Critics mistakenly evaluate Ellington's complex composition by classical European musical standards after only one hearing, and regard the music as imprecise, choppy and disjointed, confusion that is understandable given the improvised freedom of Jazz versus the controlled precision of classical music. The fact is that classical music generally emphasizes the first beat of each measure, while Jazz emphasizes the second and handles rhythm more flexibly (the swing effect). The vast difference is in instrumentation, with Jazz relying heavily on brass (particularly saxophones which are rarely used by classical composers), the "plucking" versus bowing of the upright bass and the use of slurred and "dirty" sounds that create tonal colors distinct from those heard in classical music.[57]

Ellington intentionally selects music familiar to his audience for the first half, setting the stage for the debut of his revelatory *magnum opus* before closing out the concert with more of his familiar hits. But as his premiere of *Black, Brown and Beige* begins, it is like the slow release of air from a glossy, overfilled balloon that even Ellington, the master of reading and controlling the moods of his audiences, cannot affect. Ellington's daring performance is rewarded with something to which the composer is wholly unaccustomed – thunderous, yet confused applause. After a nearly three-hour performance, Ellington's intellectually, emotionally, and physically fatigued listeners flee the concert hall just minutes before

---

56   Tucker, *Ibid.*

57   Carl Harper, "The Difference Between Classical and Jazz Music," *Our Pastimes*, updated September 15, 2017, https://ourpastimes.com/the-difference-between-classical-and-Jazz-music-12320058.html.

midnight, not knowing what to think about the pioneering *Black, Brown and Beige* sandwiched between Ellington's familiar hits.[58]

## THE CARNEGIE HALL CONCERT

Recorded January 1943 is a live album by Duke Ellington recorded at Carnegie Hall in New York City in 1943, but not released on the Prestige label in 1977.[59] All compositions and arrangements are by Ellington except as indicated below.

1. "The Star Spangled Banner" (Francis Scott Key, John Stafford Smith) - 1:12
2. "Black and Tan Fantasy" (Ellington, James "Bubber" Miley) - 6:35
3. "Rockin' in Rhythm" (Harry Carney, Ellington, Irving Mills) - 4:12
4. "Moon Mist" - 3:38
5. "Jumpin' Punkins" - 3:24
6. "A Portrait of Bert Williams" - 2:56
7. "Bojangles" - 3:17
8. "Portrait of Florence Mills (Black Beauty)" - 3:40
9. "Ko-Ko" - 2:23
10. "Dirge" (Billy Strayhorn) - 3:28
11. "Stomp" (Johnny Come Lately)" (Strayhorn) - 2:59
12. "Are You Sticking?" - 3:13
13. **"BLACK"** [First Movement of "Black, Brown and Beige"] - **21:52**[60]

---

58 The premiere of *Black, Brown and Beige* was preceded by a trio of original Ellington "new musical portraits of the historic black performers Bert Williams, Bill (Bojangles) Robinson, and Florence Mills; even the brassy instrumental "Ko-Ko," of 1940, was, Ellington told the audience, meant to portray the square in New Orleans where slaves had once come together to dance—the place where Jazz was born. Everything was designed to set off *Black, Brown and Beige*, a three-movement composition, some forty-five minutes long, that had been advertised as 'Duke Ellington's first symphony'." Pierpont, "Black, Brown, and Beige: Duke Ellington's music and race in America."

59 Description and track listing found at https://en.wikipedia.org/wiki/The_Carnegie_Hall_Concerts:_January_1943.

60 Actual tracking List for *Black, Brown and Beige* itself: *Work Song, Come Sunday, Light, West Indian Dance, Emancipation Celebration, Blues Theme Mauve* and *Sugar Hill Penthouse*.

14. **"BROWN"** [Second Movement of "Black Brown and Beige"] - **11:49**
15. **"BEIGE"** [Third Movement of "Black, Brown and Beige"] - **14:34**
16. "Bakiff" (Ellington, Juan Tizol) - 6:36
17. "Jack the Bear" - 3:19
18. "Blue Belles of Harlem" - 6:09
19. "Cotton Tail" - 3:11
20. "Day Dream" (Ellington, John La Touche, Strayhorn) - 4:02
21. "Boy Meets Horn" (Ellington, Rex Stewart) - 5:58
22. "Rose of the Rio Grande" (Ross Gorman, Edgar Leslie, Harry Warren) - 2:33
23. "Don't Get Around Much Anymore" (Ellington, Bob Russell) - 4:39
24. "Going Up" - 3:56
25. "Mood Indigo" (Barney Bigard, Ellington, Mills) - 4:38

According to American music expert Randall Keith Horton, *"[Black, Brown and Beige]* was an entirely new concept. No one had heard a programmatic, extended composition by an African American composer who was perceived as the greatest dance-band leader of his day but was nonetheless expected to stay in the performance milieu of night-clubs, theaters and the continuous retinue of "one-nighters." Neither his ardent Jazz fans nor establishment classical music critics were prepared for what they heard."[61]

The next morning, major music critics tear Ellington's *Black, Brown and Beige* apart faster than the ugly stepsisters shredded Cinderella's ball gown: "Judged as Jazz, the composition is deemed unrecognizable. Judged as classical music, it is found 'formless and meaningless,' a series of poorly connected parts that did not add up to a whole."[62] And in an

---

61   Randall Keith Horton, Stony Brook University, 2006.

62   Roth Pierpont, "Black, Brown and Beige: Duke Ellington's Music And Race In America", *New Yorker,* May 10, 201 0, https//www.newyorker.com/magazine/2010/05/17/black-brown-and-beige.

especially racially charged critique, one unidentified manager dismisses Ellington's extended-length composition as "worthless" and purportedly tells Ellington he should "get back to Nigger music."[63] Classical music critics weigh in:

### "Overreaching the limits of Jazz"
Jon Pareles, *The New York Times*[64]

### "...a series of poorly connected parts that did not add up to a whole"
and
### "...A gaudy potpourri of tutti dance passages and solo virtuoso work."
Paul Bowles, *New York Herald-Tribune*[65]

### "Such a form of composition is entirely out of Mr. Ellington's ken"
Douglas Watt, *New York Daily News*[66]

### "Mr. Ellington had set for himself a lofty goal, and with the best of intentions, did not achieve it"
John Briggs, *New York Post*[67]

---

63  Graham Lock, "Blutopia: Visions of the Future and Revision of the Past in the Work of Sun Ra, Duke Ellington, and Anthony Braxton," Duke University Press, 1999, p. 120.

64  Jon Pareles, "Review/Jazz; Re-Creating Ellington Debut At Carnegie Hall in 1943." *New York Times*, 12 July 1989, p. 14, www.nytimes.com/1989/07/12/arts/review-jazz-re-creating-ellington-debut-at-carnegie-hall-in-1943.html. Rock critic and part time Jazz critic.

65  Paul Bowles, "Duke Ellington in Recital for Russian War Relief," *New York Herald-Tribune*, January 25, 1943.

66  Douglas Watt, "The Duke has hot concert at Carnegie," *New York Daily News*, 1943.

67  John Briggs, "The low-down on Duke's concert," *New York Post*, 1943.

### "Far from being an *in toto* symphonic creation"
Robert Bagar, *New York World-Telegram*[68]

### "Discordant, inchoate and substantively empty music"
Gunther Schuller, 1989 specifically about *Beige*[69]

The African American press celebrates the spectacle and social importance of the concert even though they feel Ellington has strayed from the essence of Jazz's musical roots. Critiques of Ellington's actual music are limited in the few African American publications that exist whose reporters lack the technical training to judge it by prevailing classical European music standards.

### "...dripping in mink, silver fox and such."
(describing patrons)

and

### "Negroes don't suffer when they are publicly represented by such obvious class, poise, dignity and assurance as Duke Ellington tonight."
Dan Burley, *The New York Amsterdam News*[70]

### A "Happy Anniversary" in which Ellington "Scores" in this Carnegie Hall debut," (continuing...)

---

68    Robert Bagar, "Duke marks 20th year as musician," *New York World-Telegram*, January 25, 1943.

69    Andrew Homzy, "Black, Brown and Beige" in Duke Ellington's Repertoire, 1943-1973," Black Music Research Journal, no. 2 (1993): 87-110. Accessed September 4, 2021. doi:10.2307/779514, p. 104.

70    Scott DeVeaux, "Black, Brown And Beige And The Critics." Black Music Research Journal, vol. 13, no. 2, 1993, pp. 125–146. Autum, doi:https://doi.org/10.2307/779516. *New York Amsterdam News*, one of the oldest African-American newspapers in the United States, is a weekly newspaper catering to the African-American community of New York City.

**"Jitterbugs and Millionaires Rub Elbows to Hear Classical Concert...", "...Duke Ellington held court and earned spectacular acclaim...", "Without a doubt the greatest triumph of the significant evening was...Duke's amazingly intimate work, 'Black, Brown and Beige'."**

Alfred A. Duckett, *The Afro-American* (Baltimore. 30 January 1943)

**"Duke Kills Carnegie Cats!, 'Tone Parallel', Famed Soloists Slick, Click: Carnegie Kicked"**

*Metronome Magazine*[71]

(followed by the editorial "Reactionary Reviewers" that labeled classical critics as "condescending" and "stupid")

**"Impeccable in full-dress attire, the Duke and his musicians... stood to acknowledge the tremendous wave of tribute which swept the rafters of Carnegie."**

*Washington Afro-American*[72]

The critical reviews from the predominantly white press are a devastating rejection for Ellington, though likely an anticipated possibility, including Bowles' conclusion that "The whole attempt to fuse Jazz as a form with art music should be discouraged." According to Horton, "Bowles' comments exemplified the Euro-centric denial of the validity of the African American experience as being an integral component of American musical/cultural life."[73]

Although newspaper deadlines demand next-day content, few if

---

71    "Duke Kills Carnegie Cats!" 1943 Metronome 59 No. 2 (February): 5-7. Metronome (1881-1961) was a music magazine that focused on Jazz music, catering to musicians in marching and dance bands from the swing era.

72    Harvey Cohen, et al. "Black, Brown And Beige." *Duke Ellington's America* , edited by Harvey Cohen, Chicago Press, 2011, p. 229.

73    Randall Keith Horton, "The Performance/Recording and Critical History of Duke Ellington's "Black, Brown and Beige": An Overview, 2006, p. 5.

any critics are equipped to assess a composition as innovative and sweeping as Ellington's *Black, Brown and Beige* after only one hearing.[74] But there is one rare critic who takes a more informed approach. Mike Levin from *Down Beat*, following the sage advice of his boss to "never pan a band until you've heard them at least four times," learns of a rare, private recording of the premiere made by Ellington's manager Danny Jones. He tracks Jones down, convinces him to let him listen to the recorded concert not four, but *six* complete times before he writes his review. He concludes that Ellington is particularly wronged by critics who judge him on one, *not-too-good* hearing—most of the critics not even being familiar with the Ellington Orchestra or its previous works. "Like it or not," Jones writes, "this looks like not only a fusion of the American classical and Jazz traditions, but also the first road without a dead-end close by. It would be a tragedy to drown it in one-nighters and theater dates."[75]

Alas, anyone else hoping for a second listening of Ellington's innovative *opus* at Carnegie Hall will have to wait another thirty-four years before even a partial recording is made commercially available to the public through Prestige records (1977).[76] [77]

Yet, aside from Levin's informed review, the enigmatic Ellington, who has shattered innumerable racial, cultural and musical barriers, fails

---

74    Andrew Homzy, "Black, Brown And Beige In Ellington's Repertoire." *Black Music Research Journal*, vol. 13, no. 2, 1993, pp. 87–110. *Autumn*, doi:https://doi.org/10.2307/779514.

75    Mark Tucker, *The Duke Ellington Reader*, Oxford University Press, 1991, 170.

76    "The 1943 premiere performance was not recorded by RCA Victor, Ellington's recording company. Using the technology available at that time, a forty-five minute work would have required ten 10-inch discs or seven 12-inch discs; only classical music was commonly issued in such multi-disc albums. Fortunately, Carnegie Hall staff technicians made a private recording on 78 rpm acetate discs, bootleg copies of which circulated among collectors. Finally in 1977, Prestige brought out on LP the complete Carnegie Hall concert of January, 1943, which at last gave the public access to the music. Too many of Ellington's masterpieces have shared a similar fate. Let us hope there will be no such circumstances to report when we celebrate Ellington's bicentennial." Richard Wang, "Black, Brown & Beige," Jazz Journalists Association Library, 1999, http://www.Jazzhouse. org/library/?read=wang1.

77    Andrew Homzy, "Black, Brown And Beige In Ellington's Repertoire." *Black Music Research Journal*, vol. 13, no. 2, 1993, pp. 87–110. *Autumn*, doi:https://doi.org/10.2307/779514. "But issuing a forty-five-minute composition by a Jazz and dance band leader in 1944 may have been deemed commercially unfeasible. As it was, Ellington recorded more than eighteen minutes of excerpts from *Black, Brown and Beige* (on both sides of two twelve-inch 78 rpm discs) with a well-rehearsed band."

to receive acceptance or even appreciation for his most ambitious and introspective music to date. It is a pioneering moment in musical history that is viewed as threatening, perhaps even dangerous, presaging changes to come in the cultural fabric of America. In the biographical book *Duke Ellington's America*, published sixty-seven years later in 2010, author and historian Harvey G. Cohen lends his more informed voice to Levin's, insisting that *"Black, Brown and Beige* should not be judged by pre-existing standards —that its abrupt musical transitions are not a shortcoming but a choice—and that the composer achieved exactly what he intended."[78] Cohen goes on to defend Ellington against critics and historians who ignore the nonverbal communication behind the band and music that transform Ellington into a surreptitious race leader. The American Jazz bassist, composer, arranger, and six-time Grammy winner Christian McBride[79] gives us an even more modern take in 2019.

> First of all, you have an African-American bandleader and composer playing a piece about the history of the American Negro in 1943 at Carnegie Hall. That alone might get you a couple of bad reviews before you even play a note. I think there were a lot of critics who sort of deemed themselves experts on fine music, you know, classical music. So when you have this African-American composer using timpani *[sic]*, violins[80], but mixing it with swing rhythms, African rhythms, I'm sure a lot of reviewers had no idea what they were listening to. How do you write about something you don't know about?[81]

---

78    Claudia Roth Pierpont, "Black, Brown and Beige: Duke Ellington's Music And Race In America", *New Yorker,* May 10, 2010, https//www.newyorker.com/magazine/2010/05/17/black-brown-and-beige.

79    Christian McBride (1972) is an American Jazz bassist, composer, arranger, historian and six-time Grammy winner.

80    Point of clarification: Ellington's original *Black, Brown and Beige* does not include timpani or violins.

81    Christian McBride, "A Sprawling Blueprint for Protest Music, Courtesy of The Jazz Duke," interview by Audie Cornish, *American Anthem*, NPR, February 22, 2019, https://www.npr.org/transcripts/697075534.

"Syncopation lay at the heart of disapproving reviews on both sides," explains Horton. "Jazz purists insisted on syncopation as the defining criteria for identifying Jazz in its "authentic" musical milieu (clubs, dance halls, and so on). Classical purists insisted that such syncopation could never enter into the canon of through-composed western art music which in my view encapsulates the deep-seated assertion that the Negro must "stay in his place."[82]

In the week following the Carnegie debut, the Ellington Orchestra painfully presents two more previously scheduled performances of *Black, Brown and Beige* in Boston and Cleveland.[83] The audiences' and critics' responses mirror those from the New York premiere. It is a bitter pill for Ellington to swallow, and it is likely that he already knows he will never perform *Black, Brown and Beige* again in its entirety. Critics (and perhaps even America itself) are not ready for the Negroid characterizations exemplified in Ellington's music.[84]

Looking back in 2006, Horton provides the following insight. "A survival instinct necessitated the composer's decision to withdraw the work. Ellington's response revealed a direct relationship between his standing as an artist in American society and his competitive posture as a popular musician/bandleader whose work required commercial success. He could either enter into scraps and unfruitful debates with his detractors, risking his posture in international circles of high art, or continue to create at the highest possible artistic levels available to him and his orchestra."[85]

---

82    Randall Keith Horton, "The Performance/Recording and Critical History of Duke Ellington's "Black, Brown and Beige": An Overview, 2006, 5.

83    It is not clear if the Ellington Orchestra's performance of *Black, Brown and Beige* in Cleveland showcased the complete work despite an advertisement in the *Cleveland News* of Friday, February 19, 1943 which reads: "Tomorrow Eve. Public Auditorium.    Duke Ellington and his Famous Orchestra - Concert Program as Performed at Carnegie Hall, NY."

84    Randall Keith Horton, "A Single Beam of Light and its Transformation of my Life (Discourse from an Obscure Ellingtonian)" (unpublished manuscript, December 18, 2019).

85    Randall Keith Horton, "The Performance/Recording and Critical History of Duke Ellington's "Black, Brown and Beige": An Overview, 2006, 15.

It seems that truly pioneering ideas and art inevitably weather a period of being diminished before later being reevaluated and accorded their due. American writer Nelson Algren once observed that "if society denies someone their reality, then they'll structure their own reality." Which is precisely what Duke Ellington does. "He knows what league he is really competing in…. even when the critics and the impresarios and the managers denied it."[86] Ellington could have caved to the public's exclusive hunger for his familiar Jazz hits, but he has a more ambitious objective. As far back as 1930, Ellington is quoted as saying:

> I am not playing Jazz. I am trying to play the natural feelings of a people. I believe that music, popular music of the day, is the real reflector of the nation's feelings. Some of the music which has been written will always be beautiful and immortal. Beethoven, Wagner and Bach are geniuses; no one can rob their work of the merit that is due it, but these men have not portrayed the people who are about us today, and the interpretation of these people is our future music… The Negro is the blues. Blues is the rage in popular music. And popular music is the good music of tomorrow.[87]

But to later art critics like *Chicago Tribune* writer Howard Reich, there is a more ominous undercurrent influencing the rejection of *Black, Brown and Beige*. In his April 4, 1999 article *The Unknow[n] Ellington*, he writes,

> Yet the work never caught on with most critics or the public, and one reason is more disturbing than either the frayed state of the scores or the undeniable complexity of the

86    Ralph J. Gleason, "Farewell to the Duke," in *Music in the Air: Selected Writings of Ralph J. Gleason*, ed. Toby Gleason, Yale University Press, 2016.

87    Florence Zunser, "Opera Must Die, Says Galli-Curci! Long Live the Blues!," *New York Evening Graphic Magazine*, December 27, 1930, reprinted in *The Duke Ellington Reader*, ed. Mark Tucker, p. 45.

music... 'There's a racist position at work here among many people who dismiss this music,' adds William Russo (1999), whose Chicago Jazz Ensemble has been in the forefront of playing Ellington's large works.

Their position is that Jazz (essentially a black musical form) has to be entertaining and adorable. But this music isn't entertaining and adorable. It's profound music in the sense that Beethoven and Brahms wrote profound music. Its longer forms; it makes a bigger statement. Many people think Jazz is not supposed to do that, which is unfortunate. The anti-intellectualism in Jazz is staggering.[88]

And the same year (1999), poet Sterling Plumpp[89] chimes in on Ellington as a cultural icon, saying "Like [writer] Langston Hughes, Ellington found a great deal of vitality and inspiration in urbanity and city life, in the movement of African-Americans from the rural South to the big Northern cities. Ellington gave the highest form of expression to that movement."[90]

Missing from all of the reviews of *Black, Brown, and Beige* is any mention of the effort and risk Ellington takes, using his popularity to transform attitudes about race in America. "Based on estimates of record sales, as well as his concert touring, radio exposure, and sheet music sales, Duke Ellington is arguably the most popular African American musician between 1927 and 1943. His ability to use this popularity to gain a

---

88   Howard Reich, "The Unknow[n] Ellington," *Chicago Tribune*, April 4, 1999, https://www.chicagotribune.com/news/ct-xpm-1999-04-04-9904040144-story.html.

89   Sterling Dominic Plumpp is an American poet, educator, editor, critic, and author of several books.

90   Reich, *Ibid.*

high-profile booking at Carnegie Hall is an achievement that, by itself, has an effect on how African Americans are perceived"[91] and treated.

"I want to break away from European tradition," Ellington is quoted as saying in a 1934 *Hollywood News* article. And one year later in a *Portland Oregonian* interview he adds, "you can't stay in the European conservatory and play the Negro music... Negro music is what we are working on. Not as a component of Jazz, but as a definite unadulterated musical entity."

Ellington clearly feels he is establishing a new tradition for African American music and American music in general.

The critic who seems to best understand the pivotal significance of Ellington's *Black, Brown and Beige* is Nina Naguid, who writes the following in the *Chicago Musical Leader* magazine in her February 1943 article:

> There's a new word needed in the English language, it's a word to describe the kind of music played by Duke Ellington. Anyone familiar with it will recognize it instantly just as one does Bach or Beethoven, yet one can't apply the same standards to it that are applied to art music because Ellington writes in no established form.

Enjoying the advantage of her monthly magazine's longer deadlines, she goes on to comment on the newspaper reviews that immediately followed the music's Carnegie premiere.

> ... most of the New York reviewers concerned themselves with [*Black, Brown and Beige*]. Because it lasts 48:15 minutes, they fell into the error of thinking it had to be judged

---

91   Garth Alper, "Black, Brown, and Beige: One Piece of Duke Ellington's Musical and Social Legacy," *College Music Symposium* 51, 2011, https://symposium.music.org/index.php/51/item/16-black-brown-and-beige-one-piece-of-duke-ellingtons-musical-and-social-legacy.

according to formalistic rules. Apart from its rondo-like[92] Third movement, the work follows no definite pattern, and judged by established rules of technic [sic], it is diffuse and aimless. However, it is programmatic, and for sheer wealth of ideas, melodic and rhythmic ingenuity and creativeness, the work is an artistic phenomenon.... *Black, Brown and Beige* is the beginning of a new American music which has its roots right here and cannot be judged from European standards of composition. Its historical and sociological backgrounds put it into the category of "heart" music, or folk music if you will, and out of the super-sophisticated, intellectualized realm of art music. [93]

In other words, at least in Naguid's mind, Ellington writes music that reflects uniquely American experiences and values that are a welcome contrast to European music which some say stresses technique over feeling. Ellington is "prescient in his prediction that the blues will define the future of popular music: Rhythm and Blues, Rock and Roll, Jazz, Country/Western, Rap, and other forms of blues-influenced music." And the integration of Blues lays the groundwork for greater "racial integration and tolerance" in America. "Ellington plays an essential part in linking and advancing both of these ongoing phenomena."[94]

In the ensuing weeks, months and years, Ellington does his best to prevent *Black, Brown and Beige* from slipping into oblivion. He revisits the music throughout his career, breaking the whole into shorter excerpts and playing them between more familiar hits with the hope of making the music more palatable through repetition and familiarity.

"What I'm trying to do with my band is to win people over to my

---

92    Music scholars may disagree with Ms. Naguid's assessment of BBB as "Rondo-like".

93    Nina Naguid, "Ellington in a Class by Himself," *Chicago Music Leader* (magazine), February, 15 1943.

94    *Ibid.*

bigger composing idea," says Ellington. "That's why I pared down *BB* and *B*. You gotta make 'em listen first, listen to things like *Don't Get Around Much Anymore* and *Do Nothin' (Til You Hear from Me)*. Then, when they've heard that, maybe they'll… listen to the longer and more ambitious works and maybe even enjoy them."[95]

Ellington walks the same swaying tightrope experienced by many musicians and artists: the unforgiving, prickly lifeline between writing commercially successful music, or music that is forward-leaning and personally meaningful. It is a high wire act upon which one wrong move can prove career ending. Ellington risks his popularity and career to perform *Black, Brown and Beige* at Carnegie Hall. And although it is labeled a failure by most critics, his bold actions succeed on a far bigger stage by shifting the ways African Americans and Jazz are perceived. "By focusing on the subject of black history, dressing like a classical conductor and confidently asserting his orchestra's and Jazz's worthiness to cross yet another arbitrary barrier (and achieving it), he once again elevates the cultural standing of his race, Jazz music and the way black Americans [are] portrayed in the mass media."[96]

Ellington's career survives. And while his hopes for racial and classical parity languish against the fearsome tide of rejection, Ellington simply moves on. "There are two kinds of worries," Ellington advises, "those you can do something about and those you can't. Don't spend any time on the latter."

Ellington's popularity as a nightclub performer and songwriter unfortunately mean that his more serious pieces of music never receive their due. Instead of letting this get him down, he continues to astound audiences with his charming elegance and melodies while writing important music behind the scenes. He calls it *"Skillapooping"* and

---

95    Barry Ulanov, *Duke Ellington* (New York: De Capo Press, 1975), 274-275.

96    Harvey G. Cohen, "Duke Ellington and "Black, Brown and Beige": The Composer as Historian at Carnegie Hall," *American Quarterly* 56, no. 4 (December 2004): 1004, https://www. jstor.org/stable/40068293.

defines it as "the art of making what you're doing better than what you're supposed to be doing."[97]

It is said that people rise to the level of their incompetence, but for Ellington and so many other talented visionaries, it is perhaps more appropriately restated that people rise to the level of society's incompetence. Ellington's foray into extended-length compositions performed in venues traditionally reserved for the classical elite results in sharp rebukes to stay in his lane, the lane in which society is comfortable seeing him and other black composers/musicians, namely Jazz establishments such as bars and supper clubs. And for heaven's sake, don't waste any more of our time, attempting to write music that is beyond your (a black man's) reach and won't fit on a LP (78 RPM) record. How frustrating it must have been!

The trouble with being a pioneer is that you have to wait for the world to catch up to you, and often it doesn't happen in your lifetime. Ellington experiences the sorry province of many innovators, of somehow being plucked from the distant future and sent back in time to enlighten the world around them. With *Black, Brown and Beige*, the Maestro attempts something so unfamiliar and disquieting to his American audiences and critics, which they not only reject but also effectively seal the threatening *oeuvre*, its important messages and Ellington's watershed genius in a soundproof vault, throwing away the key, so the world will never be disquieted by it again. Or so they think.

Little do they know, at the very moments of Ellington's Carnegie Hall and Boston Symphony Hall concerts, an infant is growing up just a stone's throw from Boston Symphony Hall who will eventually stoke the smoldering embers of *Black, Brown and Beige* until they are reignited in the hearts and minds of a more progressive world.

---

97    Bill Gutman. "Praise God And Dance." *Duke: The Musical Life Of Duke Ellington*, Open Road Integrated Media, 1977, p. 11.

# HISTORICAL CONTEXT
## 1945-1950

By 1945, America's post World War II popular music welcomes returning soldiers and attempts to rekindle relationships and soothe the psychological trauma of war with romantic music sung by popular Crooners. Saxophonist Charlie Parker continues to lead the charge for Bebop, and though big bands still enjoy popularity, most do not survive the lean wartime years. Others carve out a living doing limited tours in more appreciative and lucrative European cities. Some Jazz musicians like Sidney Bechet (1920's), Dexter Gordon (1962-1976) and Johnny Griffin (1980's) actually move abroad to take advantage of Europe's more accepting environment. From their overseas vantage point, America's growing racial issues stand in sharp relief.[98]

In 1946, President Truman's Committee on Civil Rights pushes for greater racial equality and change. Truman desegregates the United States armed forces by Executive Order in 1948. Two years later, the Korean War begins, and the Ellington Orchestra makes a second tour of Europe through France, Belgium, Holland, Switzerland, Italy, Denmark, Sweden and West Germany.

Doo-Wop vocal groups singing multi-part harmonies rise in popularity, evolving from the African-American vocal groups of the 1930's and 40s (Ink Spots, Mills Brothers and later, vocal acts such as the Orioles, the Ravens and the Clovers) with saxophonist/singer Louis Jordan providing the musical pivot between late 1940's Big Bands/BeBop to the early expressions of Rhythm and Blues[99] and Rock-n-Roll in the

---

98  Samuel G. Freedman, "The Blues of Expatriate Paris: Recalling America's Jazz Exiles," *New York Times*, section 2, October 12, 1986, 1, accessed via https://www.nytimes.com/1986/10/12/movies/the-blues-of-expatriate-paris-recalling-america-s-Jazz-exiles.html.

99  Rhythm and Blues incorporated traditional gospel influences with the energy of Jump Blues, an up-tempo style of blues usually played by small groups and featuring horn instruments.

1950's.[100] Louis Jordan becomes a seminal figure in the development of both Rhythm and Blues and Rock 'n' Roll.

The appeal of African-American music, deemed "race music" (often dance-oriented), is crossing over to a growing white youth audience. With vocalist-piano players Little Richard and Fats Domino leading the way, Rock 'n' Roll music gains popularity, which in turn encourages more interracial cooperation through shared experiences.[101] Large bands with orchestral accompaniment continue to give way to smaller combos featuring [guitars], piano, bass [and drums, often with a featured saxophone solo].[102] Rock 'n' Roll creates new vocalists with unique identities and styles (Elvis Presley, Jerry Lee Lewis, Chuck Barry, Pat Boone, and others) with hit songs that are performed almost like television skits.[103] With the expansion of TV and programs such as the Ed Sullivan Show (1948-1971), the physical appearance of the artist takes center stage, and the music begins to express emotions that people rarely talk about, awakening a new American youth culture.[104]

The abolition of slavery (1865) and The Great Migration (1916-1970) facilitate the merging of blacks and whites and African and European musical traditions with European instrumentation.[105] Rock 'n' Roll, originating in the South through the influences of Gospel, Jump Blues,

100   Louis Thomas Jordan (1908-1975) was prominent in the 1940's and '50s with an astonishing 57 R&B chart hits. He was also inducted into the Rock-n-Roll Hall of fame in 1987.

101   Michael T. Bertrand, *Race, Rock, and Elvis (Music in American Life)* (Champaign, IL: University of Illinois Press, 2004), 95-6.

102   Bogdanov, Woodstra, and Erlewine, *All Music Guide to Rock: The Definitive Guide to Rock, Pop, and Soul (3rd Edition)*, p. 1303.

103   Elijah Wald, *How the Beatles Destroyed Rock 'n' Roll* (Oxford: Oxford University Press, 2009), p. 162.

104   William J. Schafer, *Rock Music: Where It's Been, What It Means, Where It's Going* (Minneapolis: Augsburg Publishing House, 1972).

105   Michal T. Bertrand, "Race And Class In Southern Juxtaposition - The Forgotten Roots of a (Rock) Revolution." *Race, Rock and Elvis (Music In American Life)*, University of Illinois Press, 2000, pp. 21–22.

Jazz, Boogie Woogie and Rhythm & Blues[106] and country music[107] (all at least partially African American-influenced genres), spreads to the North, Midwest and West as a result of The Great Migration, with earlier Jazz and Swing paving the way. Exposure to the music is accelerated among white and black audiences through live performances, records, radio, and television, building toward a cultural and racial collision and America's Civil Rights Movement.

106   Albert Christ-Janer, Charles W. Hughes, and Carleton Sprague Smith, *American Hymns Old and New* (New York: Columbia University Press, 1980), p. 364.

107   Richard A. Peterson, *Creating Country Music: Fabricating Authenticity* (University of Chicago Press, 1999), p. 9.

## CHAPTER 3

# THE HORTON AIRSHAFT

---

*"Love is indescribable and unconditional.*
*I could tell you a thousand things that it is not,*
*but not one that it is.*
*Either you have it or you haven't.*
*There's no proof of it."*
- Duke Ellington

I didn't know Randall Keith Horton as an infant, adolescent, or young adult. I meet him as a 71-year-old, distinguished gentleman in the dining car of an Amtrak train in 2013 and piece together his contributions to Ellington's extended-length compositions over hundreds of hours of conversation. The facts of his life are relatively easy to verify. It takes a bit more digging to resolve the secondary riddles; to understand the motivating forces behind his behaviors, decisions, missteps and successes... and the improbable string of events that transform him into the world's leading expert on *Black, Brown and Beige* as well as Ellington's three, equally transcendent extended-length *Sacred Concerts*.

Like most people, Randall Keith Horton's life meanders like a river, carving out its own unique path, bending around obstacles and being alternately strengthened and weakened by controllable and uncontrollable forces. And like all natural bodies of water, Horton is imbued with the essences of the people, places and times through which his life flows, beginning with those of his childhood and family in Boston's South End/Roxbury and Dorchester neighborhoods in the 1940's, 1950's, and early 1960's.

Early personal traumas temporarily entangle him in a stereotypical maelstrom of racism. He grows up living a life in sharp contrast to Ellington's. He isn't pampered as a child. He isn't a celebrated musical genius, and although he embarks on a musical career at the age of 22 at the directive of his *calling* (1964), he doesn't fully discover his life's full musical purpose until he is in his mid-40's. Yet, he consistently shares four indelible traits with Duke Ellington: love of music, faith in a Higher Power, pride in his African American roots and a strong sense of loyalty and dedication to his *calling*. These are what inform and shape much of Horton's adult life, powering him along a musical odyssey that few could have predicted.

Duke Ellington and Horton are separated in age by 43 years. When Horton is born in Boston in 1942, Duke Ellington is already at the apex of his career and on the cusp of his Carnegie Hall premiere of *Black, Brown and Beige*. It will be another twenty-three years, before the trajectories of the two men's lives cross, let alone impact one another – time enough for Horton to overcome personal challenges of his own and hone his musical skills.

The South End of Boston where Horton spends most of his childhood is one of the city's many in-fill projects designed to relieve the congestion of Boston's urban center. Between 1849 and 1880, construction in the South End alone creates a 300-acre residential neighborhood of predominantly Victorian style town homes served by more than 200 parks. Although the neighborhood initially attracts middle class families, by the turn of the century, with new housing is available in Roxbury and the Back Bay, Boston's South End slowly transitions to a low-income tenement district. Single bedroom housing caters to Irish, Jewish, African American, Puerto Rican, Chinese, and Greek immigrants and later, in the 1940's, gay men. The railway connection between Boston and Albany, completed in 1841, delivers the highest concentration of Pullman Porters in the country. By 1913 Boston's South Station is the largest and busiest train station in the world, facilitating the city's rise as an epicenter for Jazz.

Randall Keith Horton and his twin sister Joyce are the first of four children born to Lloyd Trevor "Buster" Horton, Sr. and Helen (Taylor) Horton. His parents marry and settle in Boston's South End in the early 1940's and are shaped by a potent mix of urban, cultural, racial, and economic influences. They are richly steeped in the ideals of the Harlem Renaissance, a period between 1918-1930 when African Americans sought to escape racism and discrimination and elevate themselves through education, contributions to world culture and a sense of racial pride.

Randall's father Lloyd "Buster" Horton (born in 1912 to Lillian Horton) is an intelligent and ambitious young man living in the inner city with his single mother. When she is institutionalized after sustaining severe head trauma from a tragic fall from her third-floor tenement window, 13-year-old Buster is taken in as a foster child and raised by the neighboring Paige family who have two young children of their own, Beverly and Sonny. Buster Horton becomes particularly close with Sonny Paige and grows into a gregarious young man and a respected leader in his community. He enjoys singing in the community choir and earns a role in a Broadway production as a talented young actor and tap dancer. Like many African Americans of the time, his new family emphasizes the importance of bettering oneself through education. Buster sets his sights on becoming a lawyer and ultimately becomes one of Boston's (Suffolk County) Assistant District Attorneys.

Helen Taylor Horton is born into a close-knit family of seven in 1913 and later moves to Boston's South End from Washington DC as part of the Great Migration. Helen Horton attends the New England Conservatory of Music a short bus ride from her Boston home, plays piano and nurtures her promising career as a classically trained, lyric soprano.

Buster and Helen meet while in Boston and connect over their shared love of music and respect for education, achievement and family. Their dispositions, however, contrast sharply. Where Buster is laid back and social, Helen is precise, high strung and mercurial. Their opposing strengths are at first a welcome counterbalance to one another. The two begin courting while Buster is in law school, marry a year later in 1941 and settle into a small apartment on Ottawa Street in the Roxbury neighborhood. Times are lean as Buster swims against a steady stream of racial bias, attending law school at Suffolk University and Northeastern while working for the US Postal Service. Helen hones her singing skills at the New England Conservatory of Music. In 1942 Helen and Buster welcome twins, Randall and Joyce. A third child, Lloyd Trevor "Tim" Horton, Jr. arrives three years later (May 1945), necessitating the family's move to a slightly larger apartment at One Trotter[108] Court in the Lenox Street Housing Project in a nearby Roxbury neighborhood. With three young children to raise, Helen has little choice but to put her college aspirations on hold while still attempting to nurture her musical talents.

In addition to an emphasis on education, Randall and his two siblings are raised on a steady diet of faith and music, a joyous and reliable constant in their household. Records spin on the family Victrola,

---

108  Named in honor of William Monroe Trotter (1872 - 1934), an important civil rights leader and hero to many African American, including Horton's my parents.

Buster studies law and Helen practices her arias with her own expert piano accompaniment. They expose their children to a rich variety of music, from the Boston Symphony Orchestra and the Boston Pops, to opera, church music, big band, swing and Jazz. Rhythm and Blues also fills the Lenox Street neighborhood. Randall absorbs much of it simply by listening and imitating the most popular sounds of the day. In fact, between 1915 and 1970, while the country's top black musicians' union is headquartered in Boston,[109] the South End and Roxbury neighborhoods become a mecca for Jazz and a hub for black, middle-class life and culture. Jazz greats the likes of Duke Ellington, Cab Calloway, Chick Webb, Earl Hines, and Jimmie Lunceford perform regularly at the iconic clubs that line the streets: The Royal Palms, Eddie Levine's, the Pioneer Club, Handy's Grille, Tic-Toc, Connolly's, Estelle's, The Hi-Hat, The Savoy, The Cave, Basin Street, Louie's Lounge, and Wally's Paradise.

"Some of the greatest big bands and Jazz musicians of the time frequented the Boston area," recalls Horton. "Russell Procope, an alto saxophonist and clarinetist in the Ellington Orchestra, will tell me many years later that when performing in Boston, Duke Ellington and his musicians would jam and party with such Boston notables as Sabby Lewis and his big band.[110] And I learn much later in life that it wasn't uncommon for my father to share a drink or two with Johnny Hodges, another Ellington alto saxophonist who lived next door to Harry Carney, Ellington's alto/baritone saxophonist, personal driver and the longest tenured member of the Ellington Orchestra."

---

109 The American Federation of Musicians Local 535.
110 Sabby Lewis and His Orchestra.

# 1950's Vignette: Part I

*(A dramatized version of actual events)*

A young, well-dressed woman ushers her three young children quietly into Boston Symphony Hall. Helen Horton is enraptured by the symphonic music while her three young children sit attentively in their seats. At the sound of a brightly played brass segment, young Randall perks up and sits forward with interest. Helen smiles at her son, and the two enjoy a moment of shared excitement.

"You like that?" Randall's mother asks in a whisper. Five-year-old Randall nods his head enthusiastically without taking his eyes off of the musicians.

As the family exits Boston Symphony Hall after the performance, Helen is startled by the sight of her voice coach Professor Brown. She tries to avoid him at first, but he waves her down and introduces her to his wife, who already knows a great deal about Helen's exquisite voice. Professor Brown then bends down to shake hands with each of the Horton children, asking them if they enjoyed the symphony and telling them, "One of these days you'll be able to hear your mother sing in this concert hall!"

Flustered heat and pride color Helen's cheeks as she attempts to brush off her coach's generous compliment. He raises his eyebrows, challenging her to accept the truth of his opinion, repeating, "Helen? Helen?" until she relents and self-consciously acknowledges her own vocal gifts.

"Yes, well, maybe one of these days!" she hedges, nervously toying with her neck scarf.

Professor Brown provides further detail for his wife, stating, "Helen is going to sing on a live radio broadcast next week." He turns to Helen, confirming their next meeting, "See you for your lesson tomorrow night?" He asks as he places his hand on his wife's back, signaling their departure.

"Yes, of course," says Helen. "I'll be there. Say goodbye to Mr. and Mrs. Brown," she tells her children. "Come on," she says, collecting their hands. "Let's go home and see if daddy is back from work." As the four walk hand in hand, a panoply of emotions wash across Helen's face: pride, hope, uncertainty, frustration and determination.

The next morning the Horton household chugs along in its familiar rhythms. Buster settles into his regular place on the couch to study tort law. Helen readies five-year old twins Randall and Joyce and three-year-old Lloyd for a trip to the park and then to a friend's house to create a less distracting study environment for Buster. They return later in the afternoon just as Buster is packing up his books and preparing to leave for his job at the post office.

A visibly tired and frazzled Helen reminds her husband, "Don't forget to come home right after work tonight. No unplanned stops! I have my lesson with Professor Brown at 9:00 p.m. sharp." She will be rehearsing the solo she will be singing on the live radio broadcast the following week.

"I'll be home in time," Buster assures her.

"Promise?" asks Helen.

"I promise!" Buster says, confirming the time. "8:30 p.m. at the latest."

"You won't be late?" Helen verifies as she grabs her sewing tape and takes a quick measurement of Buster's arm length before helping him slip into his coat. She grabs the lapels of his jacket, emphasizing her next words. "This is really important to me, Buster."

"I'll be home in time!" He insists, kissing her on the cheek as he scoots out the door.

The wariness Helen feels in the pit of her stomach dissipates in the busyness of the evening's activities. She cooks dinner for the kids, gives them their baths and helps them into their pajamas. When all three are finally in bed, she hurriedly changes her clothes, touches up her hair and makeup, grabs her sheet music and glances impatiently at the wall clock as she collects her purse and coat.

**8:30 p.m.**

She takes a seat at the kitchen table, training her eyes on the front door while her right foot taps out the passage of time in hurried 16th notes.

**8:45 p.m.**

*Where is Buster!* Helen thinks as she checks her watch… again. *I can still make it there in ten minutes if I hurry,* she reassures herself, trying to calm her nerves.

**9:00 p.m.**

Buster is still not home. Helen's simmering frustration blisters into anger. A furious, overheated Helen sloughs off her coat and dials her coach's telephone number. When he answers, she apologizes in a carefully controlled voice for having to cancel their lesson on such short notice.

"Helen," her frustrated coach begins, pausing for a moment before continuing, "opportunities like this don't come around often. This is a *live* radio performance! You need to prepare." There is another brief pause before he addresses the elephant in the room. "How is that husband of yours going to pass the bar if he can't even get *past* the bars?"

Humiliation globs onto the anger and resentment already growing in the pit of Helen's stomach like a snowball gathering mass and speed as it rolls downhill.

**10:00 p.m.**

She snatches a pile of brown and white seersucker fabric off the back of a kitchen chair and hunkers down at her sewing machine. She is an excellent seamstress and welcomes the distraction as she feeds the material under the presser foot with trembling hands.

**11:30 p.m.**

She is still at her sewing machine when Buster stumbles through the front door, intoxicated. The commotion wakes five-year-old Randall in his adjacent bedroom.

*Daddy's home!* The young boy thinks joyously as he scampers out of bed and cracks open his bedroom door to peer into the front room. He instinctively feels the heat from his mother's anger hiss through the vertical crack, stopping him instantly in his tracks.

"You were supposed to be home at 8:30 p.m.," Helen says to Buster in an arctic voice, "Three hours ago," (louder) "I missed my rehearsal. Again!" (shrieking)

*Mommy's mad!* Horton warns himself from experience. Seconds later, any semblance of Helen's control snaps, and her words explode with pent up ferocity.

"I stay home all day, taking care of the kids, so YOU can go to law school. I just need you to come home on time one night! One night! But where do you end up? I'll tell you where you end up! It's no secret. Everyone in the damn neighborhood knows, even my voice coach!"

Helen's voice cracks on the last three words. She raises her hand to her mouth to compose herself before continuing in a barely controlled voice.

"I will not sacrifice my singing career while you're out in the bars boozing it with your friends!"

When Buster attempts to wave her off dismissively, Helen lunges at him and strikes him on the head with the blunt end of the sewing scissors still clutched in her right hand.

From his hiding place, Randall witnesses the blow with wide eyes and a sharp intake of air as he sees blood well-up and glisten on his father's forehead.

"DADDY!" Randall cries aloud. He wants to run back to the safety of his bed, but he is rooted in place by fear.

His mother swivels and locks eyes with her small witness. The resulting shock wave jolts her son into action. Randall slams his bedroom door, jumps back into his bed and buries himself under the protection of his covers.

*I shouldn't have been spying! I shouldn't have been spying!* He admonishes himself.

Sleep eventually comes to him in fits and starts. Young Horton wakes the next morning sleepy and uncertain about his memories. Hearing the sounds of breakfast being made, he cautiously cracks open his bedroom door, experiencing a rush of *déjà vu*.

"Good morning, Randall!" his mother says cheerfully.

Randall remains silently in place, scanning the kitchen and living room for contextual clues... *Daddy's coat is on the hook; he must still be sleeping* , before venturing from the security of his doorway. As he pads hesitatingly toward his mother in the kitchen, his eyes alight on a shiny pair of scissors on the table's edge a fraction of a second before his mother casually slips them into the pocket of her robe. There is no mention of the previous night's incident.

*I must have been dreaming*, Randall rationalizes to himself, but when his father rises later in the day, Randall sees the fresh wound on his forehead.

* * *

"Our father was absent much of the time, pursuing his education and a challenging career," explains Horton almost 70 years later, "and our mother's resentment and anger over the forced abandonment of her own career aspirations sometimes boiled over in volatile and unpredictable ways. We were too young to understand the virulently racist culture in America, or the pressures and disappointments of their adult world. So, my siblings and I learned to be vigilant and attune ourselves to the slightest shift in emotions. When dust ups occurred, we assumed our actions, or inactions, were the cause. That being said, we always knew that our parents loved us, and a moment, an hour or a day later, our parents could turn around and do the kindest, most loving things."

## 1950's Vignette: Part II

*(A dramatized version of actual events)*

The following weekend, Randall's father emerges from his bedroom ready for church, dressed in a brown and white seersucker suit that Helen has sewn for him. Helen admires the fruits of her work and the expert fit of her tailoring.

"I have something for you too," she says excitedly to her son as she holds up an identical, albeit miniature brown and white seersucker suit. "Now you and daddy can match!"

Randall is thrilled! He dresses quickly and beams at the reflection of a matching father and son in the hallway mirror. As the family walks to church, neighbors fawn over their appearance. Randall is warmed with pride and an inner sense of import. The thoughtful surprise soothes his unease from the previous week's events. The identical suits connect father and son, and with each wearing, Randall comports himself with a treasured, yet fleeting, sense of confidence and well-being.

\* \* \*

"My mother was a very gifted soprano," recalls Horton. "As children, we heard her accompany herself on the piano, singing the most beautiful art songs, church and popular music on a daily basis. I vividly remember the first time I heard her sing on the radio. I was around five years old (1947). There were several of us sitting around one of those large, console-sized, Zenith Radios at our neighbor Kate Watkin's home, when all of a sudden, the beautiful clear tone of my mother's voice floated out over the airwaves. Mrs. Watkins grabbed my shoulders with both of her hands and exclaimed with the greatest pride and amazement, 'That's your mother, Randall! Do you hear that? That's your mother, singing on the radio!' Accomplishments of a single African American often became the communal property and pride of the entire black community, proof that advancement was possible despite the daily, soul-jarring, double standard of discrimination."

As the Horton children grow, young Randall develops an interest and special aptitude for music that his mother nurtures. She teaches him to play the piano by ear and for a short time manages to place him in violin lessons. They sing in their church choir and soak up the popular music of the day. They are also steeped in the ubiquitous Jazz sizzling out of the plentiful, South End clubs on a nightly basis.

"You could just walk down the street and let the gorgeous, swinging Jazz music wash over you," recalls Horton. "Once in a while, I would catch a glimpse of the musicians performing through an open door; pretty heady stuff!"

But the 1940's nightclub scene is no place for a young child, nor are the hard scrabble Boston neighborhoods, a point that is driven home to five-year-old Horton when he witnesses a young boy get run over by a horse-drawn wagon, and a man stumble out of an apartment across the street from his home with mortal stab wounds to his chest and abdomen.

"Blood on his shirt and everywhere," Horton still vividly recalls decades later. "Scared me to death!"

And there are other things that frighten Randall. Over time, the stresses of Buster and Helen's respective roles take a toll on the couple. Buster continues to turn to alcohol to escape, while Helen simmers in anger and resentment. By the time Randall is six, his parents' marriage is faltering. Perhaps because of the more negative influences of older boys in their housing project, Randall is sent to live with his aunt and her family for the next 18 months. He joins his Aunty Nona (Eleanor Brown Lee) and her husband Benjamin Lee, the stepfather to his aunt's four teenage daughters, Erma, Eloise, Elaine and Evonne, in the adjacent, slightly less economically-challenged neighborhood of Roxbury. Oldest daughter Erma has recently started working and moved out, making room for Randall. The new living arrangement allows him to attend the superior Higginson Elementary School, ("The Higgie," an adult Horton interjects as he relays the story) while Buster and Helen work to repair their relationship. Randall is only two miles away from his parents and siblings in the care of a strict disciplinarian, but it seems a world away from a child's perspective. And for Randall, it proves catastrophic.

The newly blended family of seven squeezes into their three-bedroom, one bath apartment on the second floor of a three-story Victorian tenement located at 4 Hollander Street. The first floor is rented out to an elderly woman and the third floor to a family with a 17-year-old son. The first-floor tenant is kind and caring, but the teenager on the third floor is a "predator" who quickly singles Randall out as his new prey.

Perhaps it is these damaged humans' raptorial attempt at survival... stealing pieces of innocent souls to replace the festering rot of their own. Randall is too frightened and bewildered to share the devastation of his attack with anyone. He runs away from his aunt's home and sleeps in the nearby Horatio Harris Park[111] for a night, two nights, sometimes a week, to avoid his abuser. When he returns, he receives whippings from his aunt for his incorrigible behavior. She never learns the true reason for his disappearances.

The 18-month separation from his parents and siblings produces a new baby sister Jennifer (Jann) Horton (1951), but does little to repair Buster and Helen's marriage. The family moves into a three-story home at 132 Devon Street in Dorchester near Grove Hall. Soon after, Buster discovers Randall missing from his bed. He searches for some time before finding his son asleep in the basement, tucked into a small nook behind the home's boiler. It is a logical, preemptive move in the mind of an eight-year-old based on his previous moving experience. And like his Aunty Nona before, Horton's parents never learn the reason for his proclivity for small, hidden spaces.

His parents eventually separate and divorce four years later (1955), when he is 13 years old, adding further instability to his life. Like her sister, Helen rents out two of her home's three floors and works two jobs to make ends meet. She also sends Randall, and sometimes his baby sister Jann, to his father's rented room at 59 Georgia Street each month to collect the family's $80 child support check.

"It was a 30-minute walk and a wretched task," recalls Horton. "The

---

111  As a child, Horton and many locals knew this park as Walnut Park, perhaps because of its location along Walnut Street.

two never spoke favorably about one another, and it didn't help to hear my mother repeatedly tell me, 'You're just like your father,' as I grew up."

The traumas Horton absorbs are grievous and affecting. Childhood is supposed to be a time for unconditional love and trust, and as a result, children are ill-prepared to deal with devastating betrayals of that trust. Horatio Harris, the name of the park where Horton sought refuge as a grade schooler, proves to be strangely predictive of the future role he will be called upon to play as an adult. The character *Horatio* in William Shakespeare's play *Hamlet* is Hamlet's faithful and intelligent friend who humbly accepts the world as it is and becomes the *unremarkable* person Prince *Hamlet* entrusts to interpret his actions that perplex those around him during his lifetime and tell his true story after his death. In future years, one need only substitute Ellington's spirit for Hamlet and Horton's for Horatio as a parallel to Horton's efforts to demystify and champion the late composer's equally misunderstood, extended-length compositions (*Black, Brown and Beige* and *Sacred Concerts*).

Like many survivors of abuse, Randall's mind whirls in a constant state of hyper-vigilance. He uses the limited tools available to a grade schooler and young teen to construct around himself a sense of safety and control. He builds walls of false bravado to hide his self-doubt. He drywalls over his hurt with anger. He uses his fists to hammer back his fear, and he befriends fellow miscreants because he doesn't think he deserves better.

Horton's rebellious childhood behavior escalates over the next five years as he grows into an angry teenager. He comes and goes as he pleases, hanging out on the street with friends who drift up from his old Lenox Street neighborhood to sing Doo-Wop. He eats whatever food he can secret away in his pockets from stores and fruit stands, and his absences and defiant behavior frustrate his mother and further strain their relationship.

"We weren't bad kids by today's standards," explains Horton. "We didn't carry guns or get involved in drugs. We just ran around unsupervised, listening to the latest singing groups (affecting a deep radio voice)... *The Flamingos, The Four Freshmen and The High Lows*... and getting into fisticuffs from time to time. We were searching for our identities, respect, a place to belong and something that would lift us out of our unforgiving circumstances."

For Randall and his friends, the music scene of the late 1950's beckons with the promise of just that. Hollywood films, glittering marquees and iconic record labels glamorize the giants of Dixieland, Jazz, Swing, Blues, Doo-Wop and the latest Crooners, while radio and television deliver their music and panache into the epicenter of their home – none better than Duke Ellington and his famous orchestra. With every syncopated note, every crisp tuxedo, and every exuberant performance, the Ellington Orchestra transforms and elevates the music and image of African Americans. They do so with a potent blend of musical genius, personality-driven improvisation, and heart-pumping performances, each with its signature ingredient of *danger* simmering provocatively just below the surface.

# HISTORICAL CONTEXT
## 1951 - 1960

By the end of America's Civil War (1861-1865) three Reconstruction Era[112] amendments are added to the United States Constitution: The Thirteenth (1865), abolishing slavery; the Fourteenth (1868), providing citizenship rights and equal protection under the law; and the Fifteenth (1870), ensuring (male) citizens the right to vote regardless of "race, color, or previous condition of servitude." But a series of Supreme Court decisions between 1873-1883 virtually nullify the work of Congress during Reconstruction. In 1896, the Supreme Court sanctions "legal separation of the races" in *H.A. Plessy v. J.H. Ferguson* by ruling that separate but equal facilities do not violate the Constitution's Fourteenth Amendment of equal protection under the law.[113] By the mid-1950's, the effects of the Harlem Renaissance and The Great Migration contribute to several dramatic actions that lead to growing cultural friction.

In 1954, in a unanimous decision in *Brown v. Board of Education*, the Supreme Court reverses its 1896 ruling, declaring segregation in public schools unconstitutional. The NAACP legal team representing *Brown*, led by African American attorney Thurgood Marshall, provides empirical evidence that racially separate schools are inherently unequal and psychologically harmful. Strong resistance follows, forcing President Dwight D. Eisenhower to dispatch federal troops to escort a group of nine black students (the Little Rock Nine) to their classes amid violent protests by angry white students and townspeople. The symbolism is unmistakable.

---

112  The Reconstruction Era (1863-1877) refers to the era after the Civil War that marked the end of slavery, recognized the newly free slaves as citizens with civil rights and attempted to re-assimilate the eleven Confederate States.

113  It is important to note the earlier and highly contrasting Dred Scott Decision (formally *Dred Scott v. John F.A. Sandford*) ruled on by the U.S. Supreme Court on March 6, 1857, stating that a slave (Dred Scott) who had resided in a free state and territory (where slavery was prohibited) was not thereby entitled to his freedom; that African Americans were not and could never be citizens of the United States; and that the Missouri Compromise (1820), which had declared free all territories west of Missouri and north of latitude 36°30', was unconstitutional.

That same year, while visiting his aunt and cousins in Money, Mississippi, a 14-year-old African American Chicago native named Emmett Till is brutally murdered for allegedly flirting with a white woman named Carolyn Bryant. The white woman's husband and brother order Till to take off his clothes, beat him nearly to death, gouge out one of his eyes, shoot him in the head, tie a 75-pound cotton-gin fan around his neck with barbed wire and throw him into the Tallahatchie River. His badly decomposed body is retrieved three days later and returned to his family in Chicago where his mother insists on an open casket funeral, "so the world can see what was done to my son." His vicious murder shocks the nation and the world.

Emmett Till's murderers are later acquitted in a court of law by an all-white jury even though his accuser Carolyn Bryant, the only witness, recants her story, adding, "Nothing that boy did could ever justify what happened to him." Her husband and brother later confess to the murder when interviewed for a magazine article. The death sheds national light on racism and the brutality of Jim Crow segregation in the South and is the early impetus for the African American civil rights movement.

That same year, the Vietnam War begins. Rosa Parks refuses to give up her seat on a bus to a younger, white patron, leading African Americans in Montgomery, Alabama, to stage a 381-day bus boycott to protest segregated seating. And in an ironic twist of mixed messages, the US Government funds the *Voice of America Jazz Hour* radio program (1955-2003) to broadcast American excellence and freedom by broadcasting American Jazz to 30 million international listeners. Its opening theme: The Ellington Orchestra's famous *Take the A-Train*.[114]

The Moonglows become an influential R&B singing group with several Billboard R&B and Juke Box Chart Hits.[115] An unknown lead

---

114   Ruth Ellington-Boatwright shared with Randall Keith Horton that Willis Conover, the host and producer of the Voice of America, was a highly-valued friend of hers and of Duke.

115   The Moonglows' hits include *Sincerely, We Go Together, See Saw, Please Send Me Someone To Love* and *"The Ten Commandments."* They were inducted into the Vocal Group Hall of Fame 1999 and the Rock-n-Roll Hall of Fame in 2000.

vocalist named Marvin Gaye is added in 1959. Other major artists include Sam Cooke (*You Send Me, A Change Is Gonna Come*), Johnny Ace[116](*My Song, Pledging My Love*) and Otis Redding (*These Arms of Mine, Sittin' On The Dock Of The Bay*). Early Rock'n'Roll, dubbed "race music" until 1954, is just beginning to get the world *all shook up* as Elvis Presley introduces the "new" African American sound to the screaming delight of his young mixed-race audiences. According to historian Marty Jeze, "Presley [brings] Rock 'n' Roll into the mainstream of popular culture…and [gives] the young a belief in themselves as a distinct and somehow unified generation — the first in America ever to feel the power of an integrated youth culture."[117]

The music of this decade and its accompanying freestyle is heard and seen in movies ( James Dean, Marlon Brando), magazines and television and influences Americans' lifestyles, fashion, attitudes, language and perhaps even the Civil Rights movement due to its appeal to both African American and white American teenagers.[118]

And in 1956, the struggling Ellington Orchestra makes a jaw-dropping, career-altering appearance at the fledgling Newport Jazz Festival (story to follow). One year later Ellington is awarded the Spingarn Medal, the National Association for the Advancement of Colored People (NAACP) highest honor, awarded annually in recognition of the highest achievement of an American of African descent.

---

116  John Marshall Alexander, Jr.(1929 – 1954), the "Most Programmed Artist of 1954", was a R&B singer and piano player who died at the age of 25 from an accidental, self-inflicted gunshot wound while playing Russian Roulette. Additional hits included: *Cross My Heart, Please Forgive Me, The Clock, Yes, Baby, Saving My Love for You* and *Never Let Me Go.*

117  Marty Jezer, *The Dark Ages: Life in the United States 1945-1960* (Boston: South End Press, 1982), p. 281.

118  G. C. Altschuler, *All Shook Up: How Rock 'n' Roll Changed America* (Oxford University Press, 2003), p. 35.

## CHAPTER 4

# NEW WORLD A-COMING

---

*"You can say anything on a trombone,
but you have to be careful with words."*[119]
- Duke Ellington

So how and where does Jazz, with its underlying messages of African American pride, fit into this politically charged musical landscape? Has it been forgotten? "No," says contemporary Jazz bassist Christian McBride.

I don't think it was forgotten, but I believe the message got much more visceral... you had Sonny Rollins, who recorded the *Freedom Suite*... and Max Roach recording *We Insist! The Freedom Now Suite*. So, there was a younger generation that was much more direct in their message. Duke Ellington tended to use

---

119  https://thelasttrombone.com/2017/03/22/the-trombone-and-words/.

metaphor. He always had this singular way of filtering the joys, the pains, the sorrows, the tribulations through a musical lens of hope. There was not one facet of African American culture that Duke did not embrace. His music was sort of the medicine for the cancer of racism and discrimination. I think for that reason, if hope is always going to be a factor in life, then Duke Ellington's music will always be relevant.[120]

And Ellington has no desire to stop treating America's racial afflictions with his unique brand of medicine. He has a deep-seated need to compose music that interprets what is going on around him and hear it performed the next day. It isn't a choice, but a personal necessity that supersedes celebrity, money and notoriety. And so, as other big bands slowly break up, the Ellington Orchestra maintains a grueling travel schedule of one-nighters at low paying venues, even roller-skating rinks, to scrape by and stay on the road.

"It's a matter of whether you want to play music or make money," Ellington is quoted as saying. "I like to keep a band, so I can write and hear the music next day. The only way you can do that is to pay the band and keep it on tap 52 weeks a year."

Yet to keep his "very expensive gentlemen" at his beck and call, the iconic maestro has to regularly dip into his personal royalties from earlier hits to meet the band's payroll and expenses. As a result, the Ellington Orchestra is one of the few big bands to survive intact. But something wholly unpredictable looms on the horizon that will turn the downward trajectory of the Big Band era on its ear... at least for the masterful Ellington Orchestra.

---

120   Christian McBride, "A Sprawling Blueprint For Protest Music, Courtesy Of The Jazz Duke," NPR American Anthem, February 22, 2019, 4:25 p.m. ET.

# The 1956 Newport Jazz Festival

In 1956, Ellington is set to open and close the Newport (Rhode Island) Jazz Festival, an innovative new concept in live musical performance. On the evening of July 7th, the band begins its uninspired opening set with several band members absent from the stage. The following account by Beryl Porter[121] published in 2016 captures the serendipity, magnetism and genius of Duke Ellington's ability to respond to his audience and provide a riveting and freely improvised Jazz performance.

After performances by the other groups, the remainder of Ellington's band trickled onto the onstage. *Take the 'A' Train* was followed by new compositions by Ellington-Strayhorn, *Festival Junction, Blues to Be There*, and *Newport Up*. Intended to be the showstopper, the reception to the suite was not as enthusiastic as Ellington hoped.

Following the *Festival Suite*, Duke called for Harry Carney's baritone saxophone performance of *Sophisticated Lady*. Then the orchestra played *Day In, Day Out*. Following this, Duke announced that they were pulling out 'some of our 1938[122] [*sic*] vintage': *Diminuendo and Crescendo in Blue* joined by an improvised interval, which Duke announced would be played by tenor saxophonist Paul Gonsalves.

Ellington is believed to have told Gonsalves to blow as long as he felt like blowing when the solo slot came. As performed at Newport, the experiment ended up revamping the Ellington reputation and fortune for the rest of Ellington's life. The performance culminated in a powerful 27-chorus solo by Paul Gonsalves backed only by bassist Jimmy Woods and

---

121   Beryl Porter, "What was (arguably) the Greatest Sax Solo in Jazz History?," *Beryl Porter's In One Ear*, May 3, 2016, https://inoneearnet.wordpress.com/2016/05/03/what-was-arguably-the-greatest-sax-solo-in-Jazz-history/.

122   Duke announced it as 1938, but it was actually a 1937 composition.

drummer Sam Woodyard, with Ellington himself punctuating the performance with piano chords. Band members urged him on: "Come on, Paul — dig in! Dig in!" While a stunning platinum blonde in a black dress (Elaine Anderson) dancing enthusiastically.

When the solo ended and Gonsalves collapsed in exhaustion, Ellington himself took over for two choruses of a piano solo before the full band returned for the *Crescendo in Blue* portion, finishing with a rousing finale, featuring high-note trumpeter Cat Anderson.

After (Gonsalves') performance, pandemonium took over. Duke calmed the crowd by announcing, "If you've heard of the saxophone, then you've heard of Johnny Hodges." Duke's best known alto saxophonist then played two of his most famous numbers in *I Got It Bad (and That Ain't Good)* followed by *Jeep's Blues*. Still the crowd refused to disperse, so Duke called for Ray Nance to sing *Tulip or Turnip*. The festival's organizers tried to cut off the show at this point, but once again were met with angry refusals to end the evening."

"Don't be rude to the artists," Ellington soothingly [told] festival officials who [wanted] to end the Ellington Orchestra's portion of the concert early out of fear of a riot. Instead, "Duke [told] the announcer that he would end the show and wanted to thank the audience, but instead announced [that] he had a 'very heavy request for Sam Woodyard in *Skin Deep*,' a number written by former Ellington drummer Louis Bellson. This drum solo was the final number featured, followed by a farewell from Duke over *Mood Indigo*. In his final farewell, he thanked the crowd for the 'wonderful way in which you've inspired us this evening,' closing the historic show with his trademark statement, 'You are very beautiful, very sweet and we do love you madly.'

The following month, Ellington is featured on the cover of *Time* magazine, as if its editors anticipated Ellington's powerful Newport Jazz Festival performance. Shortly thereafter, Columbia Records capitalizes on the hysteria by hastily releasing the album *Ellington At Newport*. It becomes Ellington's bestselling album of all time, alleviating his financial worries and freeing him to compose music of more personal import. According to *Time*, "The event marks a turning point in Ellington's career and gives the Jazz world something they have long hoped to hear: that the Ellington band is once again the most exciting thing in the business. It awakens Ellington from a long period of quiescence, and he is once again bursting with ideas and inspiration."[123]

Ellington revisits his extended-length composition *Black, Brown and Beige* and kicks the hornets' nest of musical innovation once again, asking Mahalia Jackson, the Queen of Gospel music and piety, to record a new Jazz album with his orchestra that reprises and expands upon portions of *Black* from his 1943 *Black, Brown and Beige*. She accepts.

It is a risk, even for a woman of Jackson's stature and reputation. She is openly criticized by some gospel purists for bringing Jazz (the devil's music) into the church.[124] In fact, it is a controversial move for both: Duke Ellington for writing slow, meditative, plaintive supplications (Jazz) for the church, and Mahalia Jackson for consorting with "the devil."

Ellington concedes that, "By and large, then as now, Jazz is like the kind of man you wouldn't want your daughter to associate with."[125] As for Jackson, when asked why she made an exception to perform with

123 "Music: Mood Indigo & Beyond," *Time*, August 20, 1956, http://content.time.com/time/subscriber/article/0,33009,891768,00.html.

124 Victor M. Parachin, "Mahalia Jackson," *American History* 29, no. 4 (1994): 42, http://search.ebscohost.com.nmu.idm.oclc.org/login.aspx?direct=true&db=khh&AN=9408241125&site=hrc-live.

125 Howard Reich, "The Story Behind the First Pulitzer for Jazz How Wynton Marsalis's 1997 Win Moved the Music Pulitzers beyond the Classical Canon." *Neiman*, Neiman Foundation, 20 June 2016. *Neiman Foundation*, nieman.harvard.edu/articles/the-story-behind-the-first-pulitzer-for-jazz/.

the Ellington Orchestra when she would not sing in night clubs or with other Jazz groups, she answers that she, "does not view Duke Ellington's musicians as a Jazz band, but a sacred institution."[126]

Mercer Ellington, Duke's son, provides further insight into the Jackson-Ellington relationship when he outlines his father's strong feelings about anything that touches on religion.

> Knowing his feelings about sacred music, Mahalia Jackson came to him once, suggesting that he be the one to produce her on records. This he couldn't do, because he thought it wrong to profit from anything concerned with the church, which is why she always had a great regard for him. She herself felt religion had no place in certain areas and refused all kinds of money to appear in Las Vegas. She would never even visit '*sin city*.' Pop was a bit different, but he wouldn't let anyone project him as a kind of Messiah. He never was a hypocrite. There were things he did that in a sense were not pure — and some *he intended to continue doing* — so he refused to be held up as a moral example of how a man should behave.[127]

The controversy swirling around his collaboration with Jackson doesn't deter Ellington in the least. Having an inherent aversion to reproducing something he previously did well, the composer nonchalantly breaks *Black* into six shorter segments,[128] adding new lyrics to

---

126  Derek Jewell, *Duke: A Portrait of Duke Ellington* (New York: W. W. Norton, 1977), as printed in Homzy, Andrew. ""Black, Brown and Beige" in Duke Ellington's Repertoire, 1943-1973." <i>Black Music Research Journal</i> 13, no. 2 (1993): 87-110. Accessed September 4, 2021. doi:10.2307/779514, p. 96.

127  Stanley Dance and Mercer Ellington, "*Duke Ellington in Person: An Intimate Memoir,*" Boston, 1978, p. 184.

128  Irving Townsend, "Liner Notes: Irving Townsend on "Black, Brown and Beige," by Duke Ellington and His Orchestra, Featuring Mahalia Jackson," Jerry Jazz Musician, November 27, 2013, http://jerryJazzmusician.com/2013/11/liner-notes-irving-townsend-black-brown-beige-duke-ellington-orchestra-featuring-mahalia-jackson/. "This performance consists of the two principal parts of the complete piece, *Work Song*, heard in Parts I and III, and *Come Sunday*, heard in Parts II, III, and IV and V. Both themes are stated, developed, and restated with new ideas and new meanings inherent in the music…"

*Come Sunday.* According to Terry Teachout, author of *Duke: A Life of Duke Ellington,* "... this recording is 'falsely billed by Columbia as a complete version of *Black*, the work's first movement, augmented by a vocal version of *Come Sunday* performed by gospel singer Mahalia Jackson, who also contributes an impromptu singing of the *Twenty-Third Psalm.*' But it is only a partial treatment; a 17:00 minute revisitation versus the original movement's complete 21:52 minute length.

Jackson arrives in Los Angeles one week before the album's first recording session and meets with Ellington each afternoon to write and rehearse the beautiful and thematic *Come Sunday.* According to Ellington's sister and long-time business associate Ruth Ellington-Boatwright, "Duke called me after the recording session with Mahalia and said, 'You know, we couldn't get it just right last night for a long time because Mahalia said she didn't sing as she had wanted to sing. So I turned out all the lights in the studio, and she was magnificent!' All the musicians played in the dark as well. They had the music memorized, which is true of the orchestra in general, because Duke dictated much of his music in the recording studio."[129]

"Like the *Sacred Concerts, Black, Brown, & Beige* remained a living, evolving work throughout the composer's life. While Ellington had not previously regarded it as such, the lyrics he wrote for Jackson's *Come Sunday* performance clearly re-rendered the piece as a sacred work."[130]

Duke also senses that his *Black, Brown and Beige* album needs a concluding number. At their final rehearsal, he asks Mahalia to bring her Bible. He opens it to the *Twenty-third Psalm,* plays a chord and asks her to sing the lyrics. Her improvised rendition with Ellington's piano accompaniment becomes just the ticket.

The album cover features a photo of Ellington seated with Jackson

129 Randall Keith, Horton and Ruth Ellington-Boatwright. "Ruth Ellington." www.randallkeithhorton.com/ruthellington,.html. Accessed 22 Sept. 2021.

130 Dr. Christopher J. Wells, "Program Notes: Duke Ellington's Sacred Concert," *Phoenix Chorale,* https://www.phoenixchorale.org/concerts/program-notes-duke-ellington/.

standing behind him with her hand on his shoulder. The message is subtle, yet explicit. "The single most powerful black woman in the United States" (Harry Belafonte), "the greatest spiritual singer now alive" (1954 *Downbeat Magazine*) and noted civil rights advocate Mahalia Jackson is endorsing Ellington and his music as reverent and worthy of acceptance in and by the (black) church.

"In 1958, when this album was recorded," states Christian Mc Bride, "I think it's safe to say that there was no more powerful a voice in the gospel world than Mahalia Jackson. And, you know, there was a contingent of gospel artists or church people who still thought Jazz is secular music, it's music that is not of the church. So I think it says something to the power and majesty of Duke Ellington's musicality to be able to have this singular artist of another so-called genre to say, I don't usually do this, but this music is so powerful, I want to help further this artistry, this majesty of this song."[131]

The recording partnership becomes yet another pioneering triumph with Ellington's expert melding of Big Band Jazz and Gospel with neither a note nor a lyric wasted. "Those self-same critics who panned the live performance of *Black, Brown and Beige* in 1943, were fulsome in their praise in 1958, proof of the vitality of the *Black, Brown and Beige* album."[132]

131 Christian McBride, NPR American Anthem, "A Sprawling Blueprint For Protest Music, Courtesy Of The Jazz Duke", February 22, 2019, 4:25 pm, EST.

132 Hallmark. Review of *Editorial Review - Black, Brown and Beige Album (1958)*, Review of *Black, Brown and Beige Amazon Music*, www.amazon.com/Black-Brown-Ellington-Mahalia-Jackson/dp/B00GIKI2OC.

# Tracking List and Descriptions

*The Black, Brown and Beige Album Featuring
Mahalia Jackson, 1958*

## Part I Work Song
**(8:17)** As in original score.

## Part II Come Sunday
**(6.14)** As in the original score minus eleven measures in the beginning and two at the end.
Carney and trumpeter Shorty Baker (on the bridge) play Hodges' original solo.

## Part III Light
**(6.26)** As in original score.

## Part IV Come Sunday
**(7.58)** Vocal version with new orchestral backgrounds by Strayhorn. Jackson "hums an extra chorus as if she were aware of the power of her performance and wanted to let it linger a moment more" (Townsend 1958).

## Part V Come Sunday
**(3.46)** Nance on violin plays an impassioned solo with yet more new instrumental backgrounds.

## Part VI The Twenty-third Psalm
**(3:01)** Jackson sings the psalm as lyrics to Ellington's newly composed music.

The passage of time and the pairing of Ellington's *unfamiliar* secular music with Jackson's familiar religious vocals, unite their disparate fan bases: Ellington's "unchurched" African American audiences and Jackson's "churched" African American congregants. It also allows Ellington to quietly revisit some of the musical themes created for this original *opus*. Critics do not rail against the album as they did Ellington's full-length performance of *Black, Brown and Beige* in 1943, but they still do not embrace it. The record album's partial treatment of the original composition rises from rejection to an only marginally better state. As groundbreaking and altar-rattling as the recording is, it does little to redefine Duke Ellington to his critics or public, in whose eyes he remains the charismatic, dapper king of swinging, short-form Jazz hits, not extended-length compositions of classical, cultural or religious merit.

\* \* \*

As the American public's general interest in Jazz wanes during the 1950's and 1960's, its popularity abroad escalates. Building upon the early international tours by American saxophonist, clarinetist, composer Sidney Bechet (1920's), Jazz saxophonist, clarinetist, trumpeter, composer, arranger, and bandleader Benny Carter (1934-1937) and Duke Ellington, Jazz producer Willis Conover[133] begins broadcasting his legendary *Voice of America Jazz Hour*[134] (1955-2003). The program opens with Duke Ellington's (and Billy Strayhorn's) *Take The 'A' Train* as its theme and airs American Jazz music throughout Europe and Asia for 40 years. The program attracts more than one-hundred million listeners and

---

133 Willis Clark Conover, Jr. produced Jazz concerts at high-profile locations such as the White House and the Newport Jazz Festival, and for movies and television. His concerts were known to be open to all races, giving him the notoriety of helping desegregate Washington D.C. nightclubs. Conover also served as a broadcaster on the *Voice of America* for more than 40 years.

134 Karl Ackerman, "State And Mainstream: The Jazz Ambassadors And The U.S. State Department," *All About Jazz*, April 27, 2018, 2, https://www.allaboutJazz.com/state-and-mainstream-the-Jazz-ambassadors-and-the-us-state-department-by-karl-ackermann.php.

is credited with keeping Jazz alive in the countries of Eastern Europe during the Cold War (1947-1953).

This primes world demand for live performances by American Jazz artists which the US State Department happily provides through its *Jazz Ambassadors Program* (1956-1972). The program is designed to counter "communist propaganda with the offshore display of American exceptionalism."[135] Jazz musicians soon begin replacing classical orchestras and ballet companies on international tours because it is felt that Jazz is a better representation of the true American experience.[136] And in an ironic twist, the *Jazz Ambassadors Program* becomes a powerful tool in 1963 for the US to downplay its own domestic social and political unrest when images of police dogs attacking African Americans and a cop pinning a black woman to the pavement in Birmingham are splashed across global newspapers and televisions. In response, the State Department quickly dispatches the Ellington Orchestra on an extended tour of the Middle East where they field numerous questions about the lack of racial equality in America.

Fortunately, according to historian John Edward Hasse,[137] Ellington is "a natural-born ambassador... and an adept politician... secure, self-confident, optimistic, prideful, aristocrat in demeanor, charming, well-mannered, easy with people from all walks of life, religious, ambitious, clever, didactically oriented, street smart, shrewd in business, restive with categories, stylish dresser, and a growing individualist. Very American indeed."[138]

And throughout their tour, Ellington and his accomplished musicians are once again buoyed by the warmth of their receptions, the lack

---

135 *Ibid.*

136 Ehsan Khoshbakht, "Far of the Middle: Ellington's 1963 State Department Tour," Take the "A" Train, January 17, 2013, https://ehsankhoshbakht.blogspot.com/2013/01/DukeIran.html.

137 John E. Hasse, *Beyond Category: The Life And Genius Of Duke Ellington.* Da Capo, 1993.

138 Ehsan Khoshbakht, "Far of the Middle: Ellington's 1963 State Department Tour," Take the "A" Train, January 17, 2013, https://ehsankhoshbakht.blogspot.com/2013/01/DukeIran.html.

of discrimination and the power of their music to bridge cultural divides. In addition to touring Europe (1933, 1946, 1950, 1955) and the Middle East and India (1963), the Ellington Orchestra makes US State Department sponsored tours through Japan (1964), Latin America and Mexico (1968) and the Soviet Union (1971). Their travels inspire Ellington to compose several exotic suites (*The Liberian Suite, Far East Suite, Togo Brava, Afro-Bossa, El Gato, Ad lib on Nippon, The Queen's Suite, Latin Suite,* and others). Yet the greatest benefit of the State Department's *Jazz Ambassador Program* featuring the Ellington Orchestra's unique brand of American music is eloquently summed up by American composer and conductor Leonard Bernstein, who says, "The point is, art never stopped a war and never got anybody a job. That was never its function. Art cannot change events. But it can change people. It can affect people so that they are changed... because people are changed by art—enriched, ennobled, encouraged , they then act in a way that may affect the course of events...by the way they vote, they behave, the way they think.[139]

The Ellington Orchestra's worldwide exposure and appeal is unprecedented. Ellington's music changes how 20th Century American-Popular music is heard, which Duke, in turn, showcases to the world. And in much the same way that he and his music come to embody *hope* for African Americans, they also symbolize the freedom and opportunity of life in America to both free and oppressed people around the globe. Ellington and his orchestra showcase, perhaps better than any other band, the unique characteristics of Jazz — "active listening, freedom, improvisation and spontaneous interaction"[140] — as a compelling voice for social change. It is, therefore, not surprising that Ellington's 1958 version of *Come Sunday* evolves into a hymn of hope and solidarity during America's Civil Rights movement, setting the tone for future "protest music."

---

139  Ackermann, *Ibid.*

140  Garth Alper, "Black, Brown, and Beige: One Piece of Duke Ellington's Musical and Social Legacy". College Music Symposium, https://symposium.music.org/index.php/51/item/16-black-brown-and-beige-one-piece-of-duke-ellingtons-musical-and-social-legacy, October 1, 2011.

It is interesting to note how prescient and predictive Ellington's 1943 *Come Sunday* melody (and 1958 re-recording with lyrics sung by Mahalia Jackson) are. They predate the American Civil Rights Movement by nearly two decades. While the noted Civil Rights leader Reverend Martin Luther King, Jr. speaks out against discrimination with peaceful yet impassioned words, Ellington deploys his own unique panacea, the beauty and persuasiveness of his music, like *a spoonful of sugar* to help the *medicine* of his civil rights statements *go down in a most delightful way*. And true to Leonard Bernstein's words, Ellington and his music help advance meaningful racial, social, and cultural change.

## The Ellington Orchestra - International Tours

*(116 Stops in 66 Countries Over 40 Years)*

| | |
|---|---|
| **1933** | Great Britain, Holland, and France |
| **1939** | France, Brussels, the Netherlands and Sweden |
| **1948** | London, Paris, Antwerp, Brussels, Geneva and Zurich[141] |
| **1950** | France, Belgium, Holland, Switzerland, Italy, Denmark, Sweden and West Germany |
| **1958** | England, Scotland, France, Belgium, Holland, Sweden, Norway, Denmark, Germany, Austria, Switzerland and Italy. |
| **1963** | Paris, Stockholm, Hamburg and Milan, Jordan, Pakistan, India, Deylon, Iraq and Lebanon |
| **1964** | London, Milan, Paris and Tokyo |
| **1965** | France, Denmark, Sweden, Germany, Switzerland and England |
| **1966** | Dakar, Senegal, Japan and France |

---

141 Ellington, Ray Nance, Kay Davis - Variety act only as the British Musicians Union refused to allow his band to join them.

| 1968 | South America and Mexico |
|------|--------------------------|
| 1969 | Caribbean |
| 1970 | Japan, Philippines, Hong Kong, Singapore, Thailand, Taiwan, Australia and New Zealand |
| 1971 | Soviet Union, Britain, France, the Netherlands, Belgium, Poland, Hungary, Romania, Austria, Denmark, Norway, Sweden, Italy, Germany and Spain, Brazil, Uruguay, Argentina, Chile, Peru, Ecuador, Colombia, Venezuela, Puerto Rico, Panama, Nicaragua and Mexico |
| 1972 | Japan, Taiwan, the Philippines, Hong Kong, Thailand, Burma, India, Ceylon, Singapore, Malaysia, Indonesia, Australia and New Zealand |
| 1973 | Paris, Stockholm, Barcelona, France, Ethiopia and Zambia, London |

## Duke Ellington's "My People" Revue

Ellington is a great admirer of Dr. Martin Luther King, Jr., and the two finally meet for the first time in Chicago at the 1963 Century of Negro Progress Exposition where Ellington writes, directs and creates the orchestration for his stage presentation *My People*,[142] ' anniversary of President Lincoln's 'Emancipation Proclamation', a musical revue celebrating the . Using a mixture of song, dance and drama, Ellington brings to life the harsh reality of life in 1863 in two parts: life *Before* Lincoln's 'Emancipation Proclamation', featuring Negros Spirituals and life *After*, using the Blues.

The composer sticks to his signature approach, emphasizing the positive achievements and contributions of African Americans. The

---

142 Century of Negro Progress Exposition in 1963 written for stage show presented in Chicago, August 16-23, 1963.

production's musical climax features Ellington's stunning tribute to Dr. King entitled *King Fit The Battle of Alabam*. It simultaneously expresses Ellington's outrage over the recent actions of Bull Connor and the police in Birmingham, Alabama, and "re-imagines King as the protagonist of *Joshua Fit the Battle of Jericho*."[143] [144] It is "an eloquent, rousing speech that is comparable with many of the speeches by Civil Rights' activists ... and a powerful, forward-looking salute not only to King, but Birmingham's courageous black residents as well."[145] Upon hearing the song for the first time in rehearsals, Dr. Martin Luther King, Jr. purportedly wept.[146]

According to Howard Reich, *Chicago Tribune* Arts Critic, "Several [recovered] passages of Ellington's original narration underscore the ferocity of [Ellington's] commitment to civil rights... The central miracle of *My People*, though," he postulated, "is that the show can address issues such as racism and class warfare without becoming heavy-handed or depressing."[147] With the passage of time and perspective, it also became clear that Ellington's *My People* helped bridge the innovations of *Black, Brown and Beige* (1943) with the mature statements of Ellington's personal faith in his *Sacred Concerts* (1965, 1968, 1973). In it we hear *Come Sunday*, reprised from *Black, Brown and Beige* with *Sacred Music* selections: *David Danced (Before The Lord With All His Might)* and *The Blues (Ain't Nothin')*.

Following his tribute to Dr. King (*King Fit The Battle Of Alabam*) Ellington thoughtfully closes his groundbreaking and popular review

143  Paul Devlin, "Duke Ellington's Tribute to Martin Luther King, 50 Years Later," *Brow Beat* (blog), *Slate*, January 21, 2013, https://slate.com/culture/2013/01/martin-luther-king-tribute-by-duke-ellington-my-people-50-years-later-video.html.

144  *Joshua Fit the Battle of Jericho* is an old African American spiritual based on the story of Joshua in the Bible. 'Fit' represents a way of saying 'fought'. The song tells how Joshua captured the city of Jericho when he ordered the Israelites to blow trumpets until the walls fell down.

145  Derek Anderson, "Duke Ellington's My People," *Dereksmusicblog*, September 30, 2014, https://dereksmusicblog.com/2014/09/30/duke-ellingtons-my-people/.

146  Harvey G. Cohen, *Duke Ellington's America*, University of Chicago Press, 2010, 395.

147  Howard Reich, "Silent for 35 Years, Ellington's Restored Musical Celebrates Black Culture, Composer's Genius," Chicago Tribune, May 11, 1998, https://www.chicagotribune.com/news/ct-xpm-1998-05-11-9805110152-story.html.

with his poignant song *What Colour Is Virtue?* Derek Anderson noted that *My People*, when released, was considered "a groundbreaking mixture of music, drama and theatre." It told the story of the official end to slavery in America when all slaves within the ten Confederate states were freed. Because of its rife subject matter, the music is "moving, poignant, uplifting, joyous and elicits a variety of emotions: sadness, anger, frustration, hope and joy."[148]

## *My People* - Album Tracking List[149]

1. (Stage Review/Album)
2. Ain't But the One/Will You Be There/99% - 5:16
3. Come Sunday/David Danced Before the Lord - 6:09
4. My Mother, My Father (Heritage) - 2:50
5. Montage - 6:54
6. My People/The Blues (Ain't Nothin) - 8:56
7. Workin' Blues/My Man Sends Me/Jail Blues/Lovin' Lover - 5:57
8. King Fit the Battle of Alabam' - 3:25
9. What Color Is Virtue? - 2:49

Now, imagine the daring and conviction it took for Ellington to write, conduct and produce an even more outspoken musical revue—22 years earlier—that was unapologetically outspoken about America's racial issue and featured an all-black cast. Ellington's highly controversial and groundbreaking *Jump for Joy* opened at the Mayan Theater in Los Angeles in 1941, two years before the premiere of Ellington's *Black, Brown and Beige* at Carnegie Hall. Despite racist backlash, death threats

148 Derek Anderson, "Duke Ellington's My People," *Dereksmusicblog*, September 30, 2014, https://dereksmusicblog.com/2014/09/30/duke-ellingtons-my-people/.

149 Recorded at Universal Studios in Chicago on August 20 (tracks 1a, 2, 4, 5b, 6a, 6c and 7) and August 21 (tracks 1b, 1c, 3, 5a and 8), 1963.

and even a cast member's beating,[150] the show ran for nine weeks with over 100 performances. Although Ellington and his collaborators wrote it with a Broadway run in mind, it was first and foremost an attempt to change the way Broadway and the film industry commonly characterized black performers and musicians as shuffling, superstitious stereotypes. According to Associated Press writer David Dishneau in 1992, "Each of its 30 songs and sketches dealt with some aspect of African-American culture, from the sweet love song *The Brown Skin Gal in the Calico Gown*, to the deceptively upbeat *Passport From Georgia* with its references to lynching and the Ku Klux Klan." Ellington later described it in 1973 as "the first 'social significance' show."

In it, he prohibits lighter skinned performers from using burnt cork on their faces to "blacken up" their skin tones. Some initially object, but eventually acquiesce and are shocked by their acceptance and success on stage. "As the audience screamed and applauded," recounted Ellington, "comedians came off stage smiling and with tears running down their cheeks."[151] Singer Herb Jeffries, confirms Ellington's abhorrence of the practice when he is asked by one of the Hollywood VIP's backstage to darken his skin to match that of his singing partner Clarence "Frenchy" Landry in the second act.

> [The VIP] called in French and the make-up man and had him match me to French with the Max Factor Egyptian #39 or something. Now it's my cue for Act 2. I'm out there singing *If Life Were All Peaches and Cream*. Duke looks up from the pit and he's horrified. I can't figure out what is upsetting him so much because I'm thinking about the song, not how I

---

150  David Dishneau, "Ellington's 'Jump for Joy' Back After 50 Years : Stage: Chicago company revives musical about black life that opened in L.A. in '41, then was lost to World War II," *Los Angeles Times*, January 4, 1992, https://www.latimes.com/archives/la-xpm-1992-01-04-ca-1149-story.html.

151  Harvey G. Cohen, Duke Ellington's America, 2010, p. 188.

look, and besides, I don't know how I look. I thought maybe my fly was open. I was afraid Ellington was going to have an apoplexy. Right after the finale, Duke storms into my dressing room, furious. 'What in the hell are you playing, Al Jolson? We don't do blackface in *Jump for Joy!*'[152]

Sid Kuller, the Hollywood writer who penned lyrics for 11 of the show's 30 songs, says in 1992 that he was proudest of his work on *Jump for Joy* over all the material he wrote for the stage, television and films. "I place it on the top of the list," the 81-year old Kuller said in a telephone interview the same year, "because of the fact that somebody had to make the statement, and we made it, and at the time it was dangerous."[153]

"Everything, every setting, every note of music, every lyric, meant something," recalls Avanelle Lewis Harris, one of the singers. "All the sketches had a message for the world. The tragedy was that the world was not ready for *Jump for Joy*."

Choreographer Joel Hall, who also worked on the revue's 1992 revival in Chicago, cites the material's continued relevance, stating, "Many young black people [today] have no idea what things were like in that period. As for the music: Duke Ellington is relevant to any time."

Author Harvey Cohen[154] states, "Ellington did not fight for civil rights in the manner of political activists, but he contributed much to that cause, most of it unrecognized because it did not fall within traditional forms of racial protest."[155] Still, Ellington faces on-going criticism back home, primarily from the black press and black audiences, who feel he is not doing enough to support the American Civil Rights

---

152  *Ibid*, p. 191.

153   David Dishneau, "Ellington's 'Jump for Joy' Back After 50 Years : Stage: Chicago company revives musical about black life that opened in L.A. in '41, then was lost to World War II."

154   Harvey G. Cohen is a Senior Lecturer in the Department of Culture Media & Creative Industries, King's College London and author of "Duke Ellington's America", University of Chicago Press, 2010.

155   Cohen, *Ibid.*

Movement.[156] Responding to historian and music critic Nat Hentoff's[157] question about this in 1965, Ellington says, "People who think that of me haven't been listening to our music... social protest and pride in the history of the Negro have been the most significant themes in what we've done... We've been talking about what it is to be a Negro in this country for a long time."

## Jump For Joy - Album Tracking List[158]

| | | | |
|---|---|---|---|
| 1 | –Duke Ellington And His Orchestra | Take The 'A' Train | 2:57 |
| 2 | –Duke Ellington And His Orchestra | Jumpin' Punkins | 3:36 |
| 3 | –Duke Ellington And His Orchestra | Blue Serge | 3:23 |
| 4 | –Duke Ellington And His Orchestra | John Hardy's Wife | 3:32 |
| 5 | –Duke Ellington | Dear Old Southland Piano – Duke Ellington | 3:28 |
| 6 | –Duke Ellington | Solitude Piano – Duke Ellington | 3:33 |
| 7 | –Duke Ellington And His Orchestra | Just A-Settin' And A-Rockin' | 3:38 |
| 8 | –Duke Ellington And His Orchestra | Chocolate Shake Solo Vocal – Ivie Anderson | 2:55 |
| 9 | –Duke Ellington And His Orchestra | I Got It Bad And That Ain't Good Solo Vocal – Ivie Anderson | 3:21 |
| 10 | –Duke Ellington And His Orchestra | The Brown-Skin Gal (In The Calico Gown) Solo Vocal – Herb Jeffries | 3:11 |
| 11 | –Duke Ellington And His Orchestra | Jump For Joy Solo Vocal – Herb Jeffries | 2:54 |

156  McBride, *Ibid.*

157  Nathan Irving "Nat" Hentoff was an American historian, novelist, Jazz and country music critic and syndicated columnist for United Media. He wrote a column in *The Village Voice* from 1958 to 2009.

158  The ten additional Ellington songs that were featured in the revue, but did not make it onto the album, include: *Sun Tanned Tenth Of the Nation, Stump Caprice (Mercer), Bli-Blip, Cindy With The Two Left Feet, Pot, Pan and Skillet, Flame Indigo, Shhhh! He's On The Seat, I've Got A Passport From Georgia, Old Fashioned Waltz* and *Sharp Easter.*

| 12 | –Duke Ellington And His Orchestra | Chelsea Bridge | 2:57 |
|---|---|---|---|
| 13 | –Duke Ellington And His Orchestra | Perdido | 3:11 |
| 14 | –Duke Ellington And His Orchestra | Moon Mist | 3:02 |
| 15 | –Duke Ellington And His Orchestra | The 'C' Jam Blues | 2:41 |
| 16 | –Duke Ellington And His Orchestra | What Am I Here For | 3:29 |
| 17 | –Duke Ellington And His Orchestra | Johnny Come Lately | 2:43 |
| 18 | –Duke Ellington And His Orchestra | A Slip Of The Up Solo Vocal – Ray Nance | 2:57 |
| 19 | –Duke Ellington And His Orchestra | Sentimental Lady (I Didn't Know About You) | 3:05 |
| 20 | –Duke Ellington And His Orchestra | Main Stem | 2:54 |

# HISTORICAL CONTEXT
## 1961-1963

The early 1960's are defined by growing friction and clashes between supporters and detractors of the Civil Rights Movement. In 1960 alone: The Greensboro Woolworth desegregates its lunch counter after six months of sit-ins; President Kennedy and his brother Robert gain Martin Luther King, Jr.'s release after his arrest in Georgia on trumped up charges and a sentencing of four months of hard labor; the Supreme Court in *Boynton v. Virginia* rules that segregation on vehicles traveling between states violates the Interstate Commerce Act. And one year later, President Kennedy orders the Interstate Commerce Commission to enact stricter regulations and fines for buses and facilities who refuse to integrate.

In 1963, Martin Luther King, Jr. writes his famous *Letter from a Birmingham Jail*; Medgar Evers, the first field secretary for the National Association for the Advancement of Colored People (NAACP) is assassinated in Mississippi; King delivers his "I Have A Dream" speech at the *March on Washington for Jobs and Freedom*; President John F. Kennedy is assassinated; and newly sworn-in President Lyndon B. Johnson pushes through civil rights legislation in Kennedy's memory. That same year Duke Ellington and Martin Luther King Jr. meet for the first time in Chicago during Ellington's performance of the previously cited stage play *My People*[159], marking the centennial of the Emancipation Proclamation.

By the 1960's Ellington's and Jackson's recording of *Come Sunday* (1958) has become a hymn of *hope* for the Civil Rights Movement and sets the stage for the development of future protest music. "[Duke Ellington] always had his singular way of filtering the joys, the pains,

---

159 'My People', was a 1963 all-black, song-and-dance revue directed and narrated by Duke Ellington in which he wrote about African-American history. It was presented in Chicago as part of the Century of Negro Progress Exposition and included a stunning tribute to Dr. Martin Luther King, Jr., in "King Fit the Battle of Alabam where Ellington re-imagined King as the protagonist of the well-known negro spiritual "Joshua Fit the Battle of Jericho."

the sorrows, the tribulations through a musical lens of hope," states American bassist, composer and arranger Christian McBride [but] there was a younger generation that was [growing] much more direct in their messages."

Protest music calling out civil rights violations, economic injustice, unpopular politics and anti-war (Vietnam) sentiments, begins to dominate the popular music scene. Young white listeners tap into folk-inspired protest music: Joan Baez's popular recording of the Civil Rights anthem, *We Shall Overcome* (1963) and Bob Dylan's *Times and They Are A' Changing* (1964). Black listeners are drawn to music rooted in the church and Negro Spirituals: Ellington's and Mahalia Jackson's *Come Sunday* (1958), Sonny Rollins' *Freedom Suite* (1958), Max Roach's *We Insist! The Freedom Now Suite* (1960), Odetta Holmes' *Oh Freedom* (1963), Nina Simone's *Mississippi Goddam* (1964), and Sam Cooke's *A Change Is Gonna Come* (1964).

## CHAPTER 5

# WRAP YOUR TROUBLES IN DREAMS

---

*"Everyman prays in his own language and
there is no language that God does not understand."*[160]
- Duke Ellington

Back in Boston in the late 1950's, Randall Keith Horton is leading
the life of a typical African American teenager. He attends high school
and works out harmonies with local Doo-Wop singing groups in the
afternoons, evenings and weekends. He is also influenced by Ellington's
music, especially his (Newport hit) *Diminuendo and Crescendo in Blue*
and images of the elegantly attired Duke Ellington and his orchestra.

"As a teenager, I enjoyed performing in the best local Boston singing quartets and banging out rhythm and blues on the piano," recalls
Horton, "listening to Crooners, Rock 'n' Roll, Jazz and classical music,

---

160  Cohen, *Ibid.*

and living much of my childhood and adolescence through the romance of song. Before long, we started our own groups: *The Regents*, *The Supreme Tones* and *The Aladdins*. Music was a huge refuge for us. Still is. And it didn't hurt that the girls liked it too!"

In an attempt to replicate the dapper attire of his fellow Doo-Wop singers, seventeen-year-old Horton is caught stealing clothing from a department store and sentenced to 90 days in jail. Instead of enrolling in his senior year of high school, he is booked into the Charles Street Jail[161] at the foot of Boston's now prestigious Beacon Hill neighborhood. His first cellmate, a boxer in his early twenties, is another *predator*, but this time an older, more street savvy Horton is able to fight off his attacker.

"He said to me afterward, 'You're a strong little S.O.B,'" states Horton with disgust, almost sixty years later. "The man had no remorse! No sense of wrongdoing!" Horton pauses to regain his composure before continuing. "Nonetheless, being able to defend myself was profoundly empowering. I was no longer the helpless six-year-old boy of my childhood."

A short time later, Horton's twin sister Joyce visits him at the jail. The two talk through a protective wall of glass while sitting at a table facing one another. Midway through their visit, Horton's cellmate catches Joyce's eye and pushes Horton aside to flirt with her. The shuffling of chairs catches the attention of a short, squatty guard who bellows, "Horton! What the hell do you think you're doing?"

The small infraction earns the seventeen-year-old ten days in solitary confinement. The good news is that he is placed with a new cellmate when he gets out. "Laughing" Bill Wilson watches Horton as he passes the hours, playing an imaginary piano keyboard on the wall by his bunk bed. Wilson eventually calls out, "Hey, kid! I see you playing that piano on that wall. You got talent. You need to get out of here, go back to school and make something of yourself!"

---

161   In 2013, the Charles Street Jail was converted into a five-star property called the Liberty Hotel.

Horton's path, like that of most African Americans, is littered with personal hardships, racial biases, economic obstacles, injudicious decisions and social injustices. It contrasts sharply with Ellington's more privileged lifestyle, which is not yet one of perfect racial equality, but atypical enough to serve as a beacon of hope for the majority of less fortunate African Americans striving to improve their own social standing. Two and a half months later, when Horton is released from the Charles Street Jail, his longtime friend and singing partner Mike Warren graciously allows him to sleep on the floor of his studio apartment.

"Mike Warren was a genius," recalled Horton. "He never finished high school, but he managed to earn his way into Harvard University. We sang together in two or three of the top Doo-Wop groups before I left high school. He became a heroin addict, attributing it to the trauma of his mother's death when he was only five years old. 'They should've never let me see her put in the ground,' he confided to me. He cleaned himself up and became a counselor for drug addicts for a time, though he eventually relapsed and died. Very tragic."

Horton lives with Warren for two months before taking "Laughing" Bill Wilson's jailhouse advice. He moves back home with his mother, returns to his Hyde Park High School for his senior year, enjoys popularity as a singing-member of a high school vocal quartet[162] and earns excellent grades. Teacher and guidance counselor John D. O'Bryant[163] takes an interest in Horton. He steps in as a father figure and helps Horton secure a $500 NAACP scholarship to study math and physics at the Hampton Institute[164] in Virginia.

In the fall of 1962, Horton moves into James Hall, his freshman

---

162  Horton credits his brother Lloyd as the "singing genius" of this group.

163  John D. O'Bryant went on to become one of Boston's prominent African American educators, the first elected black member of the Boston School Board and the first black vice president of Northeastern University. In later years, the college preparatory Hyde Park High School was renamed the John D. O'Bryant School of Mathematics and Science in his honor.

164  The Hampton Institute, now known as Hampton University, is a private, historically black university located in Hampton, Virginia.

dormitory at the Hampton Institute, and quickly finds common ground with fellow music lover Weldon Irvine[165] whose father also happens to be the dean of the college. Irvine whets Horton's appetite for Jazz, teaching him the essence of the music and the progression of chords. The two listen to bands and travel to music festivals around the area, but none of this prepares Horton for his next life-altering experience.

At the conclusion of his freshman year in the Spring of 1963, the scholarship monies are depleted. Horton returns to Boston, works by day and enrolls in evening physics classes at Boston University, mirroring his father's earlier efforts. He struggles financially through the academic year and eventually drops out to support himself as a full-time orderly at the Peter Bent Brigham Hospital in Boston. He moves out of his mother's home and into a small studio apartment in Cambridge with two fellow co-workers from the hospital. Randall soon meets a young Jewish man named Joe Velden who lives a short distance away in a Jewish/Italian neighborhood in Boston's South End. Velden and Horton hit it off and become fast friends.

"Joe never saw the color of my skin," recounts Horton, "but he did, unfortunately, experience the prejudices associated with it while hanging out with me. One day, he and I crossed paths with a young Italian girl from my high school days. We talked for a bit, and after she left, Lednicki turned to me and said, 'She's crazy about you, Horton! Are you blind? You need to stop being so shy and ask her out!' So I did, and a few nights later, Joe and I picked up our dates for a night on the town. We didn't drive far before we were pulled over by a police officer who shined his flashlight into the front and back seats of our car and pointedly asked its three white occupants, 'Do your parents know you're out

---

165   Keyboardist Weldon Irvine looms large in the pantheon of Jazz-funk, profoundly influencing the subsequent generations of hip-hop artists for whom he served as collaborator and mentor. He published over 500 songs, including his most famous "To Be Young, Gifted and Black," performed live for the first time by Nina Simone on the album *Black Gold* (1970). It has been dubbed the "official" Civil Rights anthem. It was later recorded by Aretha Franklin (1972), Stevie Wonder and Donny Hathaway. Irvine committed suicide in New York City in 2002 at the age of 58.

with this Nigger?' I was mortified and embarrassed, and I'm sure it was uncomfortable for everyone else as well."

Weeks later, Joe receives a similar warning shot across his bow when he and Horton return to find his apartment brutally ransacked. Tacked to the shredded fabric of his sofa is a note instructing him to "Keep that Nigger out of this neighborhood!"

The tumult of these assaults passes, but the residue lingers. How can it not? For the next several months, Horton's life settles into an aimless, yet predictable rhythm. He spends the summer working at the hospital as an orderly, hanging out with friends, listening to music, and on occasion, visiting the neighborhood pool halls. Then the current of his life takes a series of Charles Dickens-inspired twists. In early January 1963, Horton comes "face-to-face" with Pulitzer Prize winning poet Robert Frost, albeit postmortem, when the poet's body is brought into the Peter Bent Brigham Hospital morgue. (*The ghost of [Horton's] Past*)

A short time later, he looks up from his pool cue to find his mother staring at him from across the felted table in the pool hall. She smiles, but with an air of authority that unsettles Horton, and makes it clear that she feels her son is squandering his God-given talents in a pool hall. (*The ghost of [Horton's] Present*)

And in a nod to *The ghost of [Horton's] future*, a medical professional at the hospital where he works issues Horton a curt directive. "It has been 55+ years, and I can still picture her," recalls Horton. "She was a short, very cultured, dark-skinned, African American woman. She was writing something in a hospital chart, and she said in a very matter of fact voice, without looking up from her clipboard, 'Randall, it looks like you're trying to get your life together. Don't spend ten years doing it.'"

"It was probably the same message my mother tried to deliver in the pool hall, in her own way, but my anger and resentment toward her and the world in general prevented me from hearing it. Funny how the words of a stranger can cut through the clutter more effectively. This woman's words really pulled me up by my bootstraps. They made me ask myself, perhaps for the first time, *What AM I doing with my life?*" These *past*, *present* and *future* encounters have a preternatural effect on Randall's subconscious, readying the soil of his mind for a seed that will immediately alter the drift of his life.

"I was standing in the kitchen of our small apartment in the spring of 1964," recalls Horton, "listening to Thelonious Monk's album *Monk's Music* when a transcendent beam of light came down and commanded me to "*Go to San Francisco and study music!*" Best described, this light, similar in appearance to a laser beam, descended from directly above me, entered my physical body and silently communicated those exact words before receding as quickly and quietly as it appeared. When it vanished, I was in shock. I couldn't speak. I certainly couldn't define what just happened. I had no understanding of spiritual matters other than attending church as a young child with my mother. All I could manage to do for the next few moments was to walk in dazed circles around my apartment. I didn't understand it, but its message was very clear in my mind that I would, or *could*, do anything other than what it commanded me to do."

"I immediately bought a bus ticket, packed my bags and called my mother to tell her I was going to San Francisco to study music. She met me at the Greyhound bus station the following morning, hoping to talk me out of leaving. She didn't understand why I had to go, and I certainly couldn't explain it. I didn't even understand it myself! I just told her goodbye and boarded the bus to the next chapter of my life. She was tearful and sad, but I was so caught up in the power of the mysterious message that I was oblivious. I wasn't aware until much later in life that my abrupt departure and my failure to say goodbye even to my three siblings was confusing and painful, which I feel badly about to this day."

Four days later, Horton's bus pulls into San Francisco's downtown Greyhound Station. With only $30 remaining in his pocket, he asks the first person he sees where he can find the nearest YMCA. It happens to be an elderly black gentleman who is shining shoes on the sidewalk just outside the station. The man looks at Horton with tired eyes, puts his arm around his shoulder and mutely points up and to his right. Horton looks in the direction the stranger indicates, and sure enough, sees a large Y-M-C-A sign on the upper floors of a building just three blocks away.

Horton stays at the YMCA for several weeks while he secures a job as an orderly in the X-ray department of Kaiser Permanente Hospital on Geary Street. There he is befriended by Frank Jones who is an X-ray receptionist by day and aspiring Jazz musician by night.

Horton saves up enough money to move out of the YMCA and into a small rented room in a tenement house on Golden Gate Avenue, then eventually to a basement apartment at 709-A Broderick Street. And since he has moved to San Francisco to study music, he rents a piano.

"Like many Jazz musicians of that time, I wasn't a strong reader of sheet music, but I could play the piano pretty well by ear. When Frank Jones discovered this, he took me to the local Jazz clubs and introduced me as his pianist. He had a small record label that recorded various local musicians; most notably, *The Magicians' Why Must You Cry?*, which became a big hit in the Bay Area around that time. He eventually hired me to do a couple of arrangements for his Villa Records label."

During this time, Horton's exposure to, and interest in, jazz grows. He frequents the *North Beach* and *Both/And* Jazz clubs, getting to know the latter's co-owner Delano Dean, and soaks up the live music of Jazz greats Herbie Hancock, Miles Davis, Cannonball Adderley and Bill Evans. Horton is awed by their skills and eager to learn the chord changes, progressions and the *ins and outs* of playing real Jazz. He has the honor of playing the Blues with the famous guitarist "T-Bone Walker" at a local bar he frequents just a block from his apartment.[166] After closing

---

166 Horton later performs at the Half-Note Club with his own big band (1972).

hours, Horton and various club musicians often retire to his basement apartment and his elegant piano for jam sessions. The apartment is close to the club and the intersection of Haight and Ashbury Streets, the epicenter of the 1960's hippie movement. Local Jazz musicians frequenting the area or looking for places to hang out between gigs find a 24-hour welcome mat outside Horton's apartment door. Visitors include Donald Jordan, the pianist on James Moody's song *Cooking the Blues* and pianist Sonny Donaldson. Some try to talk Horton into shooting up with them. Others protect Horton as if he is a little brother. "I'll kill you if I ever find you doing any of that [stuff]!" Sonny Donaldson threatens Horton on more than one occasion. And of course, the specter of Horton's father's alcoholism also acts as a deterrent. According to Horton,

> But it was worth the risk hanging out with these guys because of the lessons they taught me. Dewey Redman[167] and Stanley Willis were also frequent visitors who really helped tune me up! Willis was an ingenious Jazz musician from the San Francisco area who was known by Duke Ellington, Milt Jackson of the *Modern Jazz Quartet* and other greats. He was a God-like figure to me. He also happened to be homeless at the time. In the end, they all became my early musical mentors, refining my playing, and understanding of Jazz; at times, it was a rather eye-opening education. I remember walking into my apartment one afternoon and coming face-to-face with a beautiful, bikini-clad blonde, sitting atop my piano. It took me a moment to even notice my friend Stanley Willis at the keyboard earnestly serenading her! What was I? All of twenty-two... and still pretty wet behind the ears where women were concerned! [Horton reminisces in thought for

---

167   Walter Dewey Redman (1931–2006) was a Jazz tenor (and sometimes alto) saxophonist and is the late father of modern day Jazz tenor saxophonist Joshua Redman.

a moment, before continuing] Although I *did* propose to my elementary school classmate Linda Welsh when I was six or seven years old! Actually borrowed my cousin Elaine's *real* diamond engagement ring. Pressed it into Linda's tiny hands before running off in terror without saying a word. [Horton bubbles with laughter before becoming more serious.] The engagement ring was later returned to my cousin by my classroom teacher, and I apologized *profusely* when I understood the seriousness and stupidity of my actions. I don't mind telling you that my mother put the fear of God into me where women were concerned [affecting her voice]: 'You need to respect women, Randall!' 'Treat them right!' 'Don't you ever cheat on them!'" he says, recreating the lectures he heard growing up.

Although Horton and his siblings sometimes suffered under their mother's anger and resentment over her own lost ambitions, she also instilled lessons of merit. She was an ardent advocate of women's rights. She railed against stereotypical female roles and the limited opportunities of her era. She yearned for a better life for her children, and she drummed into their heads the importance of personal and professional self-actualization. For Horton it was a childhood tangled with positive and not-so-positive messages and behaviors that would take him years of introspection and mentoring to comb through.

During one of the many jam sessions in the basement of his Broderick Street apartment, Horton meets and begins seeing a young woman with whom he fathers a baby boy named Kevin Drew Horton.

"I behaved deplorably when she came to me with the news," relates Horton. "I didn't want to believe I was the father. I shirked my duties at first, then tried to make up for it by doing what I thought was the right thing. I eventually married another woman from my neighborhood, and my new wife and I took partial custody of our son, but over the years I found myself falling into the same abhorrent behaviors of my parents. It would take decades of hard work, support from positive role models, mostly from various churches, and the *grace* of God, before I developed the skills and understanding to break free of the patterns ingrained in me. I have lived with a great deal of guilt about my ignorance and actions. But after years of reflection, prayer, and hard work, I have found a measure of peace. I stay in touch with my grown son and try to be the supportive and loving father I was ill-equipped to be in my earlier years."

Negative thoughts and behaviors, ingrained over time, require patience and persistence to break through for meaningful change – much like changes required in the misinformed white ideologies that are propelling the American Civil Rights Movement toward its painful, yet necessary flash points. The harsh reality for black musicians and entertainers of this era is that employment is largely available only in nightclubs, bars and brothels. And the African American church is the spiritual, social and political center and base. Lena Horne once said, "I learned from Ethel Waters, Duke Ellington, Adelaide Hall, the Nicholas Brothers, the whole thing, the whole schmear. [*The Cotton Club*] was a great place because it hired us, for one thing, at a time when it was really rough [for performers of color]."[168]

However, gainful employment in the clubs comes at a cost. While Jazz musicians and entertainers benefit from the clubs' epicurean atmospheres and breathing room for unfettered personal and musical expression, *cliché* performances at most venues also perpetuate black stereotypes that serve to dismiss Jazz as a *bona fide* art form.

Many Jazz musicians believe that one has to live the African American experience in order to play what is essentially the soundtrack of their history. "Music is your own experience, your own thoughts, your

---

168   Howard Reich, "Legendary singer, civil rights activist Lena Horne dies," *Chicago Tribune*, May 10, 2010, https://www.chicagotribune.com/entertainment/chi-100510-lena-horne-dies-obit-story.html.

own wisdom," renowned Jazz (BeBop) alto sax player Charlie Parker was quoted as saying. "If you don't live it, it won't come out of your horn."

While Horton finds San Francisco's music scene in the 1960's truly amazing, he finds the culture surrounding it less so – seedy venues, drugs, alcohol, exploitation, LSD-inspired Rock 'n' Roll and the everyday hustle of the music industry – everything his mother had railed against. It is a *Catch-22* simmering just below the surface for 23-year-old Horton. To learn about and play Jazz, he finds himself immersed in its acculturated lifestyle. From the outside looking in, it appears glamorous and exciting, but Randall finds it difficult to square his love for Jazz with the uncomfortable childhood memories it dredges up. A sense of disquiet begins to color his thoughts and he quietly yearns for a more transcendent experience for his musical studies.

"Looking back, it is easier to see that I was struggling," says Horton. "In my childhood, my mother exposed us to great classical music, and I longed to return to that, to music that provided a better *fit*, where I felt more at peace. My *calling* told me to go to San Francisco and study *music*. I just hoped it applied to *all* genres, not just Jazz."

# HISTORICAL CONTEXT
## 1964-1965

The *Beatles* invade America in 1964, just as the country's social climate starts to violently destabilize. America is still trying to come to grips with President Kennedy's recent assassination. The Civil Rights Movement is in full swing and racial tensions are at an all-time high. The bodies of three voter registration workers named Schwerner, Chaney and Goodman, are found in a dam. All have been shot. The African American activist Chaney is badly beaten; Congress passes the Civil Rights Act, banning discrimination in employment and public places; Malcom X founds the Organization of Afro-American Unity to unite all Americans of African descent against discrimination, and the Nobel Foundation awards the Nobel Peace Prize to Reverend, Dr. Martin Luther King, Jr.

The lack of stability leaves young Americans confused and in search of an outlet for their thoughts and emotions, which helps shift music from the happy-go-lucky tunes of the 50's and early 60's to the political-themed music of the mid-1960's to early 1970's. Protest music becomes the new soundtrack of the American experience.

In February of 1965, African American nationalist and religious leader Malcom X[169] is assassinated by rival black Muslims. On March 7, 1975 (Bloody Sunday) several civil right leaders led hundreds of peaceful demonstrators in the first of three (intended to be) non-violent marches from Selma to Montgomery, Alabama to register Southern, black voters. A 25-year old John Lewis,[170] civil rights leaders, and participants are met on this occasion (and the other two occasions, which include Martin

---

169  Malcom X (1925-1965) was minister of the Nation of Islam in Harlem, New York. As a fiery orator, he advocated self-defense and the liberation of African Americans "by any means necessary" for which he was admired by African American communities in New York and around the country who had grown weary of the lack of progress toward equality through non-violent initiatives.

170  John Lewis (1940 - 2020), a 17-term Georgia congressman, was 45 when he marched across the Edmund Pettus Bridge and was the first to be beaten by state troopers, who cracked his skull with a billy club on the date that became known as "Bloody Sunday."

Luther King, Jr.) by State Troopers who intimidate and/or attack them as they attempt to cross Selma's symbolic Edmund Pettus Bridge,[171] By the 3rd march, 25,000 thousand participants successfully arrive in Montgomery. Several voting-rights activists[172] are beaten and murdered, generating world media coverage and precipitating President Johnson's signing of the Voting Rights Act just five months later to assure African Americans the right to vote. Duke Ellington tries mightily to apply his own soothing balm to the nation's deep wounds with his first *Sacred Concert* (9/16/65 at Grace Cathedral, San Francisco) and its daring introduction of meditative, worshipful Jazz into the church with subtextual pleas for love, tolerance, acceptance, inclusion, forgiveness and the uplifting of people of all races, religions, ethnicities and socio-economic conditions.

The music and messages of Ellington's first *Sacred Concert* stand in stark contrast to the more visceral and direct protest music. Traditional and spoken Jazz are being combined with poetic and revolutionary Jazz like Gil Scott Heron's *The Revolution Will Not Be Televised* (1970), calling for more active protest. Music of this period turns increasingly away from acoustic-oriented Folk stylings to Rock-based rhythms like Barry McGuire's *Eve of Destruction*, which enters the singles charts in August 1965, and is the first protest song to reach the number one spot. The power and popularity of the Beatles helps legitimize American protest

171 Sydney Trent, John Lewis Nearly Died On The Edmund Pettus Bridge. Now It May Be Renamed For Him, Washington Post Retropolis Retropod, podcast, audio, July 26, 2020, https:// www.washingtonpost.com/history/2020/07/26/john-lewis-bloody-sunday-edmund-pettus-bridge/. "Lewis later said on his last trek across the bridge in 2020, 'On this bridge, some of us gave a little blood to help redeem the soul of America. Our country is a better country. We are a better people, but we have still a distance to travel to go before we get there.' The televised images of the bravery shown by Lewis and other protesters in the face of state violence inspired the passage of the 1965 Voting Rights Act just two months later."

172 Jimmie Lee Jackson, an unarmed African American veteran, civil rights activist and deacon of a Baptist church died (February 26, 1965) after being mortally shot by a state trooper. His murder helped inspire the Selma to Montgomery marches. Amelia Boynton, local organizer, was beaten by State Troopers with photographs of her lying wounded and unconscious on the Edmund Pettus Bridge broadcast worldwide. James Reeb, a white Unitarian Universalist minister from Boston participating in the marches was beaten by a group of white men the same evening (February 7, 1965) and later died from his head trauma.

music and shift popular music from entertainment to an effective way of organizing resistance to various issues and mobilizing entire political groups. American bands such as *Creedence Clearwater Revival, CSNY, Grateful Dead* and *Simon and Garfunkel* quickly follow suit.

**CHAPTER 6**

# IN THE BEGINNING, GOD

---

*"When I play Sacred Music, I do this for ME.*
*This is personal. This is not, career. It is!*
*It's the most important thing in my life!"[173]*
- Duke Ellington

Ellington's sister Ruth, believes that her brother concealed himself under "veil upon veil upon veil" and relied on his personal faith to see him through racial, business and personal struggles. She writes, "…after many years of observation, I concluded that the mystique of Edward Kennedy Ellington was in fact, based upon the philosophy of life in which he profoundly believed, namely Christianity." Ellington found solace in the Bible and remained a student of its teachings throughout his life. Ruth attributes "… the way in which he truly honored and loved

---

173  Robert Drew, and Mike Jackson. *On the Road With Duke Ellington*, Direct Cinema Limited/ Drew and Associates, 1974, youtube.com/watch?v=swvEsprdrh0.

his parents", his "calm equilibrium in the face of every-day hassles of frantic show biz life," his "empathy and understanding for the problems of others" and "his warm love for human beings generally" to Ellington's religious faith and conviction.

Since he uses his musical genius to interpret every sound, event and emotion swirling around him, it is only natural that Ellington eventually explores his own faith in the same manner. "He begins by examining the porous boundary between sacred and secular music in 1927 with his *Black and Tan Fantasy* which refers to the physical and spiritual yearning for equality fleetingly experienced in *black and tan* Jazz clubs that cater harmoniously to both black and white patrons. Ellington captures this unsettled state of the human soul yearning for interracial harmony in this song with the wailing, growling and praying of the unique musical voices he creates. He later combines elements of Jazz, Blues, choral and classical music with African American Spirituals and Gospel, to create his *Sacred Music* which blurs the lines between secular and religious musical genres and expands the role of Jazz. This begins Ellington's lifelong fascination with one of the central organizing principles behind African American music – its connection between Saturday night and Sunday morning. It is a lived experience for Ellington and most Jazz musicians who routinely move from their Saturday night gigs into their Sunday church jobs, where many clean up after an all-night party and re-set their chairs for the Sunday morning church service."[174]

## Ellington's First Sacred Concert

In 1935, Ellington provides a brief glimpse of his personal thoughts with the 13-minute *Reminiscing in Tempo*. It is his musical and spiritual expression of grief over the passing of his beloved mother at the age of 56.

---

174   Dr. Christopher J. Wells, Program Notes: Duke Ellington's Sacred Concert, "50th Anniversary - Duke Ellington's Sacred Concert, November 12 - 13, 2016", Phoenix Chorale, phoenixchorale. org/concerts/program-notes-duke-ellington.

The extended-length composition evolves out of a period of self-imposed seclusion and mourning. According to Ellington, the music is "a detailed account of my aloneness after losing my mother... Every page of that manuscript was dotted with smears and unshapely marks caused by tears that had fallen. I would sit and gaze into space, pat my foot, and say to myself: 'Now, Edward, you know she would not want you to disintegrate, to collapse into the past, into your loss, into lengthy negation or destruction. She did not spend the first part of your life preparing you for this negative attitude."[175] *Reminiscing in Tempo* will later pave the way for other long form works that will cement Ellington's legacy as a major American composer.

A more formal opportunity to explore his faith comes in 1963, when the Reverend Julian Bartlett reaches out to Ellington to write a sacred concert as part of the year-long dedication ceremony for the newly completed Grace Cathedral Episcopal Church in San Francisco. Given the turbulence of the 1960's and his uncanny ability to read people's wants and needs, perhaps Ellington senses it is finally time to do a sacred piece. He eagerly accepts the commission, but allows ten precious months to tick by before composing in earnest. In typical fashion, his writing is done in fits and starts, shoe-horned into the nooks and crannies of his grueling touring schedule. He composes after performances as stagehands pack up gear around him. He writes in hotel lounges to the accompanying sounds of vacuum cleaners and bars being restocked. He arranges in his hotel room on his ever-present electric Wurlitzer piano. He orchestrates during the solitude of long road trips between gigs while being driven by bandmate Harry Carney. He doodles on dinner napkins, hotel stationery, his hand, or his shirt tails.

Six months into the composing process, news of Billy Strayhorn's

---

175   David Johnson, "Reminiscing In Tempo: Remembrance In Jazz And Popular Song," Indiana Public Media, May 27, 2011, https://indianapublicmedia.org/nightlights/reminiscing-tempo-remembrance-Jazz-popular-song/.

advanced cancer diagnosis jars Ellington. And as the final notes of his *First Sacred Concert* spill out onto paper, they are imbued with Ellington's love and respect for Strayhorn. Ellington begins to come to terms with the personal and professional voids that Strayhorn's eminent death (5/31/67) will create. The *Sacred Music* that results slowly begins to draw a stranger named Randall Keith Horton into the composer's eddy.

After Ellington's attempt to desegregate Jazz and classical music with *Black, Brown and Beige* in 1943, he makes another pioneering leap in 1965. He boldly creates a new form of jazz by including elements of classical and choral music, Negro spirituals, Gospel, Blues, dance and lyrics for religious expression and worship.[176] They coalesce upon the altar under Ellington's direction, asserting the righteousness of Jazz to praise a universal God and call for common ground. And to ensure that his music glitters aurally, he writes it with the unique acoustical characteristics of the cathedral itself in mind as a living, breathing member of his orchestra.

Ellington writes this *Sacred Concert* as his personal offering to God and refuses compensation. Aware that people will likely accuse him of trying to "take the *Cotton Club* to church," Ellington heads his critics off at the pass by holding a press conference and sharing the personal import of his groundbreaking concert.

"Now, I play a lot of places," says Ellington. "I play night clubs and gambling casinos and the greatest music halls in the world with the greatest symphonies in the world and all that for a living. But when I play *Sacred Music*, I play this for _me_! This is personal. This is not career. It is! It's the most important thing in my life!"[177] And later, "Now I can say openly what I've been saying on my knees for 60 years."

News that the *Ellington Orchestra* will be performing a special

---

176  "Duke Ellington's Sacred, Spiritual Concerts: Re-Creating a Reverent Opus of Song, Dance and Jazz," NPR, March 9, 2004, https://www.npr.org/templates/story/story.php?storyId=1752678.

177  Drew, *Ibid.*

concert[178] at a church atop Nob Hill in San Francisco has Horton and his friends buzzing. Twenty-three-year-old Horton drops everything to make sure he is in attendance. He arrives two hours early at Grace Cathedral, but the church is already filled to capacity, so he carves out a spot standing next to one of the massive stone pillars leading away from the nave.

The maestro takes the stage wearing a white suit. He says a few opening remarks before leading his orchestra through a groundbreaking 48:15-minute performance. Ellington's *Sacred Concert* includes *Come Sunday* and *David Danced (Before The Lord With All His Might)*[179] from *Black, Brown and Beige* (1943), *New World A-Comin* and *Heritage (My Mother, My Father)* from *My People* (1963). And battling what the composer admits is "a certain amount of trepidation," he also performs new music: *Tell Me It's The Truth, The Lord's Prayer, Preacher's Song, Ain't But The One,* and *In the Beginning, God* whose melody is built around the first four words (six syllables) of the Bible. This final song is woven throughout the concert, either sung by the *Herman McCoy Choir* or played. It earns a Grammy Award two years later in 1967.[180]

Bunny Briggs is introduced by Ellington as "the most super levi-athanic, rhythmaturgically syncopated, tapstermaticianismist." He tap dances magically to Ellington's *David Danced.* Jon Hendricks delivers his spoken word. Ellington sidemen Paul Gonsalves, "Cat" Anderson and Johnny Hodges stun as usual. And forever the collector of shiny, new talents, just months before the concert Ellington discovers the vocal talents of a 21-year-old gospel singer named Queen Esther Marrow.[181]

---

178  The *Sacred Concert* was performed again at Grace Cathedral on its 25th and 50th anniversaries, in 1990 and 2015, respectively.

179  "David Danced" is the same "Come Sunday" melody played in 4/4 time, an up-tempo celebratory re-casting that sets the biblical text (2 Samuel 6:14).

180  Gabe Meline, "From the Club to the Cathedral: Revisiting Duke Ellington's Controversial 'Sacred Concert'," KQED, September 14, 2015, https://www.kqed.org/arts/10957761/from-the-club-to-the-cathedral-revisiting-duke-ellingtons-controversial-sacred-concert.

181  Ellington is so taken by Esther Marrow's performance and the purity of her voice that he invites her to perform with his orchestra several more times over the next four years, a juggernaut that launches the young woman's own powerful career as a singer, songwriter, entertainer and civil rights advocate.

He arranges music specifically for her voice and features her prominently in the performance.

"Ooh, I was really nervous," recalls Marrow in an interview 31 years later (1999). "Because you gotta remember, this was my first time performing, period! I had only sang in church. And to be singing with Duke Ellington and his orchestra? Oh my God.[182] The sun was shining through the stained-glass windows. It was so beautiful. Johnny Hodges was playing saxophone. I felt honored, blessed — I was performing with genius." [183] "You know, Duke was a Jazzman, but he had a connection, also, with God. And I think that he wanted to show that being a Jazz musician did not make him separate and apart from believing in and knowing God."[184]

Ellington himself purports to have read the Bible completely four times before he was out of his twenties and several more times after the death of his mother and throughout his life.[185] Although this may have been a surprise to his fans, it is not to those closest to him. Otto Hardwick, alto saxophonist and one of Ellington's earliest friends in Washington DC, recalls how Duke would come home at night and read the Bible in his bath until the water turned cold. Ellington was meticulous about saying grace before meals, and he wore a gold cross on a chain around his neck from his middle thirties, which was odd, since he had an aversion to other jewelry, and refused to wear watches or rings ..."[186] According to Horton's recollection of that day at Grace Cathedral:

> The experience of observing a live performance by the *Ellington Orchestra* for the very first time was electrifying.

182  Meline, *Ibid.*

183  Paula Span, "The Gospel According to Queen Esther," *Washington Post*, January 31, 1999, www.washingtonpost.com/archive/lifestyle/style/1999/01/31/the-gospel-according-to-queen-esther/3187b80e-5efd-46ab-a8bc-e9a88549bdd3/?utm_term=.336fecb64883.

184  Meline, *Ibid.*

185  Derek Jewell. *Duke: A Portrait of Duke Ellington.* W.W. Norton & Company, 1980.

186  Jewell, *Ibid.*

Duke Ellington led his orchestra in a very casual, minimalist manner: a flick of the wrist, a nod of his head, clapping and verbal call-outs punctuated with an occasional swooping downbeat. I stood there against the column, mesmerized throughout the performance.

At one point, Maestro Ellington looked directly at me for several seconds. We *vibed* for lack of a better term. Our eye contact carried an inner revelation, a mutual attunement and a reflection of other-worldly significance. There was, for a long moment, the illuminating presence of the same light from the *calling* that visited me in my Cambridge and Broderick Street apartment. This time, though, it filled the entire sanctuary in conjunction with the beauty and glory of the performance. Time slowed down, and I found myself in a private bubble with Ellington and his amazing musicians. I not only saw the light, I felt its ambient warmth as if my body and the entire sanctuary were *aglow*. I glanced to my left and right wondering... *Is anyone else seeing or feeling this?* The meaning in that moment, of the light and the direct, eye-to-eye contact with Duke Ellington, resonated with me on so many levels, but again, I couldn't fully comprehend it or otherwise articulate exactly what it was...to myself, or to anyone else at the time. It would take decades to fully appreciate its personal and spiritual significance.

Every note and lyric, expressing the composer's own religious beliefs, resonate deeply with Horton on a transformative level. But while Ellington's *First Sacred Concert* is stunningly beautiful for some, it is unnerving to others. Death threats are called into the church in the days preceding the performance. The concert receives a short review in the *San Francisco Chronicle* the next day which notes the atmosphere of unease. Ellington's band, according to the uncredited review, "appeared to leave many of the audience discomfited, nervous or edgy, not completely willing to accept the idea that the wild sound of a sax should pierce the austere heights of the Episcopal cathedral's nave.'"[187]

And according to historian Peter Manseau,

> ...the fascinating thing about such religious consternation concerning Jazz is that historians now generally agree that Jazz was indeed born from religious experiences — specifically from the blending of spiritual and cultural influences within the African American community. The combination of beliefs and practices that eventually led to Jazz included rituals drawing on traditions enslaved peoples carried with them from West Africa and through the Caribbean, including Yoruba, Obeah, and Islam.
>
> The transformative blending of spiritual and musical styles is what early critics of Jazz heard when they mistakenly declared it was the devil's music. In fact it was never a music lacking religion. From the beginning, it was the product of varied religious perspectives interacting in entirely new ways.... The ability of Jazz to incorporate any influence that comes its way has continued, and now includes every religious tradition that has called America home.[188]

But, a full 22 years after Duke Ellington dares to perform *Black, Brown and Beige* at Carnegie Hall and ten years after recording his 1958 album with Mahalia Jackson similarly titled *Black, Brown and Beige*,[189] America's cultural mindset remains emboldened against Ellington's

---

187  Meline, *Ibid.*

188  Peter Manseau, "Duke Ellington's Christmas Gift," National Museum of American History, December 19, 2016, https://americanhistory.si.edu/blog/duke-ellingtons-christmas-gift.

189  This album included only portions of Ellington's complete composition.

innovative efforts, steadfast in its aversion to the content, length, and venues of his daring and pioneering compositions. The critics' and public's responses to Ellington's *Sacred Concert* mirror those of his Carnegie Hall performance of *Black, Brown and Beige*. Ellington merely responds, "We write and play from our perspective, and the audience listens from its perspective. If and when we agree, I am lucky."

But Horton finds Ellington's performance transcendent and inspiring; a simultaneous revelation and conundrum. He witnesses, upon the altar of Grace Cathedral, a Jazz performance stripped of its implied baseness, dressed up in sacred intent and offered directly to God. It is so unthinkable, so bold and innovative, that it defies immediate understanding. Some quickly reject it, while others like Horton instinctively sense they have witnessed a watershed moment. The 23-year-old Horton emerges energized and inspired to further his musical studies.

Jimmy McPhail who sang vocals in the *First Sacred Concert* captures the phenomena of Duke's bold experiment 24 years later in 1989, writing "The *First Sacred Concert* was a landmark, premiering Ellington's religious music. People had never seen anything like that in church."[190]

### First Sacred Concert

*Actual Performance*[191]

*Come Sunday / Montage / Tell Me, It's The Truth / In The Beginning God / Will You Be There? / 99% Won't Do / Ain't But The One / New World A'Comin' / In The Beginning God / My Mother, My Father / The Lord's Prayer / Come Sunday / David Danced Before The Lord / The Preacher's Song*

---

190 Patrice Gaines-Carter, "Ellington, the Duke of Musical Royalty," *The Washington Post*, April 29, 1989, https://www.washingtonpost.com/archive/local/1989/04/29/ellington-the-duke-of-musical-royalty/7eee8a04-9d1d-4375-a0af-5e822b8b4e38/.

191 Ken Vail, *Duke's Diary - The Life of Duke Ellington 1950-1974*, Scarecrow Press, 2002, p. 271.

## The Pulitzer Snub

The Pulitzer Prize for Music is a prestigious annual award recognizing distinguished musical compositions of significant dimension by Americans that have their first performance in the United States during the award year. Unfortunately, as reporter Howard Reich notes, "Since the inception of the prize in 1943…every Pulitzer-winning composition [speaks] in the language of European-derived, Western classical music. As for Jazz, Blues, Gospel, Country, Spirituals, and every other genre the United States gives to the world, all has been excluded completely."[192]

Duke Ellington's *First Sacred Concert* certainly merits Pulitzer consideration, "but the jury unanimously decides that there is no major work deserving of the Pulitzer Prize." To quell the ensuing outcry, "the Pulitzer committee recommends a special citation be given to Duke Ellington in recognition of the body of his work, but the Pulitzer Board refuses even that, and in an unprecedented and reprehensible move, no Pulitzer for music is awarded this year. It is a bitter disappointment for the 66-year-old composer who outwardly downplays the stinging rebuke, stating, "Fate is being kind to me. Fate doesn't want me to be too famous too young." It will take another 32 years (1997) before a Pulitzer Prize is awarded for a Jazz composition."[193] [194]

The Pulitzer's perpetual exclusion of Jazz, perhaps America's greatest cultural invention, disturbs some Pulitzer board members and music enthusiasts. Several board members resign from the committee in

---

192  Howard Reich, "The Story Behind the First Pulitzer for Jazz", Neiman Reports https://niemanreports.org/articles/the-story-behind-the-first-pulitzer-for-jazz/.

193  The first jazz composition to win a Pulitzer Prize in 1997 was "Wynton Marsalis's 'Blood on the Fields,' an epic vocal-orchestral suite that dealt head-on with the tragedy of slavery, became not only the first Jazz work to take the highest honor in American music but the first non-classical piece ever to win."

194  Other Pulitzer recipients for Jazz include: Chicago composer, saxophonist and flautist Henry Threadgill (2016) for "In For A Penny, In For A Pound", American pianist and composer Anthony Davis (2019) for his opera "The Central Park Five" and Jazz saxophonist, violinist, trumpeter and composer, Ornette Coleman (2007) for "Sound Grammar" - https://www.pulitzer.org/prize-winners-by-category/225.

protest. But what angers Ellington most in 1965, according to Jazz critic Nat Hentoff's *The New York Times Magazine* piece "This Cat Needs No Pulitzer Prize," is what the Pulitzer rejection says about an art form born of the African-American experience, a genre of music to which (Ellington) has dedicated his life.

"I'm hardly surprised that my kind of music is still without, let us say, official honor at home," Ellington said. "Most Americans still take it for granted that European music — classical music, if you will — is the only really respectable kind. I remember, for example, that when Franklin Roosevelt died, practically no American music was played on the air in tribute to him."[195]

---

195  Reich, *Ibid.*

# HISTORICAL CONTEXT
## 1966 - 1974

In 1968 the highly unpopular Vietnam War continues into its thirteenth year. Phil Ochs captures the public's shared sense of resignation with one of the final anti-Vietnam songs, *The War Is Over*.[196] This same year, Reverend Martin Luther King, Jr. is assassinated in Memphis and Senator Robert Kennedy is assassinated in Los Angeles. US African American Olympic medalists Tommie Smith and John Carlos, Gold and Bronze medal winners respectively in the 200 Meter race at the Mexico City Olympics, hold up their clenched fists in solidarity with the more revolutionary Black Panther movement.[197] And as the world seems to be splintering, Ellington performs his *Second Sacred Concert* in New York's St. John the Divine Cathedral (1968).

In 1969 President Nixon bestows The Medal of Freedom, America's highest civilian award, on Duke Ellington at his 70th birthday celebration. The ceremony takes place at the White House where Ellington's father once worked as a food server. French President Georges Pompidou follows suit in 1973, presenting Ellington with his country's highest honor, the National Order of the Legion of Honour, the same year Ellington performs his third and final *Sacred Concert* at Westminster Abbey in London.

On the music front, there is the tragic loss of Jimmy Hendrix, Janis Joplin and Louis Armstrong (1971). The *Beatles* break up, and there is a sharp decline in the release of new protest anthems as Baby Boomers grow physically and emotionally exhausted. On a positive note,

---

196   Frank Hoffmann, "PROTEST MUSIC," *Survey of American Popular Music*, modified for web by Robert Berkline in Spring 2003, https://www.shsu.edu/lis_fwh/book/american_renaissance/Protest%20Music2.htm.

197   The Black Panther Party (1966-1982) began as a challenge to police brutality with the core practice of armed citizens patrols to monitor the behavior of police officers, known as "copwatching." In 1969, the group instituted a variety of community social programs, like the Free Breakfast for Children Programs, to address issues such as food injustice and offered community health clinics for the education and treatment of diseases.

integration is happening organically, at least in music. Elvis Presley helps transform the black musical and cultural influences behind early Rock 'n' Roll into cool forms of expression for white Americans. *Sly and the Family Stone* releases a series of ten top Billboard hits that are pivotal in the development of Funk, Soul, Rock, and Psychedelic music and make Pop Funk palatable to the masses. Music's growing appeal to integrated audiences helps open the door for Berry Gordy's new Motown sound (1959 - 1988), featuring romantic dance tunes (Soul with distinct Pop influences), which cross over and dominate popular music.[198] In 1972 alone, eleven of the top twenty albums are released by African American artists (Isaac Hayes, Aretha Franklin, Marvin Gaye, Gladys Knight and the Pips, Al Green, Curtis Mayfield and Sammy Davis, Jr. to name a few), with songs like Gaye's *What's Going On* and the Temptations' Ball of Confusion calling for greater social awareness.

Advances in LP technology bring about a return to softer, more introspective singer/songwriters whose music is better listened to on records. Be-Bop yields to the even more intellectualized Modern Jazz styles of Miles Davis, John Coltrain, Dave Brubeck, Paul Desmond, Cannonball Adderly and the *Modern Jazz Quartet.*

In 1973, the mobile phone makes its appearance. President Nixon orders the invasion of Cambodia, widening the war in Vietnam. Millions protest and four students at Kent State University in Ohio are killed by National Guard troops. The House Judiciary Committee indicts President Richard Nixon (1974) for the Watergate scandal, and Beverly Johnson becomes the first black model on the cover of Vogue or any other major fashion magazine.

---

198 Top Motown recording artists included Diana Ross, Smokey Robinson, Stevie Wonder, Marvin Gaye, Marth Reeves and the Vandellas, the Temptations, the Supremes, the Four Tops and the Jackson Five.

## CHAPTER 7

# SOMETHING ABOUT BELIEVING

*"On becoming more acquainted with the word of the Bible,*
*I began to understand so much more of what I had been taught,*
*and of what I had learned about life and about the people in mine."*[199]
-Duke Ellington

In the weeks following Ellington's first *Sacred Concert*, Horton returns to his hospital job inspired and energized. As he pushes a patient in a wheelchair to the X-ray department, he talks excitedly about the concert and his own interest in studying music. His attentive patient remarks, "If you're really interested in studying music, you need to check out the San Francisco Community Music Center (SFCMC)."

"Her words unified a number of seminal experiences for me," states Horton: "the *calling* that delivered me to San Francisco and the majesty of Ellington's *Sacred Concert* accompanied by a second manifestation of the mysterious light. They galvanized me to take the BART (Bay Area Rapid Transit) the very next day to the SFCMC which was located in a modest, two story, Victorian house at 544 Capp Street in the Mission District, a predominantly Hispanic neighborhood."

The Center was founded in 1921 with the purpose of making high quality music accessible to all people regardless of their financial means, a perfect fit with Horton's musical aspirations and modest economic circumstances. He signs up for as many classes as he can cram into his off-duty hours: piano, cello, music theory and voice. His job as a hospital orderly keeps a roof over his head, but his immersion in music at the SFCMC feeds his soul and lifts him out of the more objectionable elements of the Jazz/hippie lifestyle of the late 1960's. During one of the many jam sessions at Horton's Broderick Street apartment, the mysterious light appears again. According to Horton:

> It was late afternoon, and we were jamming in my basement apartment: Delano Dean on bass with me on my grand piano. All of a sudden, *it* was there again. Not the laser beam of light like before. No! This time, just like the *First Sacred Concert*, the entire room was transformed. It became luminous, a feeling of warmth washed over me from above, and I was no longer in control of my own hands. It was as if something or someone was moving them for me. I played out of my mind, better than ever before. Dean dropped off his instrument and stared at me in disbelief. Without saying a word, he packed up his instrument and slipped out of my apartment. They later told me the whole scene spooked them. I was beginning to get spooked myself. This was the *third* time the unexplained light seeped into my apartment... Grace Cathedral... and my body without warning.

Little does Horton know, it will not be the last.

## Horton's Fourth Calling

Horton soon begins his first formal study of "inner hearing" techniques with violinist and teacher Wynn Westover. Westover teaches him music theory through *sight singing*, a unique method of *hearing* a musical score in one's head. Before long, Horton is traveling to Westover's home in Sausalito for more advanced private lessons.

"Those weekly lessons were an amazing escape for me," relates Horton. "The 90-minute bus ride transported me out of the chaos of the city, into the calm pastoral countryside and through the door of a lovely home where I was also exposed, perhaps for the first time, to a functional and respectful husband-wife-relationship between Wynn and his wife Virginia."

The *ear training* gives Horton the skills to eventually win a conducting seminar and competition offered at the SFCMC by its executive director Dr. Paul Freeman, who goes on to become one of America's most successful recording conductors. As the co-winner of this competition, Horton is allowed to guest conduct the esteemed San Francisco Conservatory Symphony.

"I only prepared for this extraordinary experience because of the teachings of Mr. Westover," says Horton. "It was like being in a dream world. I conducted Christoph Willibald Gluck's *Iphigénie en Aulide*, submitting myself to the beauty of the score and the skills of the musicians, and I knew in that moment that I had finally found my place in the world. *This is what I am meant to do!* I thought throughout the performance. *This is who I am supposed to be!* And I was so pleased that my mother was in the audience to witness this important milestone in my life, having traveled all the way from Boston for the occasion.

"When I stepped off of the podium, Dr. Freeman said to me, 'Mr. Horton, your conducting of the symphony was unparalleled.' If I had any doubts about my ability to work toward a career in conducting, Dr.

Freeman's generous words kicked them straight to the curb! But I still had a lot of work to do, so when a janitorial job opened up at the SFCMC in 1967, I applied, even though Dr. Freeman insisted that the position was 'beneath my abilities'. But for me, the free, on-site housing meant I could quit my day job and immerse myself in the study of music."

Horton moves into the SFCMC and on to a new phase in his life. When his daily janitorial duties are complete, he studies piano, sings, and gives back to the center's younger students by founding and conducting his own *Big Band*, a string orchestra and five Doo-Wop singing groups. The *Randall Keith Horton Big Band* features a variety of local Jazz artists whom Horton conducts in performances in and around the San Francisco Bay Area. Horton's burgeoning musical skills soon earn him an opportunity to co-conduct the recently funded San Francisco Little Symphony at the San Francisco Civic Center under the direction of Dr. Freeman, in a performance of new music written by a young American composer. Then the world turns upside down.

Rev. Dr. Martin Luther King, Jr. and Robert Kennedy are assassinated in 1968. Shortly thereafter, Horton's mentor Dr. Freeman accepts a position as the Associate Conductor of the Dallas Symphony.

"He called me into his office to give me the news," states Horton. "I came in with my mop and broom, and he laughed at the very sight of me, saying, 'You know, they're talking about you down at City Hall.' He was trying to tell me I was making a name for myself, but I didn't understand at the time. I just remember sitting on the floor of the men's bathroom a short time later with my mop and broom, wallowing in self-pity, wondering what in the world I was going to do without Dr. Freeman."

A few days later, Horton receives a phone call from Sister Gertrude Patch, PhD, the president of the San Francisco College for Women, offering him a six-month paid directorship of the school's Black Madonna arts program. It is a newly funded initiative offering 300 predominantly black, Bay Area students free access to ten creative workshops (in music, writing, television, drama, art, pottery, sculpture, painting, silk screen and photography), designed to help "unleash the stifled creative energy of black America" and "breakdown racial and social barriers."

As part of the program, Horton is allowed to form and conduct the program's 35-40 piece *African American Sinfonia Chamber Orchestra*. Not long after, Dr. Freeman contacts Horton with a personal request. Freeman is set to conduct the San Francisco Little Symphony Orchestra in a performance of George Walker's[200] music at the San Francisco Civic Center Auditorium, and he reaches out to see if Horton will feature Dr. Walker in a seminar at Lone Mountain College as part of his Black Madonna program.[201] Horton does so without hesitation and considers it one of his greatest honors. Walker is one of America's most distinguished composers and the first black composer to win a Pulitzer for a classical composition (1996). Freeman brings pundits, music scholars and critics into the community audience.

"Walker spoke to my students," says Horton. "He also confided to me that he hadn't touched the piano in six months, then sat at the Steinway, played one of his magnificent pieces and tore it up!"

In a 2020 newspaper article on Walker, *LA Times* music critic Mark Swed noted, "Like many African Americans in the classical world, Walker had to endure hardships and indignities. A concert career meant facing racism on two levels. One was exclusionary. The other ... was condescending."[202] Ultimately, he finds his greatest career opportunity in the academic world, though he continues to compose.

At the conclusion of the Black Madonna program in 1969, the San Francisco Women's College becomes Lone Mountain College with

---

200  George Theophilus Walker (June 27, 1922–August 23, 2018) was an American composer, pianist, organist, and the first African American to win a Pulitzer Prize in 1996 for his music *Lilacs*.

201  Mildred Hamilton, "Black Madonna Art," *San Francisco Examiner*, July 3, 1968, p. 15.

202  Mark Swed, "Music We All Should Know," *Los Angeles Times*, January 21, 2020, E-1 and E-4.

a co-ed campus.[203] President Sr. Patch offers Horton a full scholarship. This allows him to continue his musical studies and conduct the *African American Sinfonia* (young Blacks from the Bay Area) and later, the *Lone Mountain Symphony Orchestra* (students, university musicians and members of *San Francisco Symphony*).

"I owe my profound gratitude to Sr. Patch and all of my mentors," states Horton. "They took me under their wings, believed in me, nurtured my musical aspirations and molded me into a better person. Through their help, I learned to understand and appreciate my musical gifts and apply them toward the betterment of myself and others."

So, when a part-time Music and Choir Directorship for San Francisco's Sacred Heart Roman Catholic Church opens up,[204] a more-than-qualified Horton earns the position. It is here that Horton puts his musical training into practice and discovers another gratifying passion.

"I found the teaching aspect of conducting very rewarding," says Horton, "and learned that I am at my best when I am helping others realize their potential."

At 27 years of age, Horton is earning a supporting salary doing something he dearly loves in an environment that affords the structure and moral high ground for which he has longed. Thus begins Horton's 40-year career in musical directorships for numerous denominations of churches and synagogues.

Following one of Horton's musical church services at Sacred Heart, a woman walks up, introduces herself as Agnes Albert and says, "Randall, I want you to go to *The Bohemian Club* in the Union Square District and call on Maestro Josef Krips.[205] He is the conductor of the *San Francisco*

---

203  In 1973, Lone Mountain College merged with and changed its name to the University of San Francisco.

204  Hamilton, *Ibid.*

205  Josef Krips was the former principal conductor of the London Symphony (1950-1954) and the Music Director of the San Francisco Symphony (1963-1970) and his Bohemian Club residence.

*Symphony*. He will be expecting you. Tell him I sent you, and that I would like you to attend his rehearsals."

Horton only knows Mrs. Albert as a parishioner who sits in the back of the church, but he quickly learns that she is one of the church's – and the *San Francisco Symphony's* – most ardent and generous supporters. That same afternoon he makes his way to Josef Krips' *Bohemian Club* residence in downtown San Francisco.

"I felt like the cowardly lion approaching the great and powerful Oz," recalls Horton with a smile. "I took the BART to 624 Taylor Street and entered the imposing building on shaky knees. Maestro Krips gestured to me to sit opposite him in a tall, wingback chair. I did and mustered the courage to tell him that Mrs. Albert had sent me to ask if I could audit his rehearsals of the *San Francisco Symphony*. He listened patiently to my request, took off his glasses, removed his cigar, looked me over…through me actually… and economically said, in a strong German accent, 'Ya. You come. Sit five rows back.' I followed his instructions exactly and for the next 22 years, attended the symphony's thrice-weekly rehearsals (1969-1990)."

Five years later, as Horton observes Maestro Krips rehearse the orchestra for its premiere of Kirke Mechem's *Second Symphony*, a tall, slim gentleman standing in front of the orchestra motions Horton to join him. He does and finds himself standing beside the internationally renowned composer[206] himself as he listens to his own composition being rehearsed. Mechem introduces himself and graciously offers to share his full score with Horton, so they can follow along together. The two talk briefly afterward and Mechem mentions he is a professor and composer-in-residence (1968-1973) at the nearby Lone Mountain

---

206  Kirke Mechem is an American composer of international stature whose main body of work is in opera, symphony, chamber and piano with choral components. His first opera, Tartuffe, with over 400 performances in six countries, has become one of the most popular operas written by an American. He has composed more than 250 works in almost every form which have been performed in more than 42 countries.

College.[207] Horton, who has already served as the director for the Black Madonna arts program at Lone Mountain and is matriculating in the undergraduate music program, enrolls in Mechem's class immediately and begins learning the intricate scores of Brahms, Haydn and other composers. Over time, a long-standing mentorship develops.

"My scholarship at Lone Mountain College opened the doors for me to study and explore ALL forms of music," says Horton. "I even directed a small *Gregorian Chant Choir* and enjoyed it immensely," he recalls. "And it certainly helped me ingratiate myself with the resident nuns! Everything about my Lone Mountain experience was awe-inspiring, including the campus with its castle-like architecture, its beautiful interiors and stone floors scrubbed by Russian-speaking women dressed in white uniforms; something I could truly appreciate as a former janitor myself! (chuckling) It was a startling departure from any architecture I had previously experienced."

Horton's association with Krips and Mechem leads to a meeting with the General Director of the *San Francisco Opera* Kurt Herbert Adler[208] and permission to observe Adler's rehearsals of the *San Francisco Opera* (1969 to the mid 1990's). It also leads to Horton helping to

---

207 The school was founded by the Religious of the Sacred Heart as Sacred Heart Academy in Menlo Park, CA in 1898 and became College of the Sacred Heart in 1921. In the 1930's, it moved to San Francisco, CA and was later acquired by the University of San Francisco to become USF's Lone Mountain Campus.

208 Herbert Kurt Adler (1905–1988) was an Austrian-born American conductor and opera house director who established the Merola Opera Program, a free annual opera-in-the-park performance in San Francisco. As the General Director of the San Francisco Opera, he is credited with raising the standards of the opera company and "attracting a stunning galaxy of European stars, some at the beginning of their careers, to a small city at the other end of the world, often at significantly lower salaries than New York or Chicago would offer." Thanks to him, the door was opened for Horton to meet and learn from the guest conductors and orchestra members while observing full production rehearsals (especially those including Pavarotti).

rehearse the chorus for the *Three-Penny Opera* under Calvin Simmons.[209] After Krips' departure (1963-1970), Horton continues to audit rehearsals of the symphony under conductor Seiji Ozawa[210] (1970-1977) and a revolving door of the world's top visiting orchestras and conductors. It is an immersive education of the highest order.

"The Black Madonna program and Lone Mountain College really got the ball rolling on a number of amazing opportunities," says Horton. "It laid the foundation for me to conduct and direct the *Lone Mountain Symphony*[211] as well as the *San Francisco Medical Society Orchestra*[212] (1968-1973), which resulted in a chance meeting with another icon of the arts, classical conductor Denis de Coteau."[213]

"Denis de Coteau was a conducting giant," continues Horton. "Dr. Freeman considered him an international genius. I met him when he was the Assistant Music Director of the *San Francisco Ballet Orchestra* and a frequent Guest Conductor of the *San Francisco Chamber and Symphony Orchestras*. He was later appointed Music Director of the *San Francisco Ballet Orchestra*. De Coteau casually walked into one of my Lone Mountain Symphony rehearsals one day, a stranger to me at the time, and sat down for a listen. Imagine my surprise when I introduced myself and discovered who he was! Our chance meeting and friendly

---

209  Calvin Eugene Simmons (1950 – 1982) was assistant conductor with the San Francisco Opera from 1972 to 1975, winning the Kurt Herbert Adler Award. During this time, he was the staff conductor for the Merola Opera Program of the San Francisco Opera at which Randall Keith Horton was invited to rehearse his chorus for *Three-Penny Opera* and attend the San Francisco Opera performances for several seasons. He later became the first African American conductor of a major orchestra (Oakland Symphony Orchestra). He conducted the Los Angeles Philharmonic and was a frequent guest conductor with some of the nation's major opera companies and orchestras.

210  Seiji Ozawa is a Japanese-born American conductor known for his advocacy of modern composers and for his work with the San Francisco Symphony (1970 - 1977), the Toronto Symphony Orchestra, and the Boston Symphony Orchestra.

211  The Lone Mountain Symphony was a 45 piece community orchestra composed of area students and professional musicians.

212  The San Francisco Medical Society Orchestra was composed of physician musicians mainly from Kaiser Permanente Medical Group and Hospital.

213  Denis de Coteau (1929-1999) joined the San Francisco Ballet as assistant conductor in 1968 and served as the troupe's Music Director from 1974-1998.

discussion resulted in my auditing his rehearsals over a ten-year period (1969-1978) and absorbing a great deal more about conducting."

When people do something they love, it rarely feels like work. In addition to Horton's musical direction for Sacred Heart Church and attending rehearsals of the *San Francisco Symphony*, Opera and Ballet, Horton establishes and/or conducts two community orchestras: the *Westover Chamber Orchestra, Petaluma Symphony Orchestra* (1979) and the professional *San Francisco Little Symphony*. He also guest conducts the *Berkeley Symphony Orchestra* and *Sonoma County Peace Chorus*.

During Horton's 16 years auditing rehearsals (1969-1985), he is commissioned to arrange and conduct a rehearsal of Irving Berlin's music for Arthur Fiedler, conductor of the *San Francisco Symphony Pops Orchestras* (1951-1978). It is Horton's first experience arranging for and conducting a major orchestra.[214] It comes with a huge learning curve that teaches him an important lesson about arranging for a symphony's entire arsenal of musicians.

"Maestro Fiedler was gracious in his critique." states Horton. "He said, 'You did a good job, Randall, but you need to use more of the orchestra.' It was a very nice way of informing me that my arrangement had just taken a finely tuned race car on a Sunday drive."

Understanding the educational importance of hands-on arranging and conducting experiences, Mechem secures another arranging opportunity for Horton with members of the *San Francisco Symphony*. This time Horton writes music for the full horsepower of the orchestra. Its success leads to Horton guest conducting a small ensemble of *San Francisco Symphony* musicians playing Arnold Schoenberg's *Transfigured Night* at Lone Mountain. Thus, Horton finds himself conducting members of the San Francisco and Marin Symphonies while still a freshman

---

214  Arthur Fiedler became the Music Director of the Boston Pops (1930 - 1979) and was also associated with the San Francisco Pops Orchestra for 26 summers (1949-1975).

student at Lone Mountain College. Joseph Scafidi,[215] Executive Director of the *San Francisco Symphony*, is helpful in securing this performance and Kirke Mechem also attends.

Like Ellington and most Jazz musicians of the era, Horton hones his musical craft by listening, doing, observing and practicing. Ellington, after all, dropped out of high school a few months shy of graduation to make a living by painting signs, booking bands and only later pursuing a career in music. Billy Strayhorn cut his musical chops composing music for high school plays and musical performances. Their early "college of Jazz" was on the streets, in the pool halls and night clubs where talented Jazz musicians were relegated and could be heard. It would be decades before Jazz was formally studied in American music academies.

Horton likewise enters the San Francisco music scene in 1964 on a lowly rung and slowly makes his ascent. His contacts at the *San Francisco Community Music Center* (1966-1968), result in mentorships from some of the top figures in America's classical music; two of whom will make return appearances to help him at critical future junctures: *San Francisco Symphony* benefactor Agnes Albert, who will help solidify Horton's relationship with Duke Ellington, and composer Kirke Mechem who will endorse Horton for the musical commission of lifetime, but that's jumping ahead of the story.

## Ellington's Second *Sacred Concert*

On May 31, 1967, eight short months before the scheduled premiere of Duke Ellington's *Second Sacred Concert* in New York City, Ellington is dealt a devastating blow. His composing partner of twenty-eight years, Billy Strayhorn, succumbs to his battle with esophageal cancer. The significance of the loss cannot be overstated. In musical thought, Ellington and Strayhorn moved in concert with one another like the

---

215  Joseph Scafidi was the Executive Director of the San Francisco Symphony from 1974-1978 with more than 40 years of association.

two hemispheres of a single brain. Yet in personality, they were distinct; Ellington the supreme showman, and Strayhorn quietly, yet powerfully, composing and influencing behind the scenes.

Ellington bestows some of his highest praise on Strayhorn, stating, "In music, as you develop a theme or musical idea, there are many points at which directions must be decided, and at any time I was in the throes of debate with myself, harmonically or melodically, I would turn to Billy Strayhorn. We would talk, and then the whole world would come into focus. The steady hand of his good judgment pointed to the clear way that was fitting for us. He was not, as he was often referred to by many, my alter ego. Billy Strayhorn was my right arm, my left arm, all the eyes in the back of my head, my brain waves in his head, and his in mine."[216]

Ellington clearly revered Strayhorn's musical talent and admired his honesty, humility and humanity. As Ellington composes the music for his *Second Sacred Concert*, it is steeped in his deep respect and sorrow over the loss of his composing partner and friend.

On the cold afternoon of January 19, 1968, the Ellington Orchestra assembles for the premiere of the concert at The Cathedral of St. John The Divine in New York City. It is Ellington's personal church and the largest cathedral in the world with a seating capacity of 6,000. Ellington's opening remarks include a powerful remembrance of his late composing partner Billy Strayhorn, sharing the moral code by which he felt Billy Strayhorn lived:

> He demanded freedom of expression and lived in what we consider the most important and moral of freedoms: <u>Freedom</u> from hate, unconditionally. <u>Freedom</u> from self-pity (even throughout all the pain and bad news). <u>Freedom</u> from fear of possibly doing something that might help another more

---

216 Victor Cooper, "Stories of Standards: Rain Check" by Billy Strayhorn", KUVO – "Jazz with Victor Cooper" www.kuvo.org/stories-of-standards-rain-check-by-billy-strayhorn, 2019.

*140 | Duke Ellington*

than it might himself, and <u>Freedom</u> from the kind of pride that could make a man feel he was better than his brother or neighbor.[217]

Then Ellington and his orchestra temporarily shrug off their melancholy to perform the music of the *Second Sacred Concert*.[218] This time the maestro features the prodigious talents of Swedish singer Alice Babs[219] who sings Ellington's *Almighty God (Has Those Angels)*, *Heaven* and the wordless vocal, *T.G.T.T. (Too Good to Title)* to perfection. It is her first of many collaborations with Duke Ellington who later claims that when Babs is unavailable, he has to use three different singers to perform the music written for her more-than-three-octave vocal range. Cootie Williams' "growl" trumpet is prominently featured on *The Shepherd (Who Watches Over the Night Flock)* and the concert concludes on the climactic ending *Praise God and Dance*, inspired by Psalm 150[220], which appropriately calls for the praise of God with musical instruments, song and dance. Four months later (4/26/69), Ellington repeats his Second *Sacred Concert* at Boston's Emmanuel Episcopal Church at the invitation of the Harvard Episcopal Chaplaincy.

Ellington's second *Sacred Concert* receives a somewhat warmer

---

217  Vail, *Ibid.,* p. 317.

218  No recording of the premiere of Ellington's *Second Sacred Concert* has surfaced. It was subsequently recorded on January 22 and February 19, 1968 at Fine Studio in New York, issued as a double LP on Prestige Records and reissued on one CD, minus the tracks "Don't Get Down On Your Knees To Pray Until You Have Forgiven Everyone" and "Father Forgive." All the tracks can be found in the 24-CD box set *The Duke Ellington Centennial Edition: The Complete RCA Victor Recordings (1927-1973).*

219  Alice Babs, born Hildur Alice Nilson (1924–2014), was a Swedish singer and actress who worked in multiple genres – Swedish folklore, Elizabethan songs and opera though she was known internationally as a Jazz singer. She enjoyed a long and productive period of collaboration with Duke Ellington that began in 1963. Among other works, Babs participated in performances of Ellington's second and third Sacred Concerts which he originally wrote for her voice and three octave range.

220  Praise the Lord. Praise God in his sanctuary; praise him in his mighty heavens. Praise him for his acts of power praise him for his surpassing greatness. Praise him with the sounding of the trumpet, praise him with the harp and lyre, praise him with timbrel and dancing, praise him with the strings and pipe, praise him with the clash of cymbals, praise him with resounding cymbals. Let everything that has breath praise the Lord. Praise the Lord.

response, illustrating the importance of the passage of time and greater perspective. It has been three years since he shocked the world playing *Sacred (Jazz) Music* upon the altar of Grace Cathedral (1965), eleven years since he first performed *Come Sunday* on his *Black, Brown and Beige* album with Mahalia Jackson (1958) and twenty-five-years since the premiere of *Black, Brown and Beige* (1943). The sheer scale of these extended length compositions makes them difficult to perform, and consequently, less familiar to his audiences. Ellington thoughtfully allows three additional years to transpire before writing and performing his *Second Sacred Concert in* 1968. He even blends in songs he hopes will be familiar, and perhaps less threatening, from his first *Sacred Concert, (99%* and *The Preacher's Song)*. It proves to be a somewhat effective tactic as this time, and critics find themselves torn between not wanting to offer too much criticism, or praise.

But as the decades pass and critics revisit his pioneering *Sacred Concerts*, their critiques grow increasingly generous: Applauding Ellington's *Second Sacred Concert* for its "poignant universalism and bringing the great tradition of Jazz to the church (1999)";[221] crediting Ellington with "writing three massive works that combine elements of Jazz, classical music, choral music, spirituals, gospel and dance (2004);"[222] and summing up Ellington's *Sacred Music* as "both serious and swinging ... a reverent and hip body of Jazz (2018)."[223]

221  Ear Shot Jazz,"The History of Ellington's Sacred Music", "30th Anniversary of Sacred Music by Duke Ellington," December 26, 2020, www.earshot.org/ellingtons-sacred-music/.

222  "Duke Ellington's Sacred, Spiritual Concerts, Re-Creating a Reverent Opus of Song, Dance and Jazz", The Tavis Smiley Show, NPR, March 9, 2004.

223  Earshot Jazz, "*Sold Out* 30th Anniversary Concert of Duke Ellington's Sacred Music," www.earshot.org/event/concert-of-duke-ellingtons-sacred-music2018/.

# Actual Performance[224]

*Praise God / 99% / Supreme Being / Something About Believing / Almighty God / Heaven / Freedom / Don't Get Down On Your Knees / Father Forgive / Don't Get Down On Your Knees / Meditation / The Shepherd / The Biggest And Busiest Intersection / T.G.T.T / Praise God And Dance / The Preacher's Song*

Two short years later, another icon of the Ellington Orchestra falls silent. Alto Saxophonist Johnny Hodges dies unexpectedly from a massive heart attack (5/1970). His technique and style are irreplaceable. His tone, according to Ellington, "so beautiful it sometimes brought tears to the eyes."

## "Give Me Your Number"

In the spring of 1973, thirty-one-year-old Randall Keith Horton reads a notice in the newspaper that the Ellington orchestra is set to perform on April 13th at the *Great American Music Hall*, a supper club in San Francisco's Tenderloin District. It is another live (and recorded[225]) performance that will be particularly memorable for Horton. He clears his schedule and arrives two hours early with photos of his *Sacred Heart Chamber Orchestra* (string orchestra from the church where he serves as Director of Music), his *Big Band* in performance and Doo-Wop groups tucked proudly in the breast pocket of his sport coat. He stakes out a spot, first in line outside the venue's entrance, and waits for the orchestra to arrive. Duke's son Mercer Ellington is the first man off the bus.

Horton walks up to him, introduces himself and says, "I would like to meet your father." To his surprise, Mercer casually nods and invites him to ride the band bus to their next gig at the Sacramento Civic

---

224 Ken Vail, *Duke's Diary, Part II: The Life of Duke Ellington, 1952-1974* (Lanham, MD: Scarecrow Press, 2002), p. 329.

225  Vail, *Ibid.*, p. 432.

Auditorium. It is an unexpected and surreal invitation. Horton collects himself and follows the remaining band members into the supper club. The place is empty, allowing Horton to select a table a few feet from the stage and watch as the venue fills to capacity. By the time the Ellington Orchestra starts playing its opening number, the energy in the room is electric. The maestro, making his fashionably late entrance, acknowledges his audience's enthusiastic applause, strides to center stage and with a flick of his wrist, throws the invisible switch that kicks off the evening's high voltage performance.

Channeling all of his musical training, Horton discreetly conducts the orchestra's entire repertoire with small hand gestures from his lap as if he is auditing one of Josef Krips' rehearsals: *C-Jam Blues, Don't You Know I Care?, Goof, Satin Doll, Kinda Dukish-Rockin' In Rhythm, In a Sentimental Mood, Caravan, In Duplicate, Warm Valley* and *Take The 'A' Train."* His gestures are barely discernible to those around him, but in Horton's mind, he is auditioning.

"I was trying to show Duke Ellington with every fiber of my being that I knew and understood every nuance of his music!" recalls Horton.

Ellington takes note. He makes eye contact with Horton, and his gaze returns to the young conductor's hands throughout the performance. During the second half, saxophonist Paul Gonzalves strolls over to Horton's front row table and plays his lush tenor sax right in his face. Horton clowns a bit with him, and the two share a good laugh … hipsters for that moment.

After the performance, Horton approaches Ellington who is still tinkering at his piano on stage. He has taken extra care to dress sharply in a blue tweed jacket and tie, knowing it is Ellington's favorite color.

"Hello, Maestro Ellington," Horton says. "I'm Randall Keith Horton. I'm a conductor, composer and pianist."

"Oh you are?" Confirms Ellington, looking him over. "Give me your number."

Horton doesn't have a business card, pen or paper, and not wanting to be just a number on a piece of paper anyway, offers an alternative, "Your son Mercer has invited me to travel with the band to your next stop in Sacramento," says Horton. "May I give you my contact information there?"

"Okay, we'll talk then," Duke says with a slight nod.

The next day, Horton is filled with excitement and anticipation as he makes his way to the bus parked in front of the supper club. When the musicians and equipment are packed and loaded, Horton joins Mercer and the rest of the band for the 75-mile bus trip to Sacramento. Once there, he grabs dinner with alto saxophonist Russell Procope. The two bond over stories, including Procope's memories of Sabby Lewis' Boston-based Jazz orchestra. Horton is awestruck, but quickly finds Procope both welcoming and protective in a fatherly way.

For the Ellington Orchestra's 8:00 p.m. performance at the *Civic Center Auditorium*, Horton stands in the wings, stage right, where he can watch Ellington conduct, and conversely, Ellington can stare directly at him at regular intervals throughout the performance.

"The intensity of his gaze was penetrating," recalls Horton. "It made me feel like an interloper."

At the conclusion of the performance, as Ellington walks off stage, Horton approaches. The maestro silently acknowledges his presence, and without breaking stride, motions for Horton to follow. The two continued toward the rear of the venue, up a few stairs to a 12-foot by 8-foot room where Ellington abruptly turns and asks, "Who *are* you?"

"I'm a conductor, composer and pianist," Horton answers nervously. "We met at the *Great American Supper Club* last night (pausing before continuing). Your son Mercer invited me to ride up here with the band. I have my own big band ... which I lead in your honor, of course," Horton adds hastily. "I also conduct my own chamber orchestra and singing groups. May I show you my photos?"

"NO!" Ellington says, standing erect with his head held high.

Horton is unprepared for the blunt rejection. It devastates him, and it is all he can do not to crumble. His face flushes with heat, and tears sting his eyes. Time slows down, and it is as if he can see the gears shifting in Ellington's head, testing him, assessing him and gauging his reaction. When he sees that Horton is stricken and sad, it softens him immediately. He back-peddles, asking, "Well, what do you have there?" And holding out his hand for Horton's photos.

"This is my big band, and this is my chamber orchestra from Sacred Heart Roman Catholic Church," Horton says, handing Ellington his photos and regaining his equilibrium. As Ellington looks through them, Horton takes a risk and says, "I would like to work with you, Mr. Ellington."

"Call me next week. I'll be at the Anaheim Hotel in *Disneyland*," Ellington responds, handing Horton back his photos and heading briskly down the back staircase to his awaiting car.

"Yes sir, Mr. Ellington!" Horton replies excitedly to his impeccably attired back. Then louder, suddenly emboldened, so he can be heard by the maestro's receding figure, "Yes, I think that would be in order!"

Horton boards the band bus for a second time as it heads to its next gig in Oakland. He seeks out Mercer during the trip and shares his father's directive.

"He said that?" Mercer asks, making sure he heard Horton correctly. He pauses briefly before supportively adding, "Well, you're going to have to call him at three in the morning. That's the best time to reach him."

The Ellington Orchestra performs its Sunday afternoon concert in Oakland. They drop Horton off in San Francisco before heading to their evening performance at the *Marin Civic Auditorium* in San Rafael. The following Monday, April 16, 1973, the orchestra opens a one-week engagement at *Disneyland* in Anaheim, California.

On Tuesday, April 17th, Horton calls Ellington at 3:00 a.m. as

Mercer instructed and wakes a sleeping Ellington who manages to mumble, "Call me tomorrow," before hanging up. Horton follows his directive for the next two days without success. He tries again in the predawn hours of Good Friday to no avail. Horton is stricken. Then at 6:00 p.m. the same evening (Good Friday April 20, 1973), Horton calls again. This time, Duke Ellington answers, dispenses with introductions and inquires point blank, "You're a conductor, right?"

"Yes! Yes, I am!" confirms Horton.

"Be down here tonight with a piece of original music written for my orchestra," Ellington directs him, "We go on at 8:00 p.m. Be prepared to conduct. No rehearsals." *Click!*

Horton replays his brief conversation with Duke Ellington to assure himself that the unimaginable has, in fact, just happened. His initial excitement is quickly followed by a panic attack — and a rollercoaster of emotions: "DUKE ELLINGTON just answered my call and spoke with ME!? He wants me to meet him at *Disneyland* in Anaheim (checking his wristwatch) in TWO HOURS! And conduct HIS orchestra with an original piece of MY own music! *(pride)* NO REHEARSALS!" *(terror)*

There are only a few problems: Randall Horton is still in San Francisco, more than 400 miles from Anaheim. The thirty-one-year-old not only lacks sufficient travel funds but also adequate travel time to meet Ellington's impossible deadline. Nonetheless, he pulls out every stop to make the trip. He runs down to the local liquor store on the corner of Divisadero and Hayes Streets and convinces its owner, Mrs. Robinson, to loan him money for airfare. He throws a bag together, gathers the sheet music for his partially completed song for his youngest sister entitled *Song for Jennifer* and jumps on the first plane bound for Los Angeles.

"I must have been quite a sight," recalls Horton laughing, "nervous, frazzled and frantically trying to finish my music during the two-hour flight!"

Horton blanches as the Ellington Orchestra's 8:00 p.m. performance time comes and goes while he is still *en route*. When he lands at LAX, he grabs the first shuttle to *Disneyland* which deposits him in front of the main gate around 10:30 p.m. He struggles through the cuing turnstiles, catching the strap of his bag in the process and blanketing the ground with his unfinished music. The guard on duty informs him that the park is closed. By the time Horton processes the information and gathers his sheet music, he feels the weight of his abject failure coil tightly around his neck. He pauses to collect himself for several moments before asking the guard for walking directions to the Anaheim Hotel.

Horton arrives in the hotel lobby around 10:45 p.m. and confirms that Mr. Ellington is in fact a guest. "Yes," says the front desk staffer, "but he is currently out."

Horton asks if he might wait in the lobby until his return, which the clerk graciously allows.

"Two hours later, Duke Ellington walks through the lobby doors, wearing a belted, white, Alpaca coat," says Horton. "In California! I'll never forget it. It felt like a fantasy, or a dream on many levels. I walked nervously over to him. Duke looked me up and down, and without pre-amble, demanded, 'Where were YOU?' 'I left as soon as you called,' I said, 'but I just couldn't get here in time.' Ellington sized me up for a moment then said, 'Well, come up stairs.'

"There were a couple of people who accompanied us to his room whom I did not recognize. Ellington took a seat on the edge of his bed, elbows on his knees. I pulled up a chair opposite, sitting knee-to-knee with my idol, mind a buzz. There was a woman present who sat quietly nearby throughout our conversation. She may have been connected with Ellington's forthcoming autobiography, *Music Is My Mistress* published that same year, a writer or editor perhaps? I'm not sure. For the next two hours, Ellington interviewed me, conversing as if he had known me his entire life. He looked intently at the pictures of my parents again, as if by doing so, he could glean valuable insight into my character. Of course,

Ellington had witnessed me 'conducting' his music at the *Great American Music Hall* the week prior, but his uncanny ability to accurately ascertain temperament, personality and musical aptitude was a real marvel to me. We talked about my experiences growing up in Boston, and I showed him an Irving Berlin score I had arranged for Arthur Fiedler. Then I said to him, 'I have to admit to you that I'm really scared.'"

"'Afraid?' Ellington scoffed! 'You? Not *YOU*!'"

"I *was* really scared, but the maestro's words boosted my confidence and put me at ease… more Ellington magic.

'How many horns are in your big band?' Ellington demanded with urgency."

'Twelve,' I replied, 'five saxophones, three trombones and four trumpets.' It was a test! He was testing me. My answer must have proved acceptable because he picked up the phone, called down to the front desk and reserved a room for me and informed them I'd be down shortly to pick my room key.

'Is your music ready to go?' he asked.

'Well, not entirely,' I said, 'but it's very close!'

'Well, you'd better get down to your room and finish it. We go on at 8:00 p.m. tomorrow.'

"As I headed to the door, Duke Ellington reached into the drawer of his nightstand and pulled out a fist full of blank manuscript paper; another marvel because I never mentioned that I had used up my entire supply on the plane. When I acknowledged this, he said, 'You're just like me, huh?' It was one of many details that stuck with me, perpetuating the feeling that Duke Ellington could somehow divine my inner thoughts and emotions."

Horton picks up his key at the front desk and settles into his new room. It is the first time he has ever stayed in a hotel. He has less than 20 hours to finish his music and write out the individual parts. He is hungry but doesn't have the time or money to run out for food. Then he spies a menu with sumptuous pictures of food, his first thrilling introduction to room service. He follows the instructions and orders a hearty breakfast and a pot of black coffee to fortify himself for the hours of arranging and copying that laid ahead.

"I knew each band member and his unique style of playing," continues Horton. "I had seen them up close at the *Great American Music Hall*, dined with Mr. Procope in Sacramento, enjoyed the band's full performance from backstage, read everything written about them in print and, of course, listened to the *Ellington Orchestra's* recorded music for many years. The only unknown was a young French horn player who was a late addition to the following evening's performance. Fortunately, I was able to *hear* the music in my head as I wrote it thanks to my inner ear training with Wynn Westover. I wrote out each part meticulously; knowing exactly how it would sound at the hands of each musician... and it all just *flowed*."

"Around 7:00 p.m. (Saturday), with my music finally complete, I walked over to the Magic Kingdom where my own personal fairytale was about to come true. I was set to perform during the intermission, and from the moment the *Ellington Orchestra* kicked off its evening performance, a remarkable calm washed over me.

At intermission, Duke walked over to me and asked, 'Do you have your music?'"

"'Yes sir,' I replied."

'Okay,' He continued. 'Pass the parts out on everyone's stand. You'll go on after Akioshi.'

"He meant Toshiko Akioshi,[226]" Horton clarifies. "She was—still is —an accomplished Jazz pianist who for decades led the famed Toshiko Akioshi-Lew Tabakin Big Band. While Duke introduced her and she

---

226  15 years later (1988), Horton attended a performance of Toshiko Akioshi in Yoshi's nightclub in Oakland. He sent a handwritten note back to her dressing room introducing himself as the person who played after her performance of "Take the 'A' Train" at Disneyland. Her husband, saxophonist Lew Tabakin, invited Horton back to their dressing room where the three had an enjoyable visit.

settled in to play *Take the 'A' Train*, I began passing out the sheet music for my *Song For Jennifer* on each musician's stand, then sat down to enjoy her performance. She was cookin' it! She killed it, which made me want to run home and die! *Who was I?* I thought. *Just a 31-year-old nobody with a few years of informal music study,* I told myself, answering my own rhetorical question. Self-doubt flooded in, and I wondered, *How am I ever going to measure up to her performance?*

"At the end of Ashioki's number, Duke stepped to the microphone and simultaneously motioned me over. He thanked Ashioki for her fine presentation and casually leaned over to me and asked, 'What's your full name?'

'Randall Keith Horton, performing a song I wrote for my sister called *Song For Jennifer*,'[227] I replied.

'And now, ladies and gentlemen,' soothed Ellington, returning to the mic, 'I'd like to introduce Randall Keith Horton who is going to play an original piece for you on the piano called *Song For Jennifer*.'

"I walked over and sat down at the piano, praying all the way for strength and divine guidance. I took a deep breath and started to play. The moment my fingers touched the keys, the same light that guided me three times before — in my studio apartment in Cambridge, my basement apartment in San Francisco and later filled the sanctuary at the Ellington Orchestra's *Sacred Concert* in Grace Cathedral—returned for a fourth time. It took over the movement of my hands and created a musical performance I cannot define or otherwise describe to this day. To me, it manifested the fulfillment of my being 'chosen,' and that my time on the outdoor *Disneyland* stage would serve as my unspoken audition to serve as Maestro Ellington's new composing and conducting assistant.

"Out of the corner of my eye, I saw Toshiko come around the end of the piano, open-mouthed and wide-eyed, and just stand there

---

227  Later renamed "This Light I Must Reveal" © R.K. Horton, 1992, 2020 (P) Rakeiho Publishing Company (ASCAP).

until I was done. I came back to myself just as Paul Gonzalves came over and planted a big ol' kiss on my forehead. The next thing I knew, Duke Ellington walked over to me to take his place at the piano, softly explaining that he had to play a little something to get the band back on the stage. I stood up. He sat down and started playing. Sure enough, the musicians trickled back to their seats. When everyone was in place, Ellington leaned over to me and asked, 'Did you pass out your music?'

'Yes, sir,' I replied.

'What's the tempo?'

'It's a ballad,' I replied.

"Ellington counted it off, 'One… two… three… four; one… two… three… hup!' And just like that, the Ellington Orchestra started playing my song. Not knowing what else to do as I stood there on stage, I started conducting. The way they played the music was gorgeous! Beautiful! I was gone! The only fly in the ointment was the performance of the young French horn player who had difficulties during the bridge. I tried to help him by singing his part, but it wasn't perfect, and it bothered me. When we came to the end of the piece, and not knowing precisely why I thought I could, I hollered out to the musicians, 'One more time!' Duke popped up from the piano, thinking the song was over, spun around in a complete circle to his right and remained standing as I threw my entire body into the reprise, conducting with a ballet of body movements while *The Ellington Orchestra* glorified my song, taking it straight to heaven! When it was over, there was applause. I thanked the band, and to my amazement, Russell Procope said, 'Thank *you*!'

'*Song For Jennifer*, ladies and gentlemen!' Ellington announced, concluding the intermission. 'Mr. Randall Keith Horton!'

"I took my bow and floated off the stage. The entire experience was just GLORIOUS! GLOR-I-OUS! If this was to be my audition for the great Duke Ellington, I was grateful for the light's presence and the grace and confidence it instilled in me to deliver a flawless performance."

After the concert, Horton walks over to thank Mercer Ellington, but Mercer keeps his back turned to him.[228] Horton finds it curious, but quickly forgets about it when he is allowed to ride back to the hotel with Duke Ellington in his private car driven by Harry Carney.

"I was standing by Harry Carney's car when the concert was over," recalls Horton. "When Carney and Duke Ellington approached, I asked, 'May I ride back to the hotel with you gentlemen?' Duke looked at me and nodded his head with a slight smile. There was a *light* in his eyes that surrounded his entire being. I sensed he was happy with me, and it felt like the heavens opened up. It was just beautiful. So, there I was, sitting in the backseat of the car by myself like a nervous little ant (chuckle) as the three of us drove smoothly back to the hotel... *in total silence.* No one said a word, but my thoughts were spinning.

"When we arrived at the hotel, we walked into the lobby together, at which point Duke turned towards me and asked, 'So what do you want, Randall?'

'I want to be with you and write for you,' I replied.

'MARVELOUS!' Duke said.

"We stepped into the elevator and were whisked up to his hotel room where members of his entourage and a trumpet player from Duke's *Cotton Club Day* named Freddy Jenkins were gathered. Duke introduced me as we entered the room, 'This is Randall Keith Horton! He is a great artist!'

"I felt like I had died and gone to heaven!"

Horton remains with Ellington and the group into the early morning hours, each moment unfolding as one surreal, jaw-dropping experience after another, waiting to be processed when his brain resumes its

---

228  Steve Voce, "OBITUARY:Mercer Ellington," *The Independent*, February 10, 1996, "Mercer Ellington had been in the band's trumpet section since 1965 and, although he had led his own band in the recording studios as early as 1958, he had none of the musical genius and instinct of his father. In fact their relationship was often not like that of father and son, and Duke often thrust Mercer into menial roles, elbowing him from the limelight. Another Ellington trumpeter, Rex Stewart, recalled being at an Ellington recording section in 1966 when Duke asked, 'Where's the other trumpet player?' He meant Mercer. Duke lived for his music, not for his family."

normal function. He eventually returns to his room some 46 hours after his initial summons to *Disneyland* and drops into an exhausted sleep. The next morning, Horton travels up the California coast on the band bus for their next engagement at the Miramar Hotel near Santa Barbara. Duke Ellington snaps the lapel of Horton's sport coat as he advances to the front of the orchestra to conduct the concert. Horton watches the performance from the stage wing and stays up with the band until the wee hours before falling into an exhausted sleep. Minutes later, or so it seems, Horton is awakened by three loud raps on his motel room door.

"We're rolling!" The now familiar voice of Mercer Ellington booms from just outside the door.. "Come on! Get out here and get on the bus!"

While the band heads to Phoenix for its next engagement, Horton returns to San Francisco and shares his exhilarating experience with Mrs. Robinson, the owner of the liquor store, and Agnes Albert, his new friend and mentor. Albert, already an Ellington devotee, has underwritten a previous collaboration between the *San Francisco Symphony*, Duke Ellington and Johnny Hodges. Several weeks later, to Horton's surprise, she hands him a folded note written on her personal stationery, instructing him to "Please hand deliver this to Mr. Ellington at his next engagement."

Ellington's next closest engagement is at Lovers Lane United Methodist Church in Dallas (April 30, 1973). Horton flies to Dallas on the 29th and catches the band's rehearsal the following day in the social hall of the church. Afterward, as Horton approaches Ellington, he overhears him make a sweet, flirtatious remark to a woman whom he guesses is probably in her 80s.

"My, you make that dress look so pretty," Ellington coos as he smiles warmly at her. The effect is immediate. The woman's face lights up and blushes pink as Ellington politely touches her arm and excuses himself before heading to his dressing room. Horton quickens his pace to catch up.

"Mr. Ellington?" Horton calls out.

Ellington turns toward his now familiar voice with a surprised look on his face and exclaims, "Whoa! What are you doing here, Randall? I thought you had some work to finish up in San Francisco"

"I did. I do," replies Horton, "But my friend Mrs. Agnes Albert asked me to personally deliver this note to you."

It is a folded piece of stationery sans envelope, so Horton is privy to its contents. It opens with a warm greeting followed by a simple query: "When will you and the *Ellington Orchestra* be available to come to San Francisco to work with the symphony and Mr. Randall Keith Horton?"

Mrs. Albert remains supportive of Horton for many years. When he later attends the American Symphony Orchestra League's prestigious *Essentials of Orchestra Management* seminar in New York (in 2005), Peter Pastreich, the organizer and former Executive Director of the *San Francisco Symphony* (1978-1999) during Horton's time there, confides to him, "Agnes Albert always liked you, Randall. She really wanted to help you establish your musical career." But for Horton, her note to Ellington is above and beyond anything he could ever have hoped for.

Ellington reads Mrs. Albert's note and says, "Okay. Come with me." Horton follows him to his dressing room. This time, everything feels more official to Horton. They talk, and when it is time for the band to perform, Ellington instructs Horton to meet him at his motel after the concert.

"I knocked on his motel door around 10:30 p.m. Duke called out, 'Who is it?' I identified myself, and he opened the door and invited me in. But to my great surprise, he was singularly attired in black dress socks. He nonchalantly motioned me to a chair and sat opposite me on an identical chair. We both ignored the elephant in the room and continued our earlier conversation like old friends. There was a birthday cake nearby in honor of his 74th birthday (April 29, 1973) the day before. Duke asked if I wanted any. When I said 'yes,' he made a face like he was put out, then we both laughed heartily as he cut two pieces. In between bites of cake, we talked about Agnes Albert and my experiences with the San Francisco Symphony, Opera and Ballet. Then, Ellington picked up the phone and called his personal manager.

'What's our schedule look like?' he asked Cress Courtney. 'We have an opportunity to play in San Francisco.'"

By this time in 1973, Ellington has gone six years without Billy Strayhorn, his former full time composing partner, and his loss is gravely felt. There are professional similarities between Horton and Strayhorn in their bespectacled looks, their nurturing personalities and mutual interest in both Jazz and Classical music; even their impromptu Ellington auditions parallel one another's. Perhaps it collectively fosters a sense of comfort and familiarity for Ellington. And of course, there is the spiritual connection to Ellington that Horton senses at each point of contact, punctuated by the light and warmth of his mysterious *callings*.

"Everything struck a strong spiritual chord with me," recalls Horton, "and Maestro Ellington and I conversed for some time."

"Well, Randall," Ellington eventually said. "You have to realize that no one person can do this alone. It's too much!" He pauses briefly before continuing. "This is a team. *The Ellington Orchestra* is a *team*. You're part of the team, now, Randall."

Dumbfounded and thrilled, Horton returns to San Francisco the following day and shares his electrifying news with Mrs. Albert and rejoins the *Ellington Orchestra* at its two-week residency at the Shamrock Hilton in Houston (June 7-21, 1973). Once in Houston, Duke and a handful of tenured musicians take up residence at the Shamrock Hilton while Horton and the rest of the band members check into the Ramada Inn across the street.

"It was surreal," he recalls. "I spent the first few days sitting in on rehearsals in the afternoons and watching the band perform at night. In between, I shared meals and got better acquainted with the musicians.

They were warm and welcoming, especially Harry Carney who was a fellow Bostonian. The only exception was Mercer. I sensed an increased frigidness seep into our interactions[229], but chalked it up, at first, to having to pay my dues. After all, Mercer was 23 years my senior, a well-established trumpeter, the orchestra's road manager and of course the Maestro's son."

Midway into the engagement, Cootie Williams develops a chest ailment and is sent to the San Jacinto Medical Center to be checked out. Shortly thereafter, a mobile medical bus is dispatched to the Shamrock Hotel to test the entire band.

"We all had to blow into a special device and have our vitals recorded," recalls Horton. "Nearly everyone fails the emphysema test with doctors encouraging Duke Ellington and Harry Carney in particular to follow-up with their personal physicians."[230]

Several days later, Horton receives a call from the front desk of the Ramada Inn, instructing him to come down and settle his hotel bill.

"There must be some misunderstanding," Horton tells the hotel clerk. "I am here at Mr. Ellington's request as a member of his orchestra. I'm sure Mr. Ellington can clear up any questions."

The hotel clerk replies, "We already checked with Mr. Ellington (meaning Mercer, not Duke), and he said you're to pay your own bill."

"But I don't have the money to pay this bill!' Horton responds in shock and desperation.

"Then it looks like you'll be picking peas," the clerk replies.

---

229  In 1939, 1946-1949 and 1959, Mercer Ellington led his own bands, many of whose members went on to play with his father or to achieve independent fame (Dizzy Gillespie, Kenny Dorham, Idrees Sulieman, Chico Hamilton, Charles Mingus, Carmen McRae, et al). He composed for his father (1940-41), returned to work playing alto horn in 1950, and was general manager/copyist from 1955-1959. He returned to his father's orchestra in 1965 as trumpeter and road manager. When Duke died, he took over the orchestra, traveling to Europe in 1975 and 1977 and then became the first conductor for a Broadway musical of his father's music, *Sophisticated Ladies* (1981 until 1983). Mercer's album *Digital Duke* won the 1988 Grammy Award for Best Large Jazz Ensemble.

230  "6/7/73 - This was the first sign that Duke Ellington might have a serious illness, although it is another six months before doctors detect cancer symptoms." Ken Vail, *Duke's Diary, Part II*, 435.

"The exchange really knocked my legs out from under me, remembers Horton. My mind raced with questions ... *What's going on? Is Mercer testing me? Does Duke know? What should I do now?* I ended up going directly to Mercer Ellington, who cryptically said, 'I'm neither for or against you, Randall,' but did nothing to remedy the situation. Fortunately, Paul Gonsalves was gracious enough to let me bunk in his room at the Shamrock Hilton for a couple of fitful nights until things could be straightened out."

A few nights into his stay with Gonzalves, Horton is awakened in the predawn hours by the sound of his roommate returning. He starts to slip back into oblivion when the whispers of a woman's voice jolts him fully awake. Not knowing precisely what to do, he pretends to be asleep, but of course he isn't. Horton later learns that Paul's companion is a local female Jazz singer and figures it is probably time for him to make new sleeping arrangements. He begins by approaching Ellington after one of the rehearsals as he tinkers at his piano.

"What do you need, Randall?" Asks Ellington as he looks up from his piano.

"I'd like to talk to you if you have time," Horton says.

"I don't have time right now. I have to meet with someone very important," Ellington replies. "Maybe later."

Horton's imagination takes flight, conjuring self-created demons. *Does he really have a meeting? Is he giving me the brush-off?* To Horton's relief, Ellington does indeed sit down moments later with a distinguished gentleman.[231] Nonetheless, a sense of disquiet settles upon Horton, and it is at this moment of uncertainty that he receives a fourth *calling*. As he packs up his belongings in Paul Gonsalves' room, the now familiar *light*

---

231  It is possible that Ellington met with Maurice Peress perhaps about Peress' partial, seventeen-minute orchestration of the first movement (*Black* only ) of Ellington's *Black, Brown and Beige*, which Peress published in the early '70s. Maurice Peress (1921-2018) was a conductor who worked closely with both Leonard Bernstein and Duke Ellington, reconstructing important historic concerts and marrying Jazz and classical music. Peress also published, "Dvorak to Duke Ellington: A Conductor Explores America's Music and Its African American Roots", Oxford University Press, 2004.

descends from above once again with its signature brightness, warmth and a message.

"Just as I began to sense that my time in Houston might be the last time I would see Maestro Ellington, the warm, laser-like light appeared again and imparted two brief but powerful messages, '*Don't worry,*' and '*Don't be afraid.*' The experience centered and comforted me. I went immediately to the hotel lobby and wrote a note to Duke describing my predicament, beseeching him for his intervention, and in the event that was not possible, concluding with a heartfelt statement of immense gratitude…and a rather startling closing statement."

Horton rewrites the note neatly, tucks the first draft into the breast pocket of his jacket, slips the neater copy under Ellington's hotel room door and waits. When there is no reply by evening, he beds down on a lounge chair on the hotel pool deck, using a towel as his blanket. But Jazz singer Mama Lulu (Rhona Lacey) finds out and won't hear of Horton sleeping outside. She offers him a couch in her Houston home where she introduces Horton to her friend Arnett Cobb,[232] the internationally known, Houston-based tenor saxophonist. At Lacey's urging, Horton recounts his predicament in greater detail. Cobb and Lacey listen intently and urge Horton to call Ellington to make him aware of his situation. Surprisingly, Horton reaches Ellington on the first try, but when he inquires if the maestro has received the note slipped under his door, he says, "No."

Horton hangs up the phone, believing all is lost. He crumples the draft of his note and throws it in the trash. Lacey retrieves it and begins reading. The note conveys Horton's utmost respect and appreciation, outlines his predicament with the hotel bill and closes with a reference

---

232 Arnett Cobb (1919–1989), a highly regarded, Houston-born tenor saxophonist, was known for his exuberant visceral style and big honking sound. He made his professional debut in 1933 before joining the Lionel Hampton Band as a popular soloist. Known as the "Wild Man of the Tenor Sax," Cobb returned to the Houston area in 1960, where he led his own 16-piece big band, Arnett Cobb and the Mobb, and managed a local Jazz club called The Ebony.

to his *callings*, stating, *"I believe I was chosen by God Almighty to assist with the work that He is doing through you."* [233]

It is a bold statement, especially from a young musician in the early stages of his career who was only recently welcomed into the *Ellington Orchestra* and is currently stranded in a relative stranger's living room halfway across the country. Lacey looks intently at Horton as she passes the note to Cobb who reads it and gravely nods his head in agreement. This should be reassuring to Horton, but it is not.

He endures a sleepless night on Lacey's couch before the proverbial sun comes out the following morning. A clerk from the front desk of the motel later informs Horton that Duke Ellington has settled his hotel bill.

"It was like the end of a thrilling, yet terrifying roller coaster ride," recalls Horton. "The upward and exhilarating trajectory of being chosen by Ellington himself, spending time with the band and realizing an unbelievable dream, followed by the free-falling uncertainty over my hotel bill. It was devastating and confusing."

And perhaps because of the residue left over from his childhood, Horton finds it easier to accept his "unworthiness"[234] than Ellington's seasoned assessment and selection of him for his musical talents. He clamps a tight lid on his roiling emotions, and at the end of the two-week gig, quietly returns to his pre-Ellington life at Sacred Heart Church in San Francisco.

The next four months plod slowly by. *The Ellington Orchestra* continues its rigorous touring schedule despite Ellington's declining health as he battles an invisible foe that even the maestro himself cannot out-maneuver or charm his way past. And like most situations where

---

233 This is a statement of faith by Randall Keith Horton, who has no way of knowing the future role he will play with four of Duke Ellington's most pioneering and personally important compositions: *Black, Brown and Beige* and Ellington's three *Sacred Concerts*.

234 This is Horton's interpretation of Mercer's actions at the time, which will later be altered by the amicable relationship they enjoy in future years.

Ellington is unable to affect meaningful change, he simply chooses to ignore it. After all, he has much more compelling things on his composing plate with the approaching premiere of his *Third Sacred Concert* at London's Westminster Abbey. The music is still a work-in-progress, and Ellington continues to write large portions of his third and final *Sacred Concert* while deeply contemplating both the fullness of his life and his imminent mortality.

## Ellington's Third *Sacred Concert*

Duke Ellington's *Third Sacred Concert* kicks off in London on United Nations Day, October 24, 1973, with a rather dreary introduction by UN chairman Sir Colin Crowe. A visibly weakened Ellington takes his place on the altar of Westminster Abbey in front of his musicians, a choir, three soloists and a capacity audience that includes England's Prime Minister Heath and Princess Margaret. Gone are the showbiz kick and exuberance of his *First Sacred Concert* (1965). Absent are the eclectic impulses of his *Second Sacred Concert* (1968). Ellington's third and final *Sacred Concert* is a private conversation between the masterful composer, who surely knows his time is drawing to a close, and his Maker.[235]

Ellington writes eight new songs around the skills of returning vocalist Alice Babs[236], (baritone) saxophonist Harry Carney and his own piano skills.[237] The ink is once again so fresh on the pages that Babs is purported to have sight read much of the music with little or no rehearsal. He also mixes in some of his previously written *Sacred Music*. The closing number of Ellington's third and final *Sacred Concert*, *In The*

---

235  Richard S. Ginell gave the album only three stars in an Allmusic review, claiming it was "the weakest of the sacred concerts."

236  Vail, *Ibid.*, 440-442.

237  Gary Giddins, "At the Pulpit," *Riding on a Blue Note* (New York: Oxford University Press, 1981), 159-63.

*Beginning God*[238] is one written eight years earlier as the opening for Ellington's *First Sacred Concert*. And he once again includes *99%* and *The Preacher's Song* which has the distinction of being the only song to appear in all three of his *Sacred Concerts*. In hindsight, it is clear that this final concert circles back and closes the loop on Ellington's most personally-important programmatic and composing thoughts: *Boola* (1930's)... the thematic genesis for *Black, Brown and Beige* (1943)...whose melodic theme *Come Sunday* reappears in the album *Black, Brown and Beige* (1958) and *My People* (1963)...with music and inspiration that continues to flow into Ellington's *Sacred Concerts* (1965, 1968 and 1973)...thereby progressively and indelibly linking the composer's four most important extended-length compositions (*Black, Brown and Beige* and three *Sacred Music* concerts) with *Boola* and *My People*. All of the compositions consistently embody the composer's broader, more personal and less heralded musical and cultural contributions as a humanitarian, pioneering musical genius, keen observer, iconic style/trend setter, re-brander of the American Negro, Civil Rights advocate, patriot, ambassador and showman. Unfortunately, due to the *Ellington Orchestra's* exceptional (and "acceptable") dance band persona, critics and some audiences have difficulty embracing even the slightest deviation in his musical themes, song lengths or performance venues...even after 50 years of increasingly progressive composing and a lot of cajoling.

---

238 "In the Beginning God" begins with six notes, intoning the six syllables of the four opening words of the Bible.

| SONG TITLES | Orig. BB&B 1943 | BB&B Album 1958 | My People 1963 | First Sacred Concert 1965 | Second Sacred Concert 1968 | Third Sacred Concert 1974 | Ellington-Horton BB&B 1988/2020 |
|---|---|---|---|---|---|---|---|
| *Come Sunday* | X | X | X | X | | | X |
| *David Danced* | | | X | | X | | X |
| *Tell Me It's The Truth* | | | | X | | X | |
| *In The Beginning, God* | | | | X | | X | |
| *99% / 99.5%* | | | X | X | X | | |
| *The Preacher's Song* | | | | X | X | X | |
| *Will You Be There* | | | X | | | | |
| *The Blues* | X | | X | | | | X |
| *Praise God and Dance* | | | | | X | X | |
| *The Lord's Prayer / 23rd Psalm* | | X | | X | | X | X |
| *Work Song* | X | X | | | | | X |
| *Heritage / My Mother/My Father* | | | X | X | | | |
| *Ain't But The One* | | | X | X | | | |
| *New World A Comin'* | | | | X | | | |
| *Emancipation Celebration* | X | | | | | | X |
| *West Indian Dance* | X | | | | | | X |
| *Light* | X | X | | | | | X |

Ellington prizes *Black, Brown and Beige* and his *Sacred Music* highest among the more than 6,000 published and unpublished compositions that he is estimated to have written. But "If you asked Duke's fans, or even Jazz historians, what Duke's most important work was, few would respond with 'his *Sacred Concerts*' [or *Black, Brown and Beige*]. They received relatively little commercial success. They did not elevate Duke to a new level of stardom. But for Duke, the most important thing was not the most 'successful thing.'"[239]

Ellington is quoted, asking, "Are you—am I— spending too much time focused on what is successful, rather than what is important? How can we use our time and talents to create important things, rather than just chase what we think people want? What do people *need*?"[240]

Duke spends twenty years contemplating *Black, Brown and Beige* and more than fifty years in prayer and reflection before composing his *Sacred Music*. Each requires a degree of bravery; first, to accept or ignore the professional risks, and secondly, to strip away the veils under which he has hidden himself for so long. And in daring to go beyond the dictates of the commercially successful music of the era and allowing it to unfold organically over many years, Ellington's *Black, Brown and Beige* and *Sacred Music* achieve a greater degree of truth and *authenticity*... especially as heard by more enlightened audiences. "I have to get a bang out of it, not just the money," Ellington once said. "I'm not worried about writing for posterity. I just want it to sound good right now."

---

239  Michael Wear, "Music Monday: Duke Ellington and the Important Things," *Michael Wear*, December 30, 2013, http://michaelwear.com/blog/2013/12/29/duke-ellington-and-taking-our-faith-public.

240  *Ibid.*

## Third *Sacred Concert* - Tracking List
## Actual Performance[241]

*The Lord's Prayer / My Love / Hallelujah / Is God A Three-Letter Word For Love? / The Brotherhood / Every Man Prays In His Own Language / Tell me, It's The Truth / Somebody Cares / The Majesty of God / Ain't Nobody Nowhere Nothin' Without God / Praise God and Dance / The Preacher's Song / In The Beginning God*

---

241   Vail, *Ibid.,* p. 441.

# HISTORICAL CONTEXT
## 1975 - 1979

In the mid-1970's, the Vietnam war ends, Microsoft and Apple emerge as startups and America celebrates its Bicentennial. There is a greater variety of music than ever before. The hard-edged, bluesy music of Heavy Metal gives rise to Soft Rock and Glam Rock with its gender-bending costumes and themes. There is Country Rock, Outlaw Country, Heartland Rockers, Honky-Tonk, Salsa, Jazz and eventually Disco. Punk Rock arises in the late 1970's in reaction to the greed that some feel is gutting American music.

Elvis Presley and Bing Crosby die in 1977. Race relations flare anew in South African where (black) anti-apartheid activist Stephen Biko is brutally beaten by police, driven 700 miles to Pretoria where he is thrown into a cell and later dies naked and shackled on the filthy floor of a police hospital. Biko was a medical student at the forefront of the Black Consciousness Movement who helped found the South African Students' Organization (SASO - 1968) for South Africa's black students. The purpose of the SASO is to combat the minority government's racist apartheid policies and promote black identity and the Black Peoples' Convention (BPC - 1972) to bring Black Consciousness Ideas to wider audiences. The four former white police officers responsible for Biko's death, including Police Colonel Gideon Nieuwoudt, later admit to killing him.[242]

Jazz experiences a surge of popularity in 1978 after President Jimmy Carter invites thirty Jazz musicians to play on the White House lawn, hailing Jazz as America's original music.[243]

---

242 History.com Editors, *This Day In History*, "Afrikaner police admit to killing Stephen Biko," *HISTORY*, A&E Television Networks, January 8, 1997, www.history.com/this-day-in-history/afrikaner-police-admit-to-killing-stephen-biko, February 9, 2010.

243 "1970's Music: History, Pictures & Artists," *RetroWaste*, https://www.retrowaste.com/1970's/music-in-the-1970's/.

Memorable film scores[244] develop as a sub-genre of classical music. Technological advances such as harmonizers and synthesizers lead to greater experimentation and the development of electronic music. Disco becomes mainstream. Funk, primarily an African-American genre characterized by the heavy use of bass and the "wha-wha" pedal, also carves out a sizable audience with its emphasis of rhythm over melody.

The *Jackson 5* continue as a huge pop-music phenomenon, playing chart topping hits that combine Rhythm and Blues and Pop with some Funk and Disco. Trinidadian born Janelle Commissiong is crowned the first black Miss Universe in 1977; yet it will take six more years for the Miss America pageant to follow suit with Vanessa Williams in 1983. And in 1979, music becomes more accessible and mobile than ever before with the advent of the Sony Walkman, the first truly portable audio cassette tape player with headphones.

---

244  tps://bestlifeonline.com/70s-movie-soundtracks/ by October 21, 2019.  Memorable film scores from the 1970's: *American Graffiti* (1973), *Shaft* (1971), *Love Story* (1970), *Diamonds Are Forever* (1971), *Jaws* (1975), *Star Wars* (1977), *Grease* (1978), *Saturday Night Fever* (1977), *Super Fly* (1972), *The Last Waltz* (1978), *Mean Streets* (1973), *The Rocky Horror Picture Show* (1975), *The Harder They Come* (1972), *Suspiria* (1977), *The Warriors* (1979), *Tommy* (1975), *Rocky* (1976).

## CHAPTER 8

# WHAT AM I HERE FOR?

*"Retire to what?!*[245]
*People do not retire. They are retired by others."*[246]
- Duke Ellington

Duke Ellington continues his regular touring schedule after his *Third Sacred Concert* while Horton returns to his Music Directorship at Sacred Heart Roman Catholic Church, conducting, rehearsing and booking his *sinfonietta*, Doo-Wop singing groups and *Big Band*. In fact, he is picking up flyers at a print shop in San Francisco for one of the groups' performances when he is approached by another patron making similar copies.

245  Johnson, David. "Ellington Ending: Duke Ellington 1967-1973." *Night Lights Classic Jazz*, performance by David Brent Johnson, season April, episode unknown, Public Radio, 28 Apr. 2021. https://indianapublicmedia.org/nightlights/ellington-duke-ellington-196773.php.

246  www.brainyquote.com/quotes/duke_ellington_377741.

"Are you a composer?" The stranger asks, taking note of Horton's concert flyers.

"Yes, I am." Horton replies.

"A good one?" The stranger presses.

"Well, good enough to be chosen by Duke Ellington and his Orchestra," replies Horton.

"Wow! Great! I need an arrangement for an upcoming concert," the stranger explains.

The inquiring customer turns out to be a publicist, agent and promoter for Marvin Gaye. The concert he is speaking of is Gaye's 1974 *Let's Get It On* performance at the Oakland Coliseum. The two men's serendipitous meeting results in a commission for Horton to arrange and conduct the music for a 38- to 40-piece orchestra that will accompany one of three opening acts—the same orchestra that later backs-up Marvin Gaye with Gene Page[247] conducting. The audience that evening includes Motown executives who want to know who the fresh-faced orchestrator is.

"Randall Keith Horton," the concert promoter tells them, "But you can't have him. He's mine."

"You have to meet Marvin," the promoter says. He ushers Horton backstage, past throngs of people to reach Gaye's dressing room and knocks on the door.

"Who is it?" An authoritative voice demands.

"Come on, man. It's me!"

The next thing Horton knows, two big pair of hands reach out, grab them by their lapels and yank them into the dressing room, slamming the door. And there is Marvin Gaye. He and Horton have a nice conversation.

---

247 Eugene (Gene) Edgar Page, Jr. (1939 - 1998 was an iconic American pianist, arranger, composer, conductor and producer who worked on more than 200 gold and platinum records from the mid-1960's through the mid-1980's.

"Marvin thought you were sharp," another friend tells Horton a few weeks later, as the two drive in a brand-new Porsche to a party in Los Angeles.

They check into a hotel and are freshening up when the phone rings. Horton's friend motions for Horton to answer it. "If it's Marvin, tell him I'm not here!" he says.

Horton answers and immediately recognizes Gaye's voice. Sensing friction between the two men, and not wanting to have any part of it, Horton responds truthfully to Gaye's inquiry, "Why, yes, he's right here. Just a moment," and hands the phone to his visibly shaken friend.

"From what I could gather," recalls Horton, "a dust up occurred when, instead of using funds Gaye had given him to book a concert venue in South America, the money was temporarily diverted toward a down payment on my roommate's new Porsche."

Horton watches his "friend" get so worked up trying to explain himself that he suffers a severe asthma attack.

Music industry parties are a further eye-opener for Horton: there are illicit drugs free for the taking, and a great deal of bravado and bragging about sexual conquests. It is a shocking and surreal experience. On the upside, Horton's arranging and conducting success in Oakland opens doors (through Gaye's concert promoter) for Horton to be present for meetings and rehearsals of Stevie Wonder and Smokey Robinson.

At every turn, Horton seems to possess the intriguing good fortune of perpetually finding himself at the side of notable Americans at seminal events. He enjoys friendships, working relationships and mentoring from some of the most elite individuals in their respective fields, from musical composing, promoting and performance to academic study and research. His successful orchestrating for Gaye's promoter earns him future introductions and/or arranging work with Martha Reeves (*Martha Reeves and the Vandellas*), Mary Wilson (*Mary Wilson and the Supremes*) and *M-D-L-T WILLIS*, a female quartet produced and promoted by the *Jackson Five*. Horton even stays in some of the artists' homes while working for them, which is not unusual in the early days of Motown.

But the party scenes, the exploitation and legendary double standard between men and women cause a great deal of pain to individuals and families, and are difficult for Horton to witness. He starts to withdraw, but not before a concert promoter introduces him to Joe Jackson, the father and manager of the *Jackson Five*.

The promoter drove him up to the Jackson's home in Havenhurst, a neighborhood in West Hollywood. "As we drove through the big gate, he jokingly said, 'Stick with me, Randall, and a lot more gates will open for you!' He introduced me to Joe Jackson who was looking for an arranger to help his boys produce a 45 RPM recording of the L.A. based vocal quartet *M-D-L-T Willis*. The group featured sisters <u>M</u>axine, <u>D</u>iane, <u>L</u>averne and <u>T</u>ina Willis. Joe welcomed me into his family's home, and I stayed there while we collaborated on the arrangement for the single, *What's Your Game*, eventually recording it in the small but professional-level recording studio in the Jackson family's backyard behind their pool."

Horton recalls:

When Maxine, Diane, Laverne, and Tina did a live showcase in LA in support of their single, fourteen-year-old Michael Jackson and I sat in the audience just a few tables from one another, making eye contact and nodding our heads in agreement when the performance was great, or scowling and shaking our heads in the opposite direction when it was in need of refinement.

The first mock-up of the record label didn't include credit for my arranging work. I had to really assert myself with Joe Jackson, and he ultimately credited me on the final label: *Arranged by The Jackson Five and Randall Horton*. But I had to fight for it which was, once again, just business as usual.

"The *Jackson 5* were at the height of their popularity and in the middle of their World Tour[248]," recalls Horton. "During one of their US stops at the *Cow Palace* in San Francisco (August 24, 1973), the brothers invited me to one of their preconcert rehearsals. I arrived ahead of the boys and was sitting against a wall in a gigantic backstage room. When the brothers walked in and spotted me, they broke into a run, coming over to say hello and clown with me for a bit. The gesture made me feel very welcome. I sat with the rest of the entourage for their entire rehearsal as Michael sang and covered the stage. He would smile at me when he came close then spin away in his signature style. It was quite thrilling."

Horton continued the recollection:

I got to know the entire Jackson family, but I worked with and became most friendly with Tito and Michael. We even worked out a very democratic sleeping rotation between the floor and the two twin beds in Randy and Michael's room. Every third night, one of us took his turn on the floor in a sleeping bag without complaint, like brothers. It was a lot of fun! I even unofficially "chaperoned" the young boys for an extended weekend in 1974 at Joe Jackson's insistence when he, his wife Katherine, Wally Cox and Leroy Jackson[249] went out of town to watch a professional fight. It was another eye-opening experience for me at the Jacksons' home with young girls calling the house at all hours. *Exhausting* is the memory that comes to mind.

Everyone thought Michael was meek and mild, but he was a tough kid in my experience. I remember a particular

---

248  During their World Tour (1973-1976), the Jackson 5 played over 160 concerts all over the world including Japan, Hawaii, United Kingdom, South America, Hong Kong, Australia, New Zealand, Australia, Mexico, The Philippines and the West Indies over a 4-year period.

249  Leroy Jackson was George Foreman's manager.

incident that occurred when I was standing in the family's backyard when Michael eased up to me and sucker punched me in the chest. It wasn't a meek tap. It was a strong, painful punch! Took me completely by surprise (Horton laughs good-naturedly with a palliative touch to the afflicted area). Yes, he enjoyed the great reputation of his heartthrob Motown persona, but he was also a hard scrappin' kid.

But my most vivid memory from my time with the Jackson family occurred on May 24th, 1974. I was talking with Randy and Michael in one of their bedrooms, discussing our recent MLDT release, the air time and recognition it was starting to receive, when someone from their entourage poked his head in and said in a hushed tone, "DUKE JUST DIED!"

All the blood drained from my head as I demanded to know, "*Duke who?!*"

"DUKE ELLINGTON, man!" The person replied. "It's all over the news. He just died!"

My world came crashing down. I went directly into the kitchen and told Joe and Katherine that I had to leave immediately, and I went straight back to San Francisco. Ellington's funeral was held at St. John The Divine, his family's church in New York, but I stayed in San Francisco and honored him in the best way I knew how. I readied my *Big Band* and put on a public performance of Ellington's music at a community center in the Fillmore District. And truth be told, I welcomed having a reason to leave the pop-music industry behind.

### Duke Ellington's Final Days

Ellington returns from the London premiere of his final *Sacred Concert* (10/24/73) looking tired and frail but continues to tour for five more months. He develops pneumonia and is admitted to Columbia Presbyterian Medical Center's Harkness Pavilion in New York on March 25, 1974. Further testing and surgery confirm his suspected diagnosis in Houston nine months earlier, terminal, bilateral lung cancer.

Nearly two months later (May 15, 1974), Paul Gonsalves, the premiere sideman of the Ellington Orchestra (1950-1974) who helped resurrect the band's popularity with his tenor sax solo at the 1956 Newport Jazz Festival, collapses and dies in London after a lifelong battle with alcohol and narcotics addiction. Gonsalves' death is quickly followed by bandmate Tyree Glenn, who dies of cancer on May 18, 1974. Mercer keeps the news of both men's deaths from his hospitalized father, fearing it might accelerate his decline. But it is as if Ellington already senses their departure. As his health deteriorates, a pageant of loved ones, bandmates, musicians, friends, and VIPs pay their respects with flowers, notes and brief visits. Evie (*aka* Beatrice Ellis), Ellington's long term love interest visits every day, but his most beloved *mistress*, his electric Wurlitzer piano, never leaves his bedside.

"You know how it is," Ellington once said, explaining his relationship with his cherished piano. "You go home expecting to go right to bed. But then, on the way, you go past the piano and there's a flirtation. It flirts with you. So, you sit down and try out a couple of chords and when you look up, it's 7 a.m."[250]

At 3:10 a.m. Friday morning, May 24, 1974, the international Jazz legend Edward Kennedy "Duke" Ellington slips quietly into the spiritual world he tried so mightily to explore with his *Sacred Music*. And after 75 magnificent years, the most significant and prolific composer in Jazz history and one of the most famous and prolific American composers of any genre, is no more. His body is taken to Walter B. Cooke funeral parlor where he lays briefly next to those of Gonsalves and Glenn. At

---

250  John S. Wilson, "Duke Ellington, A Master of Music, Dies at 75." *New York Times*, April 25, 1974, p. 61.

his memorial service three days later, St. John The Divine in New York overflows with more than 12,000 mourners. Tens of thousands more gather outside. Ella Fitzgerald, Billy Taylor and Ray Nance's musical tributes are broadcast to the world. Throngs of everyday Americans pay their respects to the pioneering composer who wrote the soundtrack of their identity, history, frustrations, hopes and dreams. They line the road to his final resting place at Woodlawn Cemetery in the Bronx. Millions more in the United States and abroad absorb the loss from reports on their radios, televisions and newspapers.

"There isn't a minute in the day that Ellington music is not being played somewhere in the world," said Christian McBride in 2014, "because he always wrote for the world. While he saw himself as a black composer, he also had this universality, an identification with humanity."[251]

Ellington's granddaughter Mercedes Ellington believes that, "The commonality between people is one of the things that ... he wanted to accentuate. He was always on the path of acknowledging what was really happening in the world. The idea of people being drawn together through music was his goal. He was constantly writing, every day, even when he was ill and dying in the hospital."[252]

Jazz critic Stanley Dance, a close confidant of Ellington, made the following observations about Ellington at his funeral in 1974: "Categories of class, race, color, creed and money were obnoxious to him. He made his subtle, telling contributions to the Civil Rights struggle in musical statements" and "proudly delineated the black contribution to American history."[253]

Ellington biographer Harvey Cohen noted that "Ellington's religiosity was 'unconventional in that he adhered to no denomination and

251 McBride, *Ibid.*

252

253

did not live a 'moral' life according to usual religious dictates,' but he was deeply devoted to his own version of faith, which more than anything valued freedom in all its forms: personal, political, social, and moral. He found in the Bible stories that spoke to this sensibility, and claimed to have read it cover to cover more than 20 times."[254]

At his memorial service Jazz historian Ralph Gleason called Ellington,

America's most important composer. The greatest composer this American society has produced... Ellington has created his own musical world which has transcended every attempt to impose category upon it and has emerged as a solid body of work unequalled in American music." ...His songs have become a standard part of the cultural heritage, his longer compositions a part of the finest art of our time and his concerts and personal appearances among the most satisfying for an audience of those of any artist. Every music honor this country can bestow is little enough for such a musical giant as this man.[255]

Among the messages of condolence is one from President Nixon that says, "The wit, taste, intelligence and elegance that Duke Ellington brought to his music have made him, in the eyes of millions of people, both here and abroad, America's foremost composer. We are all poorer because the Duke is no longer with us ..."[256]

254 Peter Manseau, "Duke Ellington's Christmas Gift", National Museum of American History, December 19, 2016.

255 Wilson, *Ibid.*

256 Jack Jones, "From the Archives: Jazz Great Duke Ellington Dies in New York Hospital at 75," *Los Angeles Times*, May 25, 1974, www.latimes.com/local/obituaries/archives/la-me-duke-ellington-19740525-story.html.

Jazz singer June Norton[257] who worked with Ellington in 1949, 1950 and 1960, was among the friends who journeyed to see him one last time. "I thanked him and told him I loved him," she said before continuing, 'Most people are contented to walk the earth, but you, you thrust your feet down and planted seeds for all the world.' He looked at me, grabbed my hands and kissed me."[258]

257 June Norton was the first black artist to break the television race barrier, especially in Washington which had a population that was estimated at more than 50 percent African American at that time. The commercial's sponsors – the Beautycraft Plastics Company – reported that June Norton was the first African American woman in the mid-Atlantic region to appear on TV commercials beamed at the mass market in Southern states. In 1993, June Norton, along with other former Duke Ellington vocalists Adelaide Hall, Joya Sherrill, Kay Davis, Maria Ellington Cole, and Dolores Parker, received a lifetime achievement award from the Smithsonian Institution. Information taken from "Remembering June Norton: Sang with Duke Ellington, Broke TV Race Barrier," *Park View, D.C.*, January 23, 2015, parkviewdc.com/2015/01/23/remembering-june-norton-sang-with-duke-ellington-broke-tv-race-barrier/.

258 Gaines-Carter, *Ibid.*

# HISTORICAL CONTEXT
## 1980's

The 1980's start off on a devastating note with the murder of *Beatles* legend John Lennon outside his New York City home on December 8, 1980. Urban Pop acts like Tina Turner, Lionel Richie, Michael Jackson, Donna Summer, Paul McCartney and Diana Ross find renewed success as solo artists. New technology (cassette tapes, CDs) continues to make music more portable (boomboxes and Sony Walkman) and easier to listen to. MTV comes into existence (1981), catapulting the visual images of musicians and bands even further to the forefront, shifting the cultural influence from music and lyrics to fashion and theatrics. This helps perpetuate the public's growing appetite for celebrity news and propels Pop artists like Michael Jackson, Prince, Whitney Houston and Madonna to superstardom with unprecedented earnings.

A period of economic income disparity emerges along with a cultural preoccupation with affluence. Megastars find ways to counter music industry excesses by calling attention to important world issues and performing charity concerts (*Band Aid, Live Aid, We are the World,* and so on.) New genres of music also emerge: New Wave/Hair Metal and Hip Hop/Rap, the latter originating in African American communities in New York. Under pressure, MTV finally begins airing videos of African American artists, spiking their popularity and helping to pave the way for videos by Hip-Hop/Rap artists (Run DMC and LL Cool J to Usher). These videos provide white middle class Americans with their first glimpses of African American inner-city culture, which becomes the driving cultural force in America as well as a global phenomenon.

During this decade, America falls in love with the Rubik's Cube and the Pac-Man video game. Michael Jackson releases his *Thriller* album and later moonwalks on national TV for the first time. The Internet is born. President Ronald Reagan makes Martin Luther King Jr.'s birthday a federal holiday. Then, on Black Monday in 1987, the stock market plunges 22.3 percent, a larger drop than the crash preceding the Great Depression in 1929.[259]

Hard Rock remains popular among new groups (*Van Halen, Guns and Roses*) along with the successful re-emergence of older rockers (*Aerosmith* and Alice Cooper). Music choices abound with Alternative Rock (*R.E.M.*), Punk-mixed Folk music and mainstream music influences, Heartland Rockers (Springsteen), Folk Rockers (Stevie Nicks) and Contemporary Rhythm and Blues, with its disco-like beats, high-tech production, and elements of Hip-Hop, Soul and Funk, making R&B more danceable and modern.

259 "Music Played in the 1980's Popular Music From the 80s," The People History, http://www.thepeoplehistory.com/80smusic.html.

## CHAPTER 9

# TELL ME IT'S THE TRUTH

*"What I do tomorrow*
*will be the best thing I've ever done."*
-Duke Ellington

Ellington's untimely death leaves his loyal Horton in a state of confusion. A blur of musical opportunities presents itself.[260] And while he begins working in the presence of some of Motown's brightest stars, the experiences leave him feeling empty and tinged by sadness. He tries to fit in, turn a blind eye and embrace the lifestyle, but it cuts too close to the bone of his unwelcome childhood memories. He finds himself retreating into his shell emotionally.

---

260 Horton conducts a few local performances in San Francisco with his big band at the Oakland Museum and several churches. He hits his stride a short time later after moving north to Petaluma where he attended Sonoma State University, joined the Church of the Open Door, played engagements at the Petaluma Cafe and founded the Petaluma Symphony Orchestra and Chorus Association. His Petaluma Symphony Orchestra later performed with American folk singer/ songwriter Kate Wolf.

He recalls:

I was floundering in the toxicity of the music industry, a dysfunctional marriage and my own self-doubt. And as I had done many times throughout my life, I reached out to a family friend Catherine Guy-Buchanan for guidance. Mrs. Buchanan was a black woman of West Indian/Jamaican descent, who lived just across the street at 137 Devon Street during my adolescent years in Boston. She had her hands full with three sons and three daughters of her own, but always made time to listen and talk with me. I would sit in her kitchen just to soak up the warmth and unconditional acceptance that emanated from her.

I came to be her "son number four," and she and her hard-working husband Maurice Buchanan were, indeed, surrogate parents to me. While my family experienced the travails of divorce, the Buchanan family, whatever their challenges, remained intact. Right up until her passing at the age of 98, I would call her from all over the country to complain about life and absorb some of her healing perspectives and advice. She would speak of faith, of the importance of believing in and trusting God. I can still hear her saying in her sweet, "singing" West Indian accent, "Rahndee, there is always something to pray about!" I will always love her and keep precious memories of her and her children.

My father was also supportive in later years. I remember him coming out to visit me in California on two separate occasions (1975-1977) to offer his love and guidance during my most difficult times, which meant a lot to me.

Horton is ultimately interviewed by Mary Wilson for the musical directorship of *The Supremes* in her suite in San Francisco's Fairmont

Hotel. Motown is preparing to move their base from Detroit to L.A., and Wilson's music director is initially reluctant to relocate. It would be a plumb assignment, but Horton already senses it is a career path for which he is not suited. It is a turning point. When Wilson's music director eventually relocates, the directorship opportunity evaporates. Horton and his wife divorce, and he embarks on a 40-year career in musical directorships for various denominations of churches and synagogues in California, Texas and New York. And it is here in the spiritual and musical environments similar to Lone Mountain College that Horton finds a rewarding and comfortable sense of belonging.

For the first time in several years, his life begins to settle down, and as it does, he starts to contemplate the significant moments in his life: the challenges of his upbringing, his mystifying *callings*, the generosity of his mentors and his brief yet seminal time with Duke Ellington. It stirs a tsunami of questions for Horton:

> There were certainly others with greater musical talent, better business acumen and stronger nexuses to Duke Ellington. So, why did it all happen to me? Why!? My search for understanding led me to make an audacious phone call to New York in 1984 to Duke Ellington's long time business manager and sister Ruth Ellington-Boatwright.
>
> I called, introduced myself and asked for her help in understanding my experiences with her brother. I told her about my *callings* which led me to San Francisco to study music and to her brother's *First Sacred*

*Concert.* I told her about my *Disneyland* audition and the magic of Duke *choosing* me as his assistant in Dallas. She acknowledged knowing about my time with her brother, and she grew increasingly attentive when I told her of my forsaking the music industry in favor of a career directing church music. A subtle barrier evaporated, after which she said, "Please come to my home and tell me more about your experiences."

I traveled to New York via Amtrak and took a taxi to her elegant, four-story brownstone at 333 Riverside Drive in Manhattan. It was a beautifully appointed home that was originally Duke Ellington's primary residence. I was greeted by a woman to whom I introduced myself. "Oh, yes," she said, "Ruth is expecting you. Have a seat. She'll be down shortly."

I sat there in Duke's former living room in total awe as Ruth floated down the stairs impeccably coiffed and attired like her brother. She welcomed me and said she had spoken with one of the band members about me. Then she sat down in her floor-length gown and jewels, and we began to talk. Our conversation was a wonder. She helped me consider my experiences and *callings* as signposts, directing me on my intended path, adamant that my experiences were part of God's plan for me. Her words were reassuring and encouraging.

It is around this time that Horton changes the name and musical focus of his *Big Band* from secular to religious music, renaming it the *Randall Keith Horton Gospel Orchestra*.[261] The orchestra's first two performances under its new identity are at the Oakland Museum of Art (the garden) and the Cathedral of St. Francis de Sales.

---

261  Horton founded Gospel Orchestra while he was the live-in custodian at the San Francisco Community Music Center in the late 1960's. Horton featured this orchestra in most of his concertized performances of Ellington's *Sacred Music* (1984 - 2007) and for two performances of his *Ellington-Horton Black, Brown and Beige* (Sacramento, 1988 and Dallas, 1999).

In the meantime, five years earlier in 1979, Ruth Ellington married the talented American operatic Bass-baritone McHenry Boatwright, whom she met in 1974 when he sang at her brother's funeral. Shortly after her meeting with Horton, Ruth and McHenry move to a new apartment at 750 Park Avenue (1984) where her guidance and mentoring of Horton continued. Over time, Ruth and Horton discover shared religious beliefs, and for some twenty years, enjoy a deep, abiding friendship. Horton is privileged to attend some of the Sunday *soirees* held in Ruth's home that are an important part of her social life. He particularly enjoys meeting Brooks Kerr, a blind piano prodigy who had played with Ellington and taken part in the 1969 star-studded Jazz concert celebrating Ellington's seventieth birthday in the East Room of the White House with President Nixon. Kerr later invites Horton to his home to become better acquainted and discuss all things Ellington.

Horton continues to make trips to New York for some of Ruth's birthdays (July 2), to clubs or to dine with Ruth and her husband at *Tavern on the Green* (their favorite). Over time, Horton also befriends Ruth's two sons.

Says Horton:

Ruth's oldest son from her first marriage, the late Michael James, was the encyclopedic Ellington philosopher. We would sit up all night in his Midtown Manhattan apartment, watching one-of-a-kind videos and getting an *Ellingtonian* schooling that no university could have provided. We had street smarts in common and had many laughs together. In later years, Ruth's younger son Steven James, suave, sophisticated and worldly, honored me by inviting me to play the piano and sing an impromptu performance of *My Love* for his late brother Michael James' memorial service (2007). Steven remains a protector of his late uncle's legacy.

During this same period (2008-2013), Horton also studies under choral conductor James John at Queens College. He develops his sight—reading and score—skills, teaches sight-singing to members of the Queens College Choral Society and records his choral tribute to folk-music Kate Wolf with Dr. John's professional choral ensemble, Cerddorion (and other artists).

He tells Horton that the famous choral conductor Robert Shaw could not read sheet music at first, but when Arturo Toscanini heard the magnificent sound Shaw was able to coax from his choir, he hired him to conduct a choir performance of Beethoven's *Ninth Symphony* with the *NBC Symphony Orchestra*. John tells him that Toscanini didn't care whether or not Shaw could read music. He hired Shaw for his unparalleled skill in teasing out exceptional choral performances. But John's words get Horton thinking about classical choral music: *What are my gifts? What do I uniquely bring to composing and conducting?*

Horton already knows in relation to his Ellington calling: In his recollections, he travels to Boston in 1984 to visit his family and calls on Ruth. He updates her on his work in his musical ministry in California, and she asks him to join her and McHenry for lunch or dinner that same day. Horton apologizes, stating he is booked on a return train trip to the West Coast in a few short hours. Ruth urges Horton two more times to come to her home. Taking the not-so-subtle hints, Horton changes his travel plans. Their reunion unfolds in its usual manner with lively conversation before taking a startling turn. Ruth informs him that she is authorizing him to concertize and lead her brother's *Sacred Music*.

Horton recalls:

I was deeply flattered, and shell-shocked. I responded with the thought foremost in my mind. "Ruth, you honor me, but I don't know that I am qualified to do what you are asking of me." To which, with Ruth's nodding approval, McHenry

Boatwright responded in his deep, booming, baritone voice, "You are qualified!"

Ruth is adamant in her selection of Horton because of his unique combination of skills: his composing and conducting experience, his selection by Duke, his compatible religious beliefs, his musically saturated understanding of the Bible, Negro spirituals and church music, his earnestness, his lack of ulterior motives and his loyalty; gifts that she lets Horton know in no uncertain terms that he uniquely possesses. In short, Ruth trusts Horton to approach the task with the sensitivity, skills and purity of purpose of which her brother would have approved.

Ruth Ellington-Boatwright
750 Park Avenue
New York, NY 10021

October 12, 1994

Members of the Board of Directors
Rohnert Park Symphony Orchestra
Spreckels Performing Arts Center
5409 Snyder Lane
Rohnert Park, CA 94928

Dear Members of the Board:

This is in support of Mr. Randall Keith Horton's interest in serving as Music Director and Conductor of the Rohnert Park Symphony Orchestra.

We know Randall to be a friend and an outstanding conductor. My brother, Edward Kennedy (Duke) Ellington, invited Randall to conduct the Ellington Orchestra, directing his own music, in a concert in 1973. At my request, Randall has directed some of the Duke Ellington Sacred Concerts (since 1984) and was very successful in composing and conducting his own concerto-grosso symphonic orchestration of my brother's "Black, Brown and Beige".

Randall Keith Horton is certainly a musical asset to the Ellington musical legacy. We highly recommend him for the musical directorship of your orchestra.

Sincerely,

Ruth Ellington-Boatwright

In 2017, acclaimed Jazz critic Gary Giddins affirms Ruth's insightful selection of Horton, stating, "As an experienced composer of church music, Mr. Horton possesses a singular understanding of Ellington's *Sacred Music* and the composer's intentions. He would appear to be ideally suited to revive and conduct the *Sacred Concerts*, which Ellington justifiably prized high among his achievements."[262]

Horton accepts Ruth's appointment with trepidation and immediately begins to thematically curate Ellington's sacred melodies into a single, two-phase performance: Phase I - *The Majesty of God*, with songs drawing upon lessons from the *Old Testament*, featuring *Sacred Music* selections that express a non-personal or non-intimate worship of God.[263] And Phase II - *The Love of God*, featuring songs with themes from the *New Testament*, expressing a more personal, loving relationship between God and the individual.[264] Horton conceives his *Highlights of Ellington's Sacred Music*[265] with briefly spoken religious/musical anecdotes to introduce each song to help orient its listeners. Ruth is pleased with Horton's sensitive treatment. It becomes a labor of love for Horton who continues to perform and consult on *Sacred Music* performances even after Ruth's death in 2004. In total (to date), he faithfully raises funds to conduct or consult on more than thirty-two *Sacred Concert* performances, more than any other individual or institution.

---

262  Gary Giddins, phone conversation with author, 1/27/2017.

263  Musical selections included in Phase I "The Majesty of God" include: The Sonnet of the Apple, In The Beginning, God, T.G.T.T., Will You Be There, Ain't But The One, Freedom Suite and David Danced.

264  Musical selections included in Phase II "The Love Of God include: My love, Something 'Bout Believing, Come Sunday, Heaven, Father Forgive!, Don't Get Down On Your Knees To Pray (Until You Have Forgiven Everyone) and the "Finale" Praise God and Dance (150th Psalm).

265  "Highlights of Ellington's Sacred Music" is not to be confused with the sheet music for *The Best of Ellington's Sacred Music* also published by G. Schirmer. Randall Keith Horton's concertization of Ellington's three *Sacred Concerts* was premiered by Horton at the Morton H. Meyerson Symphony Center in Dallas in 1999. It was performed from sheet music given to him by Ruth Ellington-Boatwright while it was still under the control of her Tempo Music Publishing Company. She later sold Tempo Music to G. Schirmer.

## Sacred Concerts Performed By Randall Keith Horton

*32 Performances for a total audience of 33,550 people*[266]

| | |
|---|---|
| 1984 | Sonoma State University, Rohnert Park, CA |
| | Three performances in small auditorium x 2 |
| | Audience of 600 |
| 1985 | Luther Burbank Concert Hall, Santa Rosa, CA |
| | Sponsored by "100 Black Men of America"[267] |
| | Audience of 1,200 |
| May 2, 1986 | United Methodist Church, San Francisco, CA |
| | Audience of 200 |
| May 4, 1986 | Allen Temple Baptist Church, Oakland, CA |
| | Audience of 600 |
| 1986/1987 | Hamilton Community Center, Novato, CA |
| | Audience of 100 |
| February 22, 1987 | Morris Dailey Auditorium, San Jose State University, San Jose, NM |
| | *The Sacred Concerts of Duke Ellington* |
| | Audience of 400 |
| October 18, 1987 | St. Bartholomew's Church, New York, NY |
| | Ellington Alumni Orchestra, produced by Ruth Ellington, narrated by Douglas Fairbanks, Jr. |
| | Audience of 850 |
| February 28, 1988 | Hiram Johnson H.S. Auditorium, Sacramento, CA |
| | The "Ellington Horton Black, Brown & Beige" with the Camellia Symphony Orchestra |
| | Audience of 1,200 |

266 See appendix "A" for copies of programs and attendant newspaper articles.

267 100 Black Men of America is a men's civic organization and service club formed in 1963 to help educate and empower African-American children and teens by improving the quality of life within our communities and enhancing educational and economic opportunities for all African Americans.[1] Mottos "Real men giving real time" and "What they see is what they'll be" capture the organization's goal of providing positive role models and leaders to guide the next generation of African Americans and other youth.

| April 28, 1989 | Marin Covenant Church, San Raphael, CA |
| | Audience of 500 |
| April 30, 1989 | St. Francis de Sales Catholic Cathedral, Oakland, CA |
| | Audience of 800 |
| 1993 | Washington National Cathedral, Washington, D.C. |
| | Music Consultant |
| | Audience of 3,200 |
| June 26, 1993 | Luther Burbank Center, Santa Rosa, CA |
| | *The Duke Ellington Sacred Concert* |
| | Audience of 1,200 |
| February 16, 1997 | Lover's Lane United Methodist Church, Dallas, TX |
| | *Duke Ellington Sacred Concert*[268] |
| | Audience of 800 |
| October 5, 1997 | The Gem Theater, Kansas City, MO[269] |
| | *Duke Ellington's Sacred Concert* |
| | Audience of 1,400 |
| February 12, 1999 | The Palace Theatre, Grapevine, TX |
| | *The Sacred Concerts of Duke Ellington* |
| | Audience of 300 |
| March 2, 1999 | Morton H. Meyerson Symphony Center, Dallas, TX |
| | Highlights of the *Duke Ellington Sacred Concerts* |
| | and the *Ellington-Horton Black, Brown & Beige* |
| | Audience of 2,500 |
| October 28, 1999 | Lover's Lane United Methodist - Church Dallas, TX |
| | *Duke Ellington's Sacred Music - In celebration of New* |
| | *Jerusalem United Methodist Church* |
| | Audience of 800 |

---

268   Horton dedicated this *Duke Ellington's Sacred Concert* to 'Mother Barron', his beloved mother-in-law Leona Maxine Barron who died two days prior on February 14, 1997.

269   Reopening celebration for the historic 18th & Vine District known as one of the cradles of Jazz (Charlie Parker) and a historical hub of African American businesses in the 1930's and 1940's. A $30 million redevelopment in the 1980's led to its "reopening" in 1997 during which Horton's performance received thunderous applause.

| | |
|---|---|
| Dec 9-12, 1999 | Jazz At Lincoln Center, NY, NY |
| | Horton was guest Music Consultant on Eight |
| | performances of *In His Solitude, The Sacred Music of* |
| | *Duke Ellington* |
| | Audience of 14,000 |
| 2000 | Lover's Lane United Methodist Church, Dallas, TX |
| | "A Sacred Calling" |
| | Audience of 1,000 |
| April 28, 2004 | St. Peter's Lutheran Church (The Jazz Church), |
| | New York, NY[270] |
| | *n Evening of Duke Ellington's Sacred Music* |
| | *(Improvise!* Festival) |
| | Audience of 250 |
| 2007 | St. Peter's Lutheran Church (*The Jazz Church*), |
| | New York, NY |
| | Audience of 150 |
| March 22, 2009 | Riverside Church, New York, NY |
| | *The Sacred Music of Duke Ellington* (Horton piano solo) |
| | Audience of 100 |
| December 14, 2013 | Colden Auditorium, Flushing, NY |
| | *The Best of...Duke Ellington's Sacred Concerts* |
| | Queens College Jazz Ensemble and Choral Society |
| | Audience of 200 |
| January 17, 2017 | Boston University, Boston, MA |
| | *Hope, Despair and The Blues* |
| | BU Symphony Orchestra, Inner Strength Gospel |
| | Choir, Soloists, Dancers |
| | Audience of 1,200 |

---

270  A collaborative performance between the American Composers Orchestra (ACO), the Duke Ellington Society (TDES) and the Juilliard Jazz Orchestra to celebrate Duke Ellington's 105th birthday.

In the early 1980's, Horton also envisions the creation of an educational television series to explore and celebrate the history of American music. While taping the initial pilot for this project, the person he is interviewing suggests another potential guest, a nun located in San Rafael who founded the first library documenting the earliest forms of American music. Horton reaches out to Sister Mary Dominic Ray[271] at her American Music Research Center[272] (AMRC) in nearby San Rafael, California, He introduces himself and his television program and asks if he might interview her about her mission to preserve, study and reintroduce forgotten and unknown music from America's musical heritage. She declines. But according to Horton,

> The third time I called was the magic charm. She agreed to film a segment about early American Pilgrim music with a performance of the music, featuring a 60-member gospel choir, my 16-piece *Big Band*, experienced singers of Pilgrim music and a Hebraic dance ensemble. It was magnificent, and our working relationship soon blossomed into a friendship and mentorship. Sr. Dominic Ray introduced me to American Colonial music and planted additional seeds of appreciation for American music history. She created a research position for me at her center and helped me grow as a person through her examples of hard work, devotion, joy, her sense of humor and consideration for others. She introduced me

---

271 Sister Mary Dominic Ray was a pianist and musicologist whose private collection of Pilgrim hymnals, California mission music, Samuel Felsted's *Jonah*, music of the gold rush and comic operas became the basis for the AMRC's collection devoted to the preservation, study and performance of America's musical heritage, one of the few such centers in the United States.

272 The American Music Research Center is the oldest center for the study of music of the American continents in the United States. It was originally located at Dominican College in San Rafael, California until 1989, at which time the Center, its name and its collections were purchased by the University of Colorado and moved to Boulder as a joint venture between the College of Music and the University Libraries. Its archives include extensive collections of popular sheet music, silent film music, sacred hymnals and tune books, big band and swing era music as well as music from Colorado and the American West.

to internationally recognized scholars in what was known at that time (1985-1987) as The Sonneck Society for American Music (now the Society for American Music or SAM). It was through the teachings of Sr. Dominic and the encouragement of the iconic music scholar H. Wiley Hitchcock[273] that my vision for my *American Music* Educational TV Program was nurtured and refined.

In 1987, in addition to his musical directorships and his research for his *American Music* TV program with Sister Dominic Ray and H. Wiley Hitchcock, Horton prepares another *Sacred Concert* at St. Bartholomew's Church in New York. He is privileged to rehearse, conduct and interact with the *Duke Ellington Alumni Orchestra* featuring Savion Glover tap dancing and Douglas Fairbanks, Jr.[274] narrating. Also in attendance is Jazz guitarist Kenny Burrell, who seeks Horton out for a chat at intermission.

In 1990, Horton rehearses his big band, choral and dance ensembles for a *Sacred Concert* (his eleventh) at Grace Cathedral in San Francisco under Ruth Ellington-Boatwright's authority and guidance. But during one of the final rehearsals, he is pulled aside and informed that his conducting services and Gospel Orchestra are no longer needed. Horton makes a frantic call to Ruth to clear up the misunderstanding, only to discover there is no misunderstanding. Ruth casually informs him that she accepted a sizable sum of money to turn the entire concert over to a local established concert producer who plans to record it, featuring the *Duke Ellington Alumni Orchestra* with Mercer Ellington conducting.

---

273  H. Wiley Hitchcock was an American musicologist who founded the Sonneck Society (1971), later renamed the Institute for Studies in American Music at Brooklyn College of the City University of New York (CUNY). The Institute was later renamed the Hitchcock Institute for Studies in American Music in his honor.

274  Douglas Fairbanks, Jr. (1909 – 2000), son of movie star Douglas Fairbanks Sr.,was an American actor and producer, who appeared in more than 100 movies and TV shows, including *The Prisoner of Zenda* (1937), *Gunga Din* (1939) and *The Corsican Brothers* (1941) and was married to Joan Crawford.

Regrettably, she neglects to share her decision with her good friend. "Darling," Ruth explains to Horton by phone, "what did you expect me to do?"

After six years of loyally championing and performing Duke's *Sacred Concerts* under her direction, Ruth's indifferent explanation delivers a *coup de grâce*. It is a business decision for her of course, but for Horton, it is a deeply personal slight. His skin has thickened over the years, but not enough to withstand this. Ruth's actions rupture his trust, along with their long-standing friendship. He returns home, binds up the original *Sacred Music* lead sheets loaned to him for his (uncompensated) concertizing of Duke's *Sacred Music* and drops the priceless bundle off with Ruth's doorman. A period of wounded estrangement ensues.

Two years later, additional performance opportunities for the *Sacred Music* lead to a reconciliation between Horton and Ruth. He travels to Ruth's home in New York at her invitation, and their friendship is reestablished.

> While I was there, Ruth took a call from Kenny Burrell, the same Jazz guitarist who attended Horton's *Sacred Concert* performance at St. Bartholomew's Church in New York in 1987. He was well aware of my estrangement from Ruth and the underlying reason for it. So I heard Ruth tell Kenny, 'Mr. Horton is in my home. We're talking.' Her acknowledgement of our reconciliation melted away all the hurt I had felt over the last two years.

But just as Horton and Ruth Ellington-Boatwright's friendship is mended, a sizable rift develops between Ruth and her nephew Mercer, who posthumously gifts his father's collection of music, business papers and memorabilia to the Smithsonian Institution and sells additional materials to what was known at that time as the Duke Ellington Project Partnership for "pennies on the dollar."

The Smithsonian Institution's *American Historical Museum of Music* develops a traveling exhibit for its newly acquired Ellington materials.[275] Horton and Mercer Ellington travel to Washington, DC from California and from Copenhagen, Denmark, respectively, for its official opening. While there, Horton reaches out to the collection's Smithsonian curator John Edward Hasse to propose a concert tour of Ellington's *Sacred Music* to accompany the Ellington exhibit at each of its stops. Although Hasse is initially open to the idea, the concept never comes to fruition. Says Horton,

> It was unfortunate. A concert of Ellington's *Sacred Music*, whether I or someone else conducted it, would have brought Ellington's traveling exhibit to life and provided a terrific opportunity for community outreach. Nonetheless, I was invited to conduct a *Sacred Concert* at the Gem Theater in Kansas City, Missouri, when the exhibit traveled there in 1997, and it was a rafter-raising night of music!

---

275 Duke Ellington Collection. Archives Center, National Museum of American History, Washington D.C. https://sova.si.edu/record/NMAH.AC.0301.

## CHAPTER 10

# ELLINGTON-HORTON BLACK, BROWN & BEIGE

*"It is becoming increasingly difficult to decide where Jazz starts or where it stops, where Tin Pan Alley begins and Jazz ends, or even where the borderline lies between classical music and Jazz. I feel there is no boundary line."*[276]

\- Duke Ellington

It is difficult to predict how introductions and connections at various points of one's life might eventually bear fruit in seemingly unrelated areas. Horton has no way of knowing that his successful concertizing of Duke Ellington's *Sacred Music* will lead him to an even weightier Ellington commission three years later. Nor can he fathom how his time working with Sister Mary Dominc Ray at the *American Music Research Center* (1983-1987) will expand his knowledge and perspective on music and

---

276 *The Cambridge Companion To Jazz*, Edited by Mervyn Cooke and David Horn, Cambridge University Press, 2002, 153.

bring him in contact with the leading scholars and experts in American music: H. Wiley Hitchcock, PhD, founder of the *Institute for Studies in American Music* (ISAM), Richard Crawford, PhD,[277] co-founder of the *Society for American Music* (SAM), Mark Tucker, PhD, music scholar and author specializing in Duke Ellington and Daniel Kingman, PhD,[278] conductor of the *Camellia Symphony Orchestra* (Sacramento, CA). Horton is enlightened by each of them and conversely imparts his own music experiences: being invited to conduct the Ellington orchestra at *Disneyland* and appointed by Ruth to lead her brother's *Sacred Music*. As a direct result of these experiences and interactions, Dr. Daniel Kingman lunches with Horton at the 1985 conference of the *Sonneck Society for American Music* and tracks him down again in 1987, brandishing a review by noted Jazz critic Gary Giddins.[279]

In it, Giddins offers a strident critique of orchestrator/conductor Maurice Peress'[280] (17-minute) "lacunary interpretation" of the first movement (*Black* only) of Ellington's *Black, Brown and Beige*, stating, "*BB&B*, and not just *Black*, is a rich, buxom work. Its stirring, affirmative self-confidence, proliferation of melodies and rhythms, and command of moods can only benefit *Symphony Hall*: subscribers bored with the romantics and weary of the *avant garde* should find it intriguingly

---

277  Dr. Richard Crawford (1935) is an American music historian who authored, published and edited a number of books on American music, including the seminal book on the subject, titled *American Musical Landscapes* (2001), *The Business of Musicianship from Billings to Gershwin* (2000) and *America's Musical Life: A History* (2005). He was also Mark Tucker's advisor during his PhD dissertation at Michigan State University.

278  Dr. Daniel Kingman was the Conductor of the Camellia Symphony from 1979-1981 and made it his mission to program seldom performed American music as well as recently composed music, including some of his own. Under his direction, the Camellia Symphony won its first ASCAP award. He was also a professor, composer and author of the *American Music: A Panorama* (1979). This best-selling survey text describes American music as a collection of distinct strains of music--including popular, folk, sacred, classical, blues, Jazz, and rock music - that have evolved into a musical panorama reflecting the nation's unique character.

279  Gary Giddins is an American Jazz and film critic, author, director and former contributor to *The Village Voice*.

280  Maurice Peress, the "very important person" Duke Ellington likely met with in Houston during the Ellington Orchestra's two week engagement at the Shamrock Hilton Hotel in 1973. It is possible that the two met to discuss Peress' partial orchestration of "*Black*" from Ellington's 1943 *Black, Brown and Beige*.

new, yet accessible. But until a conductor with as intransigent a vision as Ellington's is commissioned to prepare *Black, Brown and Beige* for performance, it will have to be done in the Ellington manner. So far, no one from the Jazz or symphonic worlds has measured up."[281]

Kingman implores Horton to contact Mercer Ellington immediately and offer his services as the obvious architect for the definitive, full-length, *concerto grosso* orchestration of Ellington's *Black, Brown and Beige* for which Giddins begs. Kingman feels strongly that Horton is uniquely qualified to interpret and create an incisive orchestration that fully embraces Duke's symphonic vision for his big band *opus*. Kingman's entreaty catches Horton off-guard. He experiences a moment of *déjà vu* and the same sense of shock and awe that a *second* expert, this time the esteemed conductor Dr. Daniel Kingman, might deem him qualified for another lofty Ellington-related assignment.

"The very suggestion that I should reach out to Mercer Ellington to arrange his father's *magnum opus*...and that he would even endorse me...was unthinkable at that time," states Horton. "You have to remember that my last interaction with him centered around the settlement of my Houston motel bill fourteen years earlier in 1973."

When Horton demurs, Dr. Kingman takes matters into his own hands. He contacts Mercer himself, shares Giddins' review and proffers Randall Keith Horton as the most qualified person to faithfully and competently orchestrate Ellington's *magnum opus*. Mercer concurs and authorizes New York music publisher G. Schirmer to set the commission in motion. G. Schirmer, unfamiliar with Horton's composing and conducting credentials, asks for samples of his writing and a recording from his *Randall Keith Horton Gospel Orchestra*.[282] The music publisher also seeks additional references and receives an endorsement of Horton

---

281  Gary Giddins, "In Search of Black, Brown and Beige," *Riding on a Blue Note*, Oxford University Press, 1981, p. 169.

282  Randall Keith Horton Gospel Orchestra.

from one of its own esteemed composers and longtime Horton mentors, Kirke Mechem. Mechem "wholeheartedly" recommends Horton for the commission, noting his lengthy association with him (twenty years), his familiarity with the quality of his composing and conducting as well as Horton's direct work with Ellington and his orchestra, his concertizing of Ellington's *Sacred Music* at Ruth Ellington-Boatwright's behest and his association with the Ellington family.[283] The second to last paragraph in Kirke Mechem's 2014 letter references his and the Ellington family's concurrent endorsement of Horton for the 1987 commission to G. Schirmer Publishing.

Dr. Kingman further cements the deal, offering his own *Camellia Symphony Orchestra* to premiere the completed orchestration under Randall Keith Horton's baton. The endorsements assuage any hesitations by the music publisher. And when Mercer Ellington's written approval (see signature on G. Schirmer letter) is eventually received, the publisher and copyright owner of Ellington's original *Black, Brown and Beige*, approves Randall Keith Horton to write the full-length orchestration in October of 1987.

G. Schirmer executives direct Horton to compose and hand write the conductor's score from which they agree to pay a separate copyist to extract the individual parts for the *Camellia Symphony Orchestra's* premiere. It is a monstrous undertaking, an estimated 340 pages (1400 measures) of new symphonic music written for 128 orchestral instruments to accompany and enrich Ellington's original 16-piece, big band score (144 total individual parts). For his efforts, Horton is offered a small work-for-hire fee.[284]

---

283  See similar wording in the final paragraph of the 2014 endorsement letter for Randall Keith Horton written at a later date by Kirke Mechem on the following page.

284  A work-for-hire contract gives the subcontractor/orchestrator a one-time fee for his musical contributions and prohibits the same subcontractor/ orchestrator from claiming any future earnings from royalties generated by from the recording, performance or (mechanical or synchronization) licensing of the orchestration.

Comprehending the magnitude of the work, and the paucity of the terms, Horton knows he should reject the commission. But in the absence of an agent or legal representation, he indulges himself a few moments of quiet reflection on the improbable string of events that have positioned him for this momentous opportunity:

- Being *called* to study music in San Francisco (1964)
- Attending Ellington's *First Sacred Concert* (1965)
- Learning to conduct and compose classical music in San Francisco (1965 - 1985).
- Auditing rehearsals for the San Francisco...Symphony, Ballet and Opera (1969-1974, 1979- 1985)
- Arranging classical music for the *San Francisco Symphony* and its conductor Arthur Fiedler with Kirke Mechem as his mentor (1973).
- Conducting *The Ellington Orchestra* at *Disneyland* (1973)
- Being chosen by Duke Ellington as his assistant composer, conductor and pianist (1973)
- Arranging orchestral music for *The Del-Tones* and pop music for Martha Reeves and *MDLT Willis* and *The Jackson 5* (1973 - 1974)
- Absorbing Ellington insights and mentoring from Ruth Ellington-Boatwright (1983 - 2004)
- Being chosen by Ruth to concertize her brother's three *Sacred Concerts* (1984)
- Directing religious music for numerous churches and synagogues (1969 - 2005)
- Understanding Biblical teachings, religious hymns and the history of Negro Work Songs, Spirituals, Jazz and early American music.

"And now, at the age of forty-three, to be asked to 'complete' Duke Ellington's *magnum opus* as the Maestro himself envisioned...please!" exclaims a present-day Horton still in disbelief. "It was an otherworldly opportunity that triggered the same old internal questions: *What's happening? Why me?* But my self-doubt slowly transitioned to an abiding sense that if this is God's plan, how can I *not* accept?"

Horton views the commission as the fulfillment of his *calling* and his personal obligation to Duke Ellington. He commits himself to the commission in late 1987, asks for a small advance to get started, and waits. When advance monies from G. Schirmer are not forthcoming, Horton reaches out to Ruth for guidance. She provides Horton with a telephone number, cryptically instructing him to call and share his dilemma with the person who answers: "If he has any questions," she says, "tell him that I asked you to call."

Horton calls the number and is shocked when Lou Levy, the renowned music publisher, agent, concert promoter and part owner of G. Schirmer Publishing, answers the phone. He listens to Horton, dispenses with any questions and promptly writes him a personal check for $1,000 to get the project started. Mercer Ellington provides Horton with the handwritten manuscripts of his father's original *Black, Brown and Beige* (lead sheets) with the implicit instructions to, "Stay as true to my father's original music as possible and compose a symphonic tapestry to blend with and unify his original writing." And that is exactly what Horton does.

**G. SCHIRMER, INC.**

*& Associated Music Publishers, Inc.*

A Division of Music Sales Corp.

*Executive Offices: 24 East 22nd Street, New York, New York 10010*
*Telephone: 212•254•2100 Telex: 428351 Telefax: 212•254•2013*

16 October 1987

Mr. Daniel Kingman, Music Director
Camellia Symphony Orchestra
600 Shangri Lane
Sacramento, CA 95825

Dear Mr. Kingman:

Thank you very much for your letter and material of October 1.
I have had a chance to meet with Randall Horton and review his
plans and sketches for an arrangement of Ellington's Black,
Brown and Beige.

We are prepared to proceed with your proposal to perform this
new arrangement subject to the following conditions:

1.  You are granted permission to premiere a new
    arrangement of Ellington's Black, Brown and Beige, the
    copyright of which is owned by G. Schirmer, on February
    27, 1988.

2.  The rental and premiere performance fee will be waived,
    providing that the performance actually takes place
    before June 1, 1988.

3.  An appropriate credit line, such as "Premiered by The
    Camellia Symphony Orchestra, Daniel Kingman, Music
    Director" or "Commissioned for The Camellia Symphony
    Orchestra, David Kingman, Music Director" will appear
    on the title page of all copies of the full score.

4.  Upon approval by Mercer Ellington, G. Schirmer will
    engage Randall Horton to arrange this work for a flat
    fee of ▮▮▮▮. Mr. Horton must provide G. Schirmer with
    clear, legible full score masters of the arrangement,
    including all corrections and revisions made in
    preparation for and subsequent to the premiere
    performance. Mr. Horton and G. Schirmer will sign a
    separate agreement for this arrangement.

5.  The Camellia Symphony will engage a copyist to extract
    the parts for this arrangement. Samples of the
    copyist's work must be submitted and approved by G.
    Schirmer. Upon receipt of vellum masters of the parts,

continued...

including all corrections and revisions, G. Schirmer
will reimburse The Camellia Symphony Orchestra the
actual cost of extraction or $3000, whichever is lower.

6. We will print two scores and one set of parts to be
placed on "permanent loan" with The Camellia Symphony
Orchestra. This set of parts remains the property of
G. Schirmer and is for the exclusive use of The
Camellia Symphony Orchestra. It may not be copied,
rented, or loaned to anyone without written permission
from G. Schirmer.

7. The waiver of Rental and Performance fees will only
apply to performances before June 1, 1988 and does not
apply to broadcast, television, or commercial
recording. Future performances must be reported to
ASCAP and a rental fee must be paid.

8. In the event an archive recording of a performance by
The Camellia Symphony Orchestra is made, you must
provide G. Schirmer with a quality cassette copy of the
performance.

The return of three copies of this letter signed by Randall
Horton, Mercer Ellington, and The Camellia Symphony will
constitute a binding agreement between us.

Sincerely,

Stephen Culbertson
Director of Rental and Performance


Accepted and agreed to:
The Camellia Symphony Orchestra

by: _____

Accepted and agreed to:                    Accepted and agreed to:


by:_____                         by:_____
Mr. Mercer Ellington                       Mr. Randall Horton

**G. SCHIRMER, INC.**

*& Associated Music Publishers, Inc.*

A Division of Music Sales Corp.

Executive Offices: 24 East 22nd Street, New York, New York 10010
Telephone: 212•254•2100 Telex: 428351 Telefax: 212•254•2013

October 26, 1987

Mr. Daniel Kingman, Music Director
Camellia Symphony Orchestra
600 Shangri Lane
Sacramento, CA 95825

Dear Mr. Kingman:

I am writing to inform you of the situation regarding your plans to perform a new arrangement of Ellington's Black, Brown and Beige.

After meeting with Mr. Horton and discussing his plans for the arrangement, G. Schirmer is willing to go ahead with the arrangement subject to the enclosed letter. You will see in the letter that the approval of Mercer Ellington is also essential.

After the letter of agreement was drafted, I tried on several occasions to contact Mercer, and even had five copies of the letter sent up to him. I emphasized that his approval and signature was needed before we could go ahead.

To date, I have not received the letters with Mercer's signature, and I understand that he is now out of the country until the middle of November.

In an effort to give you a definite answer by November 1, I'm afraid that we cannot grant you permission to arrange and perform a new version of Black, Brown and Beige because Mercer Ellington has not approved the project.

I am sorry to bring you such unhappy news, but wish you the best for the continued success of the Camellia Symphony Orchestra.

Sincerely yours,

Stephen Culbertson
Director of Rental and Performance

cc: Barrie Edwards
Randal Horton
Mercer Ellington
Yolanda Blum
Michael Sukin
Lou Levy

*This is the OK for Randle Horton Black Brown & Beige arrangement ...*

## The *Ellington-Horton Black, Brown and Beige* Takes Shape[285]

Immediately following Ellington's 1943 premiere of *Black, Brown and Beige*, critics from both Jazz and classical persuasions are in agreement (albeit for a variety of different and misapprehended individual reasons) that Ellington's original *Black, Brown and Beige* is "not successful."

Paul Bowles, music critic for the *New York Herald Tribune* writes an article discrediting Ellington's "countless unprovoked modulations... recurrent climaxes that impede the piece's progress." Exactly three decades later (1973), composer Maurice Peress' seventeen-minute symphonic interpretation of *Black*[286] (first movement only) is dismissed by Jazz critic Gary Giddins as "an unwitting parody" of Ellington's unique musical style. Giddins further states that "until conservatory-trained virtuosos are willing to embrace Ellington's music and study its unique instrumental stylings, they may reproduce Ellington's melodies, but not Ellington's music."[287]

The critique throws down the proverbial gauntlet, calling for a full-length orchestration and preparing the soil for Randall Keith Horton's commission. In fact, Giddins elegantly demands it.

Though Horton is guilelessly unaware of all but Giddins' critiques of *Black, Brown and Beige* when he begins his orchestration in 1987, his research and subsequent study of the composition reveal that Duke is, in fact, unapologetic about the piece's "abrupt, disorienting changes in form." He does, however, obliquely acknowledge some of the

---

285 Information for this section is taken from "A Single Beam of Light and its Transformation of my Life (Discourse from an Obscure Ellingtonian)" by Randall Keith Horton, Stonybrook University, Long Island, NY, 2019, and "The Performance/Recording and Critical History of Duke Ellington's *Black, Brown and Beige*: An Overview" by Randall Keith Horton, Brooklyn College, 2006.

286 Maurice Peress's seventeen-minute orchestration of Duke Ellington's first movement only (*Black*) curiously titled *Black, Brown* and Beige, was published in 1970 and later performed and critiqued by Gray Giddins and other Jazz experts. It was recorded by the American Composers Orchestra on June 27, 1988, for which Mr. Horton was present.

287 McBride, *Ibid.*

composition's structural challenges through his revisitations of portions of his *opus* throughout his life, most notably in his 1958 album *Black, Brown and Beige,*[288] where he adds lyrics for Mahalia Jackson's exquisite rendition of *Come Sunday* and composes new music for her improvised singing of the *Twenty-Third Psalm*.

In a Tower Records store in Berkeley, Horton discovers Mahalia Jackson's singing on the *Black, Brown and Beige* album. As he combs through Ellington's original lead sheets and repeatedly listens to the *Ellington Orchestra's* Carnegie Hall recording and the *Black, Brown and Beige* album, he experiences an epiphany: Jackson's vocal interpretation of Ellington's 1958 lyrics to *Come Sunday* and newly created music for the *Twenty-Third Psalm*, when interpolated into the third movement of the original *Black, Brown and Beige*, reinforce *Beige's* structural integrity. It is a seminal and exhilarating discovery. Horton shares his postulation with Ruth, who affirms its appropriateness. Excited and energized, he can hardly write the notes to his symphonic orchestration fast enough. The newly integrated materials fall neatly into place as Ellington, in Horton's estimation, likely foresaw and intended. Horton smiles to himself, experiencing firsthand the wisdom of one of Ellington's adages: *Don't Push It. Let it Fall.*

> The connection just came to me. There was no question of the songs' fit: *Come Sunday* with Mahalia's exquisite singing of Ellington's superb new lyrics, (demonstrated by Horton *in-voce*) ["*Lord, dear Lord Above,/God almighty/God of love/ Please look down and see my people through*"] ... and here, it is imperative to note that when Ellington wrote "*my people*" he meant ALL people. ALL of us[289] and the *Twenty-Third Psalm*, which is universally revered.

---

288  Duke Ellington and the Duke Ellington Orchestra, *Black, Brown and Beige*, with Mahalia Jackson (vocals), recorded February 4-5 and 11-12, 1958, Columbia Records, 1958, 33 rpm. Despite the album's title, it was not a recording of the complete 45-minute compositions performed in 1943.

289  Confirmed by Randall Keith Horton through conversations with Ruth Ellington-Boatwright at the time of his orchestrating (1987).

With the overarching structure of the third movement fortified, Horton directs his attention to writing the symphonic orchestration, which according to music critic Bruce Nixon in 1988, "Ellington probably would have loved...Ellington envisioned an accompanying orchestral arrangement for *Black, Brown and Beige*, but never returned to it himself. "He was obsessed through much of his late career with the idea of combining Jazz and orchestral music to create an American high-art form." [290]

From the very beginning of this new musical assignment, Horton enthusiastically re-assumes his brief mantle as Ellington's assistant composer and begins writing the orchestration from his personal familiarity with the *Ellington Orchestra* and, according to Horton, "in the spiritual presence of the Maestro." He works around the clock to write and carefully weave the expansive threads of a richly sustaining, symphonic fabric around Ellington's Big Band parts to help smooth transitions and enhance connectivity. To Horton, it is far more than a musical commission, it is his personal encomium to Ellington.

## The *Ellington-Horton Black, Brown and Beige*[291]

"My guiding thought from the technical standpoint," explains Horton in his October 9, 1987 letter to the music publisher G. Schirmer, is to mold the arrangement so that the contours of what Ellington wrote originally can be heard and seen in their greatest possible representation. For example, the portion of the score ... while emphasizing the African rhythmic qualities and the conversant expressiveness ... very gradually

---

290 Bruce Nixon, "Camellia Symphony Gives Ellington A Rich Revival," *The (Sacramento) Bee*, February 28, 1988.

291 Information on Randall Keith Horton's orchestration, discoveries and contributions is paraphrased from interviews with Horton and the following: program notes of the March 2, 1999 University of North Texas Symphony Orchestra performance of the full-length *Ellington-Horton Black, Brown and Beige* at the Morton H. Meyerson Symphony Center, Dallas, TX as conducted by Randall Keith Horton; and Horton's "A Single Beam of Light and its Transformation of my Life (Discourse from an Obscure Ellingtonian)."

leads up to the spiritual theme *Come Sunday*." He notes that Ellington makes it clear that the seven-note *Work Song* motif and spiritual theme *Come Sunday* are "closely related." There is no gradual contrapuntal development (in his original score) that dramatically depicts that close relationship. This represented an opportunity for the symphony orchestra to develop the motivic shape of *Come Sunday* early in the score, so that when the actual theme appears, it is much more effective. Horton notes, "Throughout the composition, my symphonic orchestration built upon and enhanced Ellington's contours, carrying out various shapes, harmonies rhythms, effects, etc., to their logical conclusions, extensions, and implications, and created unity by treating important movements and passages collectively (for example, in *tutti*, through orchestral-symphonic/big band-unison, etc)."

The following is Randall Keith Horton's movement-by-movement exposition of his insights and contributions to the *Ellington-Horton Black, Brown and Beige*.

### Black - 1st Movement

*In Maestro Ellington*'s 1943 Carnegie Hall debut, he proclaims that *Black, Brown and Beige* tells a story. In the first movement *Black* a brief trombone solo quotes the *spiritual Swing Low, Sweet Chariot*. The Ellington orchestra immediately transitions to the sound of a rapidly moving railroad train. The Underground Railroad comes to mind whenever I listen to these musical allusions. Since my first hearing, they have inspired me as storytelling. In my *Ellington-Horton Black, Brown and Beige* score, they are seen on page 25, at measures 243 –'44 (and continuing).

Soon after, I discover the potential for thematic transformation in the first-movement *Work* theme (part 2). Starting in the embedded strings with winds and brass (p.6, from measure 49), my setting of *Didn't My Lord Deliver Daniel?* grows naturally from the *Work* theme. These spirituals speak of slaves' hope, by faith, for the Lord's deliverance from slavery and from the toil of their work. After much thinking, I went back to page 23, mm. 223-225 and inserted the Spiritual *The Gospel Train's A' Comin!*[292] to precede Ellington's *Swing Low, Sweet Chariot*" with its powerfully, rapidly-moving train rhythm in Ellington's saxophone writing...now the Gospel train! Thus, the first-movement story begins and continues until reaching the pinnacle of Mr. Ellington's sacred, thematic melody, *Come Sunday* (m.288), thus concluding the first movement in an emotionally triumphant fashion.

*Black, Brown and Beige* unfolds like a riveting novel. Ellington does a masterful job in the first movement, conveying the voyage of enslaved Africans to the shores of America with Sonny Greer on trap drums evoking the sound of tribal/jungle drums. Thanks to Horton's unique knowledge of African American history and Negro spirituals, he identifies Ellington's never-before-remarked-upon sampling of *Swing Low Sweet Chariot* [293] which he clearly embeds to help transport his listeners to the movement's appropriate time period and emotional tenor.

As a result, Horton is empowered to introduce and expand upon the original underlying spiritual in other portions of the first movement

---

292 "The Title of the spiritual is: "*The Gospel Train's A' Comin!*", otherwise known by its formal title: "*Get On Board, Little Children" (There's Room For Plenty-A-More)*. Then, of course, comes Ellington's Swing Low..., then the big-band sound of the powerfully/rapidly-moving train (in Ellington's saxophone writings) is heard (The GOSPEL train!). So in the symphony orchestra, I am quoting the part of the spiritual's melody that says: *GOSPELLL TRAINNNN:* p. 23, mm. 223-225; Trumpet 1 and French Horn 1. At that point, that motif is in counterpoint to the first introduction of the quiet *Come Sunday* melody (solo violin/solo cello). Then, at the pickup to measure 232, p. 24 of the score, the four French Horns very prominently state: *GOSPEL TRAIN'S A' COMMINNN!"*...then the trumpets join the French Horns when that motif is restated (mm. 236-237); the trumpets repeat it (mm. 239-240). By preceding and setting the stage for Ellington's *Swing Low, Sweet Chariot*, the added and repeated Spiritual injects a building energy into the orchestration.

293 The sampling of *Swing Low Sweet Chariot* appears on page 25, mm 243-244 of the *Ellington-Horton Black, Brown and Beige.*

with the attendant melodies of *Didn't My Lord Deliver Daniel*[294], *Deep River*[295] and *Oh, What a Beautiful City!* to help balance the faith-inspired hope of the slaves.[296] It is important to note that the lyrics of these spirituals were (and continue to be) familiar to most African Americans who relied upon them to cope with the brutality of their forced labor. The samplings, though brief, effectively convey the cultural importance and emotion rooted in each song. In addition, Ellington's epochal melody *Come Sunday*,[297] originally written in 1943 for Ellington's lead alto saxophonist Johnny Hodges, sets up a lovely contrast for Horton's later interpolation of Ellington's 1958 version of *Come Sunday* (with lyrics) in the third movement. Modern-day Jazz bassist, composer and arranger Christian McBride iterates the importance of the church and church music throughout African Americans history in a 2019 interview for National Public Radio, stating, "I think *Come Sunday* was [Ellington's] musical portrait of what the Gospel meant to the African-American community."[298]

The careful merging of Horton's symphonic orchestration with Ellington's big band writing adds depth and dimension to the powerful saga of the African American experience. It also adds contrast between

---

294   Horton's sampling of *Didn't My Lord Deliver Daniel*, begins on page 6, measures 49-59 of the *Ellington-Horton Black, Brown and Beige*. Lyrics from the sampled melody: Didn't my lord deliver Daniel, deliver Daniel? Didn't my lord deliver Daniel? Then why not every man?  He delivered Daniel from the lion's den, Jonah from the belly of the whale and the Hebrew children from the fiery furnace.  Then why not every man?  Didn't my lord deliver Daniel, deliver Daniel, deliver Daniel? Didn't my lord Deliver Daniel? Then why not every man? I set my foot on the gospel ship, and the ship began to sail. It landed me over on Canaan's shore, and I'll l never come back no more. Didn't my lord deliver Daniel, deliver Daniel, deliver Daniel? Didn't my lord deliver Daniel? Then why not every man?

295   Lyrics from the sampled melody *Deep River* - Deep river, my home is over Jordan. Deep river, Lord, I want to cross over into campground. Oh, don't you want to go, To that gospel feast, That promised land, Where all is peace. Deep river, my home is over Jordan. Deep river, Lord, I'm gonna cross over into campground.

296   The sampled melodies of *Deep River* and *Oh, What a Beautiful City!* can be found on page 38, measures 386-398 of the *Ellington-Horton Black, Brown and Beige* score.

297   *Come Sunday* (melody only) is heard on page 29, beginning in measure 288 of *Black* of the *Ellington-Horton Black, Brown and Beige* score.

298   McBride, *Ibid.*

the principal duality of work and religious musical themes that reflected the essence of slaves' suffering and their hope for a more universal human experience.

## Brown - 2nd Movement

Ellington's spoken introduction at Carnegie Hall cites the Emancipation Proclamation and tells of freed slaves' plaintive stories, and loss of romantic love in The Blues. Horton explains:

> My orchestration contributes two new interpretive elements: I score the *West Indian Dance* for a trio of steel drums. And leading up to a musical contrast set in the third movement *Beige*, I set *The Blues* (second-movement song) as a duet plaintively sung by a mezzo soprano and a bass baritone (previously a solo interpretation). Duke is telling the story of the lowdown, mean, ugly blues! Together, the two soloists become the musical exponents of the cultural depression and oppression that at times affected the entire African American community, even after their hard-won freedom had been secured.

Duke Ellington changes the color and tone of his music in Brown with the addition of West Indian stylisms. Horton adds to the dramatic effect by scoring the opening West Indian Dance for a trio of West Indian steel drums,[299] transporting listeners across the vast Caribbean waters for an aural encounter of North American slaves' liberation from the brutality of their enslavement. The ensuing Emancipation Celebration is an important theme in this movement, but Ellington's music in Brown also depicts the hopelessness of the freed, elderly slaves who worked hard throughout their lives only to have no means for self-support. The plaintive voices of Horton's two soloists convey Ellington's lyrics about

---

299  West Indian steel drums begin on page #2 of *Brown*, mm15 letter A of the *Ellington-Horton Black, Brown and Beige*.

the blues as a "a dark cloud marking time," and "a one-way ticket from your love to nowhere." It is here where the second movement reaches the nadir of its downward trajectory; however, a more uplifting aspect of African American history awaits to be told in the final movement.

### *Beige* - 3rd Movement

Critics were most highly unfavorable of Ellington's third movement. Horton recalls:

> When I set the symphonic music in 1987, I was unaware
> of such criticism; instead, sensing exciting opportunities to
> interpret Mr. Ellington's introductory comments. Ellington
> informs his audience of the resiliency of the Negro community.
> His implied focus is Harlem. My sense is that when he spoke
> from the Carnegie Hall stage in 1943, he referenced his own
> upbringing, as well as my own and that of the best aspirations of
> the Negro. His spacious writing in the opening of *Beige* invited
> my supplemental interpolations of his popular songs: Very
> brief samplings of *Cotton Tail* (mm. 35 -38 and beyond), *Don't
> Get Around Much Anymore* (starts in mm. 39 – 46), *Take the 'A'
> Train* (mm. 39 – 44 and 55 – 67) and *East St. Louis Toodle –o*
> (previously set by Mr. Ellington in the first movement *Black*; set
> here, in *Beige, in mm. 23 – 28*) comprise my *"Harlem Montage"* as
> complementary music to Duke's writing.[300] *Stompin' at the Savoy*
> (mm 50 – 54), the sole non-Ellington song, is also referenced
> here. This is image-heavy music, which brings the listener into
> a sense of what it was like to celebrate early-twentieth-century
> life in Harlem. Finally, the storytelling in this orchestration
> culminates with two songs interpolated here from the Duke

---

300  It is important to note that at the time of Horton's arranging, these Ellington songs were owned by Tempo Music which was managed by Ruth Ellington-Boatwright and presented little if any licensing issues.

Ellington 1958 collaboration with Mahalia Jackson on an album also entitled *Black, Brown and Beige* which featured Jackson's impromptu singing of *Twenty Third Psalm* and newly written lyrics to *Come Sunday*. Both are included in my orchestration in *Beige* (pp. 37 – 45, mm 391-438 and 439 - 483 respectively). Ruth confirmed to me that her brother viewed these two songs as an addendum and an essential capstone to his original composition. The appropriateness of strong Biblical references in each song reinforce the hope and sustaining power of faith and spirituality from which African Americans drew strength while navigating their newfound freedom.

Ellington's objective for the final movement is to musically personify the acculturation of African Americans into American Society during the Harlem Renaissance (circa 1918 -1930 and beyond) where great optimism characterizes the period despite widespread lynching, murder and other atrocities during that era and the approaching Great Depression (beginning in 1929). Ellington's chosen setting for *Beige* is Harlem in the early twentieth century, and he features the upbeat, exuberant tempos of that era to convey African Americans' optimism and hope for a better life. But some critics hypothesize that *Beige* sounds less developed than the composition's first two movements, because Ellington ran short of time to adequately complete it.

In 1989, American composer, performer, conductor, teacher, and writer Gunther Schuller[301] asserts, "There is no doubt that it [was not developed properly]. I know it because friends of mine were at the rehearsals in the days before the concert. That last movement was thrown

---

301  Gunther Schuller, (1925-  2015), American composer, performer, conductor, teacher, and writer noted for his wide range of activity in both Jazz and classical music and for his works embracing both Jazz and advanced 12-tone elements. He coined the term *third stream* to describe the confluence of Jazz and classical techniques.

together in such a frantic hurry…"[302] Schuller's 1989 comments not only exhume the forty-six-year-old dismissive critiques of Ellington's *Black, Brown and Beige*, but also single out perceived structural inadequacies in *Beige* with particular gusto, opining, "Like a cluttered living room furnished in too many styles, *Beige* displays its too many undigested lumps of musical bric-a-brac, and instead of prime Ellington we are left with too many handed-down prosaic musical commonplaces… *Beige* starts with a discordant, inchoate and substantively empty music… and ends with an equally fustian patriotic mélange that sounds thrown together and tacked on."[303]

Ouch!

But Ellington is not trying to emulate European models for composing. He is staying true to the folk roots of American Jazz and his own pioneering musical style that challenge the prevailing "cultural hierarchies that exalt European classical music as high art and disdain popular American and African American forms."[304] As for the "abrupt changes," Ellington insists that, "conservatory theories can't be 'applied' to the 'Negro idiom.' You've got to realize that the Negro is emotionally different," he explains. "He makes extreme and sudden transitions of mood and you'll find that in the music."[305]

In 2006, Horton submits a paper for one of his master's level classes at City University of New York (CUNY) entitled "The Performance/ Recording and Critical History of Duke Ellington's *Black, Brown and Beige*: An Overview." In it he calls for "a reduction in the hierarchical approach to music criticism… in evaluating music," noting that "a values-based approach to criticism has permeated critical thinking

---

302  Alper, *Ibid.*

303  Randall K. Horton, "A Single Beam of Light and Its Transformation of My Life - Discourse from an Obscure Ellingtonian." *Stony Brook University*, 2019.

304  Cohen, *Ibid.*

305  Ayer, "Duke Ellington Is Versatile Entertainer"; Riley, "Ellington's New Tone Poem."

regarding the birth and evolution of music in America since its inception." Horton's comments continue with specific reference to Ellington's *Black, Brown and Beige*:

> Is one style or folk origin 'better' than another or just 'different' and totally appropriate to its own source of creation (i.e. the culture from which it came forth)? ... Certainly Ellington was implying that new criteria, based on the consideration of American Negroid sensibilities, needed to be established. Just as Jazz, since its inception, has been a marriage of Euro-based melodic/harmonic and even formal lineage with African and African American sensibilities, criticism still faces the challenge of balancing an acceptance of the musical roots of this art form with Eurocentric standards of analysis, thus, American music was also in need of non-judgmental, balanced criticism... The Euro-centric model for analysis has survived the test of time.[306]

Of course, Duke Ellington's response to all of this analysis, criticism and evaluation is that all of this kind of talk just "stinks up the place." And Louis Armstrong cautions similarly that we need not "worry about what it *is*; if it sounds good, just enjoy it." While I realize that a non-judgmental criterion is what I am in support of, I tend to agree with Mr. Ellington and Mr. Armstrong. Analysis and music are not necessarily closely related. True folk music was not (is not) created through theoretical/analytic considerations; just as in European music, composers often wrote for decades (centuries) before a theory relating to their music was (fully) developed, even until and

---

306  Randall K Horton, "The Performance/Recording and Critical History of Duke Ellington's Black, Brown and Beige: An Overview." *Stony Brook University*, 2006.

through the work of Schenker.[307] The relationship of music and analysis sometimes mutually exclude one another. At minimum, criticism needs to reject its own tendency to place one musical practice "above" another. Its constructive contributions can call an artist to accountability without judging the merit of the creative efforts of that artist.[308]

With the passage of time and greater perspective, a 2011 article on *Black, Brown and Beige* by Dr. Garth Alper, Coordinator of Jazz Studies at the *University of Lafayette School of Music*, submits a somewhat more open-minded assessment of Ellington's third movement, stating, "While *Beige* may not equal the compositional excellence found in *Black* and *Brown*, it holds some compelling ideas."[309]

Fortunately, the timing of Schuller's 1989 critique has no effect on Horton's 1987 orchestral setting. Horton simply focuses his energies on channeling Duke Ellington's long simmering intentions for a full-length orchestration of his Big Band composition. Studying Ellington's unfolding conceptualizations for *Black, Brown and Beige* between its premiere in 1943 and the composer's death in 1974, Horton senses the potential to reinforce the connectivity and continuity between *Beige* and its previous two movements through thematic transformation. Ellington wants listeners of *Beige* to be immersed in the high-energy and fervent rhythm of city life during that particular period of the golden age of Jazz: the hot Jazz of the 1920's "Jazz age" transitioning into 30's romantic, swinging, Big Band dancing and romancing through the depression era and eventually to 1940's Bebop, exemplified by Charlie Parker's more intellectual, swinging, soloistic Jazz that is no longer meant for dancing. Ellington

---

307  Heinrich Schenker ( 1868 -1935, Vienna) was a music theorist, music critic, teacher, pianist, and composer, known for his approach to musical analysis by demonstrating the organic coherence of the work by showing how it relates to an abstract deep structure or *Ursatz*.

308  Horton, "Performance," *Ibid.*

309  Alper, *Ibid.*

wants them to sense African American's palpable optimism and excitement for even the *possibility* of opportunity, equality, and advancement.

The "Ellington-Horton" *Beige* continues the composer's story of Harlem life from the early 1920's with era-specific samplings of Ellington songs, then reaches into the mid-twentieth century with the interpolation of *Come Sunday* and the *Twenty-Third Psalm* in anticipation of the mid twentieth century American Civil Rights era. Horton's embedding of three additional Negro spirituals and five Harlem song samplings now underpin each of the three movements, broadening elements of connectivity, consistency, richness, meaning and cinematic quality that some critics argue were particularly lacking.

It is in *Beige* where Horton feels Ellington's musical intentions most powerfully. The Maestro's 1958 *Black, Brown and Beige* album and spacious writing at the opening of *Beige* inspires Horton's supplemental interpolations, fortifying the movement's structure and allowing the entirety of *Black, Brown and Beige* to resolve on a more satisfying and uplifting note. The augmented materials also provide a soothing period of aural calm, for listeners to more deeply absorb the music and messages of Ellington's main expository piece.[310]

Although Horton is commissioned to write the full-length *concerto grosso* orchestration of Ellington's *Black, Brown and Beige*, he also applies a judicious measure of Ellington-inspired *Skillapooping*,[311] carefully folding in contributions that he feels confident that Ellington contemplated and explored, but never fully integrated into his *opus* before his death.

Other composers may have enjoyed longer and perhaps better-known nexuses to Duke Ellington, but few possess Horton's requisite knowledge. The now 54:00 minute, newly orchestrated *Ellington-Horton Black, Brown and Beige* demanded an author, arranger, and orchestrator

---

310   Bruce Nixon. "Camellia Symphony Gives Ellington A Rich Revival." *Sacramento Bee*, 28 Feb. 1988.

311   Gaines-Carter, *Ibid.* Skillapooping was a term created and defined by Duke Ellington as "the art of making what you're doing better than what you're supposed to be doing."

with an array of traditional and unexpected skills. As a result, the *Ellington-Horton Black, Brown and Beige* is as close as the world is ever likely to get to a definitive, full-length, orchestration that Duke Ellington envisioned…and Mercer Ellington demanded of Horton.

## The Premiere of the *Ellington-Horton Black, Brown and Beige*

In early 1988, with the bulk of his arranging complete, Horton asks for and receives the balance of his compensation. G. Schirmer then pays a copyist from the San Francisco Bay area to extract the individual parts from Horton's completed score, and the next two months are spent polishing the music for its premiere by the *Camellia Symphony Orchestra*, with Randall Keith Horton conducting.

"The copyist worked very hard to generate the sheet music for the parts," says Horton. "He used the latest (for its time) computerized engraving software and dot matrix printing. It was much faster, easier to correct, and in my opinion, a vast improvement over handwritten parts."

The premiere is scheduled for February 28, 1988 at *Hiram Johnson High School Auditorium*, the elegant 800-seat auditorium and home of the *Sacramento Ballet*. On the evening of the concert, Music Director, Conductor and Horton-advocate Dr. Daniel Kingman warms up the audience with his *Camellia Symphony's* "polished, even-handed performance of Brahms' *Piano Concerto No. 2* with soloist Robert Bowman."[312] Following intermission, Kingman passes his baton to Randall Keith Horton to conduct the debut of the *Ellington-Horton Black, Brown and Beige*. It is a high-density ensemble: a fifty-piece symphony orchestra augmented by an expanded percussion section of African and steel drums, the *Randall Keith Horton Gospel Orchestra* and two vocal soloists – mezzo soprano Diane Moffett and bass-baritone Johnny Staton.[313]

---

312  Nixon, *Ibid.*

313  See Appendix A for concert program.

No words are spoken from the stage at the opening of the premiere to orient the audience to the significance of the performance, to Ellington, African Americans, the evolution of Jazz, America's Civil Rights efforts, Horton, or Ellington enthusiasts. But perhaps it is not entirely necessary. Horton recalls:

> It was gratifying that there were very few surprises or hiccups. The music flowed from the talented musicians almost exactly as I heard it in my head as I committed the notes to paper. Afterward, people asked me if it was an exhilarating experience. It wasn't. The commission both thrilled and terrified me. It was massive, and the self-imposed pressure to honor Duke's musical and extra-musical objectives was so staggering that there was little time to revel in the beauty or historical significance of it. In every beat of the 54:00-minute premiere, there were musicians to cue, passages to interpretatively conduct, new tempos to introduce and manage, musical subtleties to convey and spirituality, emotions and subtextual messages to communicate. It required my complete attention. All my energies were laser focused on delivering a performance worthy of its composer and his musical legacy. All for a commission I continue to cherish, but never asked for.

The Sacramento audience's responds to the final flourish of Horton's conducting baton with a standing ovation. The genre and theme of the music no longer scandalous, its African American co-composer and conductor no longer viewed as overstepping his intellectual or cultural bounds; proof that progress in the cultural fabric of America has been made. Horton sends Ruth and Mercer recordings of the premiere and receives their congratulations on the quality of his orchestration and conducting.

This of course meant a great deal to me. In the final analysis, I felt a sense of exhausted satisfaction and relief. The orchestration was complete, "test driven," beautifully received and at last ready for publication. I felt I had fulfilled my *calling* and could finally lay down the enormity of my spiritual obligation to Maestro Ellington and the weight of the commission from Mercer Ellington and G. Schirmer Publishing. I had done all that I could.

In reviewing the performance for *The (Sacramento) Bee* newspaper, music critic Bruce Nixon stated:

> From the first to the last downbeat, the piece maintains the majesty and weightiness of Ellington's original... Horton stuck close to a big, exciting, colorful, theatrical wall of sound that Ellington probably would have loved. There was no musty historicism here. The rather cinematic quality[314] of the work gives it a Pops flavor, but the scope and the scale have a majesty and weightiness, which Horton clearly sought to maintain. It worked. In all the size and sound, there is a feeling of the richness of life, the sense of a world and its people. The concert drew a near-capacity audience, which offered a standing ovation at its conclusion."[315]

"There is another way in which Ellington's music is like the movies," Jazz critic Gary Giddins says in 1989. "It's prohibitively expensive to perform as he wrote it. The great irony of big band music is that it flourished during the Great Depression and faded in the Age of Affluence."

---

314 The cinematic quality to which Nixon referred, alluded to Ellington's use of thematic transformation in *Black* and Horton's insightful reintroduction of the technique in Brown, and most notably, in *Beige*.

315 Nixon, *Ibid.*

| Reappearance of Ellington's "Black, Brown & Beige" and "Sacred Concerts" Compositions | Orig. BB&B 1943 | BB&B Album 1958 | My People 1963 | First Sacred Concert 1965 | Second Sacred Concert 1968 | Third Sacred Concert 1974 | Ellington-Horton BB&B 1988/2022 |
|---|---|---|---|---|---|---|---|
| *Come Sunday* | X | X | X | X | | | X |
| *David Danced* | | | X | | X | | X |
| *Tell Me It's The Truth* | | | | X | | X | |
| *In The Beginning, God* | | | | X | | X | |
| *99% / 99.5%* | | | X | X | X | | |
| *The Preacher's Song* | | | | X | X | X | |
| *Will You Be There* | | | X | | | | |
| *The Blues* | X | | X | | | | X |
| *Praise God and Dance* | | | | | X | X | |
| *The Lord's Prayer / 23rd Psalm* | | X | | X | | X | X |
| *Work Song* | X | X | | | | | X |
| *Heritage / My Mother/My Father* | | | X | X | | | |
| *Ain't But The One* | | | X | X | | | |
| *New World A Comin* | | | | X | | | |
| *Emancipation Celebration* | X | | | | | | X |
| *West Indian Dance* | X | | | | | | X |
| *Light* | X | X | | | | | X |

Horton's mounting of the *Ellington-Horton Black, Brown and Beige* is even more remarkable in light of the added scope and cost of the symphonic accompaniment. Ellington may have figuratively written himself into *Black, Brown and Beige* in 1943, but in 1988, Randall Keith Horton added his indelible fingerprints.

Frustrated and fearing his arrangement may never be published, Horton reaches out to Jesse Rosen, Executive Director of the *American Composers Orchestra* (ACO)[316] to blow off steam. They talk about Horton's successful performances of the *Ellington-Horton Black, Brown and Beige* in Sacramento. Rosen expresses interest in the music. He invites Horton to sit in on the ACO's (June 26, 1988) recording of Maurice Peress'[317] orchestration of *Black* from Ellington's *Black, Brown and Beige*, originally published by G. Schirmer Publishing in 1970. It is music that Horton knows only too well, for it is the very arrangement that set his own *Black, Brown and Beige* commission in motion – the direct result of Gary Giddins' review. Coincidence? It seems there is nowhere Horton can turn without coming face-to-face with Ellington's extended length works.

Arriving early at the New York recording studio, Horton settles unobtrusively into a vacant chair and waits for the recording session to begin. His presence is noticed by Peress, who walks over and asks Horton who he is. Horton introduces himself as a guest of Jesse Rosen and a fellow Ellingtonian. Horton mentions the recent premiere of his full-length orchestration, Ellington-Horton *Black, Brown and Beige*.

Fast forwarding twenty years (2010/2011), and in yet another

---

316 American Composers Orchestra is an orchestra administratively based in New York City, specializing in contemporary American music, and is the only professional orchestra in the world dedicated to the creation, performance, preservation, and promulgation of music by American composers.

317 Maurice Peress (1931-2018) was a conductor who worked closely with both Leonard Bernstein and Duke Ellington, and whose twin passions for Jazz and classical music were reflected in his penchant for reconstructing important concerts from the past. He was the "very important person" whom Duke Ellington alluded to having a meeting with when the young Randall Keith Horton asked to speak with him about his hotel bill in Houston in 1973.

coincidental twist, Peress, Horton and Giddins enter parallel and intersecting orbits at *Queens College Aaron Copland School of Music* in New York. Horton enters as a student pursuing a master's in music theory (which he later completes in 2013), Peress as an adjunct music professor and Giddins as one of Horton's professors at the CUNY Graduate Center in Manhattan. Horton introduces himself to Giddins and the two become friendly walking to and from class. Horton eventually relays the Jazz critic's pivotal role in manifesting his commission for the *Ellington-Horton Black, Brown and Beige.* It is a revelation to Giddins who expresses his appreciation at learning about the positive influence of one of his musical critiques.

# —THE—
# Ellington-Horton
# *Black, Brown and Beige*

### Full-Length Concerto Grosso Orchestration
For Big Band, Symphony Orchestra, Mezzo Soprano and Bass Baritone

### Original Big Band Composition by Duke Ellington
### Symphony Orchestra Arrangement by Randall Keith Horton

Includes vocal settings of *Come Sunday* and *Twenty Third Psalm*
from the 1958 Columbia album (CK 65566), *Black, Brown and Beige*

Commissioned by G. Schirmer, Inc., through Mercer Ellington

Randall Keith Horton with Mercer Ellington, Duke Ellington's Son
at the Smithsonian Institution*

### Commissioned for the
### Camellia Symphony Orchestra, Sacramento, CA
Daniel Kingman, Music Director
(World Premiere, February 27, 1988; Conducted by Randall Keith Horton)

### Rakeiho Publishing Company (ASCAP)
Chrysler Building, 405 Lexington Avenue, 26th Floor
New York, New York 10174 • info@RakeihoPublishing.org

*Photo image courtesy Smithsonian Institution, Washington, D.C., 1993

# HISTORICAL CONTEXT
## 1990's - 2010's

The 1990's is a decade of relative peace and prosperity in America: The US economy rebounds from the Black Monday stock market crash of 1987. The fall of the Soviet Union hastens the end of the Cold War (1949-1992). The first Iraq War (a.k.a. Desert Storm) begins in 1991. And the birth of the internet hints at radical advancements to come in communications, business, and entertainment.

For African Americans still in search of equality, the decade is a time of both progress and setbacks. According to Femi Lewis, a writer and teacher specializing in African American history, "[African American] men and women break new ground by being elected as mayors of large cities, members of Congress, federal cabinet positions as well as leadership roles in medicine, sports and academics. But when Rodney King is beaten by police in Los Angeles (1991) and riots break out in Los Angeles after the officers are acquitted (1992), [it] is a signal that the continuing search for [equality and] justice is still an ongoing concern."[318] Three years later (1995), O.J. Simpson is found not guilty of double murder in the "Trial of the Century." These events challenge America to think deeply about race and privilege.

In the world of music, fashion and superficial images are no longer the driving forces. Grunge, a mix of Metal and Punk, takes center stage (epitomized by *Nirvana's Smells Like Teen Spirit*) and expresses growing feelings of alienation, personal estrangement from the social order and a discomfort with their success and the commercial exploitation of their artistic messages. In its purest form, it is one of the last times we see musicians openly suggest that 'being famous is one of the last things desired,' to paraphrase Kurt Cobain.[319]

---

318  Femi Lewis, "African-American History Timeline: 1990-1999," ThoughtCo., updated May 24, 2019, https://www.thoughtco.com/african-american-history-timeline-1990-1999-45447.

319  Andrew Gumble, "Cashing in on a Rock Icon: Bigger than Elvis, the Lucrative Legacy of Kurt CobainIn." *Independent* , 22 Oct. 2011, www.independent.co.uk/news/world/americas/cashing-in-on-a-rock-icon-bigger-than-elvis-the-lucrative-legacy-of-kurt-cobain-421631.html.

The number of Hip-Hop and Rap hits explodes in the 1990's, influencing how people dress, talk and act. Songs from artists like Dr. Dre (*The Chronic*), Snoop Dogg (*Doggystyle*), Tupac (*All Eyez on Me*), The Notorious B.I.G. (*Ready to Die*), The Wu-Tang Clan (*Enter the Wu-Tang*), and The Fugees (*The Score*) capture the emotional response of an entire generation to the issues surrounding them. But some listeners fear that the sometimes violent and sexually explicit lyrics are reinforcing long held black stereotypes. Censorship abounds: Some lyrics are ruled "obscene," requiring parental warning stickers. Pop stations only play non-threatening rap (DJ Jazzy Jeff and the Fresh Prince's *Parents Just Don't Understand*) when they play it at all. Black stations restrict Rap airplay to nighttime and weekends, and clubs in New York shut out live Hip-Hop performers to avoid the violence that sometimes accompanies the crowds they attract.[320] As one black clergyman says, "This presentation of Hip-Hop allows whites to see us as animals in a zoo. The sad part is that we are delivering the message to them ourselves… .it tears down the progress of decades of hard work and devalues and simplifies an entire people."[321]

Yet, British research conducted on Billboard Hot 100 between 1960 and 2010 shows that "Hip-Hop, more than any defining genre of the 1990's, proves to be more durable to the sound of Pop music than even the dawn of Classic Rock. More than the British Invasion or the brief tyranny of 1980's drum-machines."[322]

The Million Man March on Washington, D.C. (1995), led by

---

320   Paul Cantor, "9 Things That Almost Killed Hip-Hop in the '90s," Complex, January 4, 2016, https://www.complex.com/music/2016/01/9-things-that-almost-killed-hip-hop-in-the-90s/.

321   Thomas Murphy, 2016, comment on John H. McWhorter, "How Hip-Hop Holds Blacks Back," *City Journal*, Arts and Culture; The Social Order, Summer 2003. https://www.city-journal.org/html/how-hip-hop-holds-blacks-back-12442.html.

322   Derek Thompson, "1991: The Most Important Year in Pop-Music History," *The Atlantic*, Culture, May 8, 2015, https://www.theatlantic.com/entertainment/archive/2015/05/1991-the-most-important-year-in-music/392642/.

Minister Louis Farrakhan, and the Million Woman March[323] on Philadelphia (1997) seek to peacefully convey to the world a vastly different picture of African Americans. These movements unite them in self-help and self-defense against the economic and social ills plaguing them, insufficient prenatal care, inferior educational opportunities, jobless parents, funding cuts to inner city schools and Head Start programs and disproportionate incarceration rates.[324] Secondary goals include elevating these issues to the nation's political agenda, registering/mobilizing black voters and combating the negative racial stereotypes in the American media and popular culture.

And while African Americans find an avenue for expression in Pop music, the classical music world remains an almost exclusively white club. Research conducted in 2014 shows less than 2 percent of musicians in American orchestras are African American. Conductors fare only marginally better at 4.3 percent, and Black classical composers remain marginalized.[325] The reason, according to author Joseph Horowitz[326] is twofold: Decades of institutional racism and provincialism. Americans don't value American music and feel they need the pedigree of classical European music. But if they would embrace the country's native vernac-

---

323 Million Man March National Organizing Committee (January 1996), "Million Man March Fact Sheet," in Haki R. Madhubuti and Maulana Karenga (eds.), *Million Man March / Day of Absence: A Commemorative Anthology: Speeches, Commentary, Photography, Poetry, Illustrations, Documents* (Chicago: Third World Press, 1996), p. 152.

324 At the time of the march, African Americans faced unemployment rates nearly twice that of white Americans, a poverty rate of more than 40%, and a median family income that was about 58% of the median for white households. More than 11% of all black men were unemployed and for those aged 16 to 19, the number of unemployed climbed to over 50%. The United States House of Representatives also slashed funding for the nation's poorest public schools and early education preschool programs. Environmental hazards were also seen as making the lives of urban blacks unstable. Black men were murdered at a rate of 72 per 100,000, a rate significantly higher than the 9.3 per 100,000 attributed to white men. Some black activists blamed aggressive law enforcement and prison construction for leaving "two hundred thousand more blacks in the jail complex than in college" and devastating leadership gaps within black communities and families. Event organizers were further infuriated by a perceived gap in prenatal care for black women and children caused, in part, by the closing of inner-city hospitals.

325 James Doeser, "Racial/Ethnic and Gender Diversity in the Orchestra Field." *League of American Orchestras*, Sept. 2016, www.ppv.issuelab.org/resources/25840/25840.pdf.

326 Joseph Horowitz is the author of 10 books, including "Classical Music in America" and "Artists in Exile." He is the executive director of the Post Classical Ensemble, based in Washington, D.C.

ular of Slave Songs, Spirituals, and Jazz, "classical music in the United States today would be indigenous rather than imported."[327] There are a handful of talented and determined African Americans who manage to break into the classical music world through the years, but their musical contributions receive limited acknowledgement and even fewer performance opportunities.

- Composers: Duke Ellington, William Grant Still Jr., Florence Beatrice Price, William Levi Dawson, T.J. Anderson, Tania León, Anthony Davis, Carman Moore, Henry Threadgill and George Theophilus Walker
- Conductors: Duke Ellington, Paul Freedman, Calvin E. Simons, Dean Dixon, Henry Lewis, Tania León, Julius P Williams, James Anderson DePriest and Coleridge-Taylor Perkinson
- Opera singers: Mary Violet Leontyne Price, William Caesar Warfield, Paul Leroy Robeson, Jessye Norman, Kathleen Deanna Battle, Marian Anderson and Roland Hayes (lyric tenor)

On a brighter note, more than thirty years after the Pulitzer committee refused to award Duke Ellington its 1965 prize for his first *Sacred Concert*, the award is finally bestowed on an African American composer, pianist, and scholar George Walker (1996). One year later, Wynton Marsalis receives the first Pulitzer Prize for *Blood on the Fields*, a two-and-a-half-hour Jazz oratorio[328] about a couple moving from slavery to freedom. It is the first Pulitzer Prize ever awarded for a Jazz composition.[329]

---

327  Tom Huizenga, "Why Is Classical American Music So White" NPR, September 20, 2019, https://www.npr.org/sections/deceptivecadence/2019/09/20/762514169/why-is-american-classical-music-so-white.

328  An oratorio is a large musical composition for orchestra, choir and soloists.

329  The first Pulitzer for a Jazz Opera, "The Central Park Five" by Jazz artist and composer Anthony Davis (with libretto by Richard Wesley) and composer Henry Threadgill was awarded in 2020. Horton became acquainted with Davis during his performance of Ellington's Sacred Music with the Juilliard Jazz Orchestra in 2004.

## CHAPTER 11

# BLOW BY BLOW

*"There are 2 rules in life: Number #1: Never quit.*
*Number #2: Never forget rule Number #1."*
- Duke Ellington

Some people such as Duke Ellington step into the limelight through sheer genius. Some demand it with aggressive tactics, and some, like Strayhorn and Horton, are more comfortable on the periphery of the spotlight at the intersection of composing, conducting, teaching and being of service to others.

No one has said the world is a fair or even hospitable place. Throughout his fifty-year career, even the inimitable Ellington endures blistering criticism and the rejection of the music he considers the most ambitious and important music he ever wrote. During times of turmoil and stress, Ellington cloaks himself in his faith and immerses himself in composing. Horton similarly finds equilibrium and renewal in his faith and music; two of the few constants in his rather tumultuous early childhood. In later years, his personal interactions with Ruth Ellington and her family also provide a soothing and reliable balm. Horton's life is becalmed, but he is about to encounter a powerful new undertow.

Following the Sacramento premiere of his orchestration, Horton makes corrections for *errata* and submits his handwritten score to the music publisher (March 1988). Less than a week later, he receives a reply insisting that the score be rewritten "more neatly" and resubmitted. It is a demoralizing response for many reasons, least of which is the lack of additional funding. Horton's progress on the rewrite slows considerably as he works full and part time jobs to support himself as a Musical Director for several area churches.[330] When G. Schirmer Publishing does not receive Horton's completed rewrite by December 31, 1989, Schirmer's Director of Rentals and Performance demands repayment of the money related to his commission for the piece or "face immediate litigation from their legal department for its immediate recovery." The archived letter contains the executive's signature, but with no acknowledging signature from Horton, it is unclear whether it is ever sent or received. Having no record of it himself, Horton simply continues his work on the rewrite.

In 1991, because of Horton's association with Duke Ellington, his successful music ministry at Marin Covenant Church (in upscale Marin County north of San Francisco) and his guest conducting work with the St. John's Baptist Church choir,[331] the *Sacramento Symphony* taps Horton to conduct their Martin Luther King Celebration and gives him the freedom to select an appropriate piece of music. Horton quickly calls mentor and composer Kirke Mechem for permission to conduct selections from his highly successful *John Brown* opera, utilizing the voices of

---

330  Horton became the music director for The Marin Covenant Church, Congregation Shomrei Torah Jewish Synagogue (San Rafael), Christ Church (Santa Rosa) and committed to a non-paying consultancy with St. John's Baptist Church, a large and influential black church in Sacramento.

331  St. John's Baptist Church is a large and influential black church in Sacramento, California.

the *Sacramento Symphony Chorus*. Mechem is more than happy to oblige, as this will mark the first performance of his choral suite *Songs of the Slave* with full orchestral accompaniment.[332] Mechem's inspiring music, the musicians' performance and Horton's nuanced conducting earn a standing ovation from the sold-out audience.

*The Sacramento Bee Newspaper's* music critic William Glackie previews the concert, writing, "The third excerpt in the suite is called *Songs of the Slave*, a recitative and aria set to words drawn from (Frederick) Douglas' autobiography. The suite will be conducted by Randall Keith Horton, Bay Area composer and music minister whose background includes classical study with Mechem as well as arranging and conducting for Duke Ellington, Michael Jackson, Marvin Gaye and Martha Reeves."[333]

And in a follow-up review in the same paper, reporter Mike Dunner writes, "Kirke Mechem, the distinguished Bay Area composer, was represented by the first orchestral performances of a suite of three pieces from his opera-in-progress, *John Brown*, with another Bay Area composer, Randall Keith Horton, a former Mechem student, conducting with infectious fervor."[334]

By 1992, Horton re-copies enough of the *Ellington-Horton Black, Brown and Beige* score to send several sample pages to the publishing company for their review and approval before continuing. G. Schirmer responds that Horton's sample pages are acceptable and that he should continue the rewrite to completion "even if the (note) stems are crooked." Horton does as instructed and continues his work on the score, albeit at a snail's pace, due to issues in his personal life.

"My marriage was failing at this time, and I hated my existence,"

---

332   Previous performances of Kirke Mechem's *John Brown* opera, including the suite *Songs of A Slave* were performed by soloists and chorus with piano accompaniment only.

333   William Glackin, "Gospel Concert to Honor King," *The Sacramento Bee*, January 13, 1991, EN6.

334   William Glackin, "Remembering A Dream - 300 Voices In Unison Fill The Night With Powerful Songs Of Joy And Peace," *The Sacramento Bee*, D1 - Scene, January 21, 1991.

Horton reveals with sadness. "When it finally became untenable, I resigned my Musical Directorship at Marin Covenant Church, filed for divorce and relocated to Santa Rosa."

Once in Santa Rosa, Horton is befriended by the late philanthropist Ms. Anna Cherney[335], in whose home he serves as a temporary caretaker before once again securing Musical Directorships at a local synagogue and a Methodist church. Before long, he is hired as the Music Director and Conductor of the *Sonoma County Peace Chorus*. In his continued struggle and search to regain his footing, he discovers a university in North Texas with a renowned jazz program that he feels will be a perfect place for him. He focuses his waning energy, packs his belongings into his car and takes a leap of faith. He sleeps in his car, sometimes in 18-degree weather, until he secures full and part-time Musical Directorships at the Eastridge Park Christian and Lovers' Lane United Methodist churches respectively, and a rented house. Once settled, he forwards his new address to G. Schirmer and assures them of his continued commitment.

"I did not touch the *Black, Brown and Beige* score during those difficult transitional years," relates Horton. "The most I could do was ensure its safety, which was critically important to me at the time. I felt a great deal of guilt about that and how irresponsible and unreliable my inaction must have appeared to the publisher."

Horton's divorce and relocation eventually usher in a period of personal renewal and growth. In addition to directing church music, Horton enrolls as a part-time student at the University of North Texas (1996–2003), studying Music Theory, Orchestral and Operatic Conducting, Radio and TV. He shares his knowledge of American music history, hosting the local KNTU Radio programs *Drive-Time Jazz* and *Music From North Texas* (classical music) programs and eventually ascends to

---

335 Anna Cherney underwrites an Ellington Sacred Concert for an audience of 1,200 at the Luther Burbank Center in Santa Rosa (6/26/93).

the position of Music Director for the station. He also lectures as an adjunct instructor within the UNT Music Department and plays piano at a restaurant in downtown Denton fittingly named *Ellington's On The Square* to help make ends meet.

"My new home in Denton wasn't big enough to accommodate my grand piano," explains Horton, "so I convinced the owner of *Ellington's On The Square* to take delivery of it and hire me as their weekend entertainment."

While teaching at the university, a couple of students approach Horton to see if they can help him create a computerized score of his orchestration. It sounds like a win-win proposition to Horton. The students will get hands-on engraving[336] experience, and he will have a publishable score that will likely be completed and edited faster than his handwritten rewrite. Horton agrees, and the students go to work. Several months later, Horton sends samples of the computerized engraving to Schirmer for their consideration. The publisher rejects the students' engraving as "unpublishable," instructing Horton to return to his rewrite. Around this same time, Horton makes an important connection. He is walking through the Student Union after class one day, looking more like a professor than a 50-year-old life-long student, when a young man in his late twenties stops him.

"Hey!" the tall, thin stranger with shoulder-length hair says in a voice just loud enough to catch Horton's attention. "You're the guy who worked with Duke Ellington, right? You play the piano up at *Ellington's On The Square* on the weekends."

"Yes," replies Horton, wondering what is coming next.

"I've been looking for you," the stranger says placidly as he extends his hand. "I'm Roy Fletcher."

"Randall Horton. Nice to meet you, Mr. Fletcher," replies Horton.

---

336 Music engraving is the art of drawing music notation at high quality for the p    pose of mechanical reproduction.

"I'm a music student here, a bass player... electric bass," Fletcher continues. "I want to learn about Jazz. How to play it, compose it, arrange it, mostly arrange."

"You're a guitar player?" Horton confirms as the gears start spinning in his head.

"Yeah," replies Fletcher in an understated way.

Fletcher grew up in a poor family under challenging circumstances. Like Horton, he possesses a natural aptitude for music which also brought him solace amid the chaos of his early years. When Fletcher discovered his innate ability playing the guitar, it created a glimmer of hope and a tangible means by which to change the trajectory of his life. He joined a Rock-n-Roll band, dropped out of high school and began touring.

According to Fletcher:

> As a kid, I discovered that my guitar might be my best ticket out of my difficult childhood, so I started listening to every genre of music and taught myself to play. I played every waking hour... by myself, in a few bands... and dreamed of becoming a rock star. So when the Dallas Celtic rock group *The Killdares* heard me and asked me to replace their existing bass player, I dropped out of high school and started living my dream. I also naively embraced the lifestyle for about five years, which nearly killed me.

Fletcher finally eventually extracts himself from the Rock-n-Roll lifestyle, enrolling in classes at UNT and stumbling upon Duke Ellington's *Ellington At Newport* album, featuring the Ellington Orchestra's career-altering performance at *The Newport Jazz Festival*. Something clicks.

> Everything Ellington and his orchestra played on that album, everything they did... just resonated with me on so

many levels. It's hard to explain, but after listening to that album many, many times, I knew I had to find this Horton guy and to my amazement, he was somewhere on the UNT campus. I knew he could teach me about Jazz…the magical ingredients of Ellington's Jazz in particular.[337]

"Well," Horton suggests, continuing his introduction to Fletcher, "why don't you sit in with me this Friday? We can figure things out from there."

"Yeah? Great!" says Fletcher, nodding. "Yeah! This Friday? Okay!"

"See you there, Mister Fletcher!" Horton confirms before continuing on his way.

When Fletcher enters *Ellington's On The Square* with his bass a few days later, he finds Horton with a female drummer from Germany and two horn players also setting up; a band! This is familiar territory for Fletcher. He is comfortable playing in a band. According to Fletcher:

> The first song Horton played on the piano that night was *April in Paris*. We played various versions of the same song over and over; speeding it up, slowing it down, throwing in chord changes. Then, as Horton started in on a smoking piano solo, he nodded at me. His message was clear. *You're on, Mr. Fletcher. Show me what you can do!* So I closed my eyes to better absorb what he was playing and tried my best to keep up, though I feared the worst, given my limited jazz experience.[338]

At the end of the night, Horton tactfully tells the drummer that she is a good funk drummer, but needs to spend some time in the woodshed honing her technique if she wants to become a good Jazz drummer.

"I'm so sorry, Randall!" Fletcher blurts to Horton as he approaches, trying to cut his own critique off at the pass.

---

337 Karen Barbera. "Roy Fletcher Interview." Sept. 2019.

338 Fletcher, *Ibid.*

"What are you apologizing for?" Horton asks, rhetorically. "You're playing was exceptional. I'll see *you* back here next week."

Fletcher returns to *Ellington's* the following weekend. This time, it is just the two of them, and they begin by playing a single Jazz standard for an hour straight, improvising through time signatures and lead changes, experimenting with different accompaniments and adjusting to multiple chord changes.

> Randall showed me that Jazz is not a spectator sport. It's something you step directly *into* and *feel* until you find your own personal connection to the music and fellow musicians.
>
> Jazz isn't about rigidly replicating notes from a sheet of paper. It's about finding and expressing an intuitive or spiritual attunement to the music and its message.[339]

"Playing piano at *Ellington's On The Square* was one of my best decisions as well," adds Horton with a happy chuckle. "I not only got to jam with Fletcher, who is a knowledgeable and accomplished musician in his own right, but I also met the beautiful Fort Worth, Texas native Andréa Renee Barron who became my wife and business partner. My fortunes changed through our shared life together.[340]

Several years later (2003), the happily married couple relocates to New York. Thereafter, Fletcher and Horton's friendship and musical discussions continue at regular intervals by phone.

"I've worked with some really great musicians," says Fletcher in 2019, "but none with whom I could discuss and analyze music in the same depth and breadth that I continue to enjoy with Randall."

Horton's ongoing study of Radio and TV at UNT supports his long-standing dream to produce an educational public television series

---

339 *Ibid.*

340 Randall Keith Horton and Andrea Barron meet at *Ellington's on the Square* in 1996 and are married in 1998.

to celebrate the creation, performance, scholarship and contributions of American music. To that end, Horton records a handful of videos, featuring Ruth Ellington-Boatwright and Sister Mary Dominic Ray, with his future educational television series in mind.[341]

"I produced the first polished episodes of the *American Music* educational television series as part of my course work at UNT," explains Horton. "It evolved as a talk show format with documentary and performance components that allowed me to bring all of my skills and knowledge to bear as a musician, composer, conductor, music historian and educator to celebrate our country's amazing music."

The next time Horton travels to New York to visit Ruth, he stops at the *Institute for Studies in American Music* (ISAM)[342]and shares a pilot video of the TV program with its director. H. Wiley Hitchcock offers direction and enthusiastic support, noting the dearth of any such programming at that time. Following up with a letter of encouragement[343] to Horton on April 1, 2001, Hitchcock writes,

> This is to essentially confirm in writing what I have told you previously – namely that I am enthusiastically supportive of your plan to develop a large-scale multipartite television project, the working title of which is *American Music*... I am deeply impressed by your vision for such a series of programs adding up to a comprehensive portrayal of the history of our nation's musical development... That vision which is clearly suggested in your demonstration video tape, which I have viewed, includes music itself (folk, popular and classical) by composers and performers of all our races, in lively and attractive performance, interviews with American music specialists

---

341  Produced in the mid 1980's.

342  The Institute for Studies in American Music (ISAM) was later renamed the H. Wiley Hitchcock Institute for Studies in American Music or HISAM.

343  H. Wiley Hitchcock Letter to Randall Keith Horton dated 4/1/2001.

and more general historians and – most importantly – cultural and historical contexts to make clear the environment and the social, political and economic forces that have conditioned American music's extraordinary development.

Which brings us back to Sister Mary Dominic Ray and the enormous debt of gratitude Horton owes her and the research center she founded. In addition to helping him explore multiple aspects of American music, she created a paid staff position[344] for Horton in 1985 that allowed him to realize his own musical gifts and introduced him to some of the country's leading music scholars, historians and authors: H. Wiley Hitchcock, Richard Crawford[345], and Mark Tucker, a Jazz historian and author with a special interest in Duke Ellington and his music.

In 1996, the news of Mercer Ellington's death at his home in Copenhagen, Denmark[346] reaches Horton. There is a memorial service there, but Ruth, who is eighty-one-years-old at the time, does not attend. One year later, Horton organizes, rehearses and conducts his 17th *Sacred Concert* in Kansas City, Missouri[347] at the Gem Theater, which underwrites the entire cost of the large scale concert. Horton rehearses 120 choir members from several churches, the 17-piece *Randall Keith Horton Gospel Orchestra*, eight praise dancers, soloists and the two McFadden

---

344   Randall Keith Horton was hired as the Assistant to the Director (Sister Mary Dominic Ray) of the American Music Research Center from 1985 until 1987 when the center was acquired by the University of Colorado and moved to its campus in Boulder.

345   Richard Crawford is an American music historian, formerly a professor of music at the University of Michigan. His *American Musical Landscape* is one of the seminal works of American music history, published in 2001.

346   Mercer Ellington Dies At 76." *MERCER ELLINGTON DIES AT 76*, 10 Feb. 1996, www. washingtonpost.com/archive/local/1996/02/10/mercer-ellington-dies-at-76/9d9d6b40-4c2c-474f-8bc7-afec5b9f4152/.   "Many American Jazz giants, including saxophonist Ben Webster, Dexter Gordon and Johnny Griffin and pianist Bud Powell believed they found refuge in Denmark from racism and musical obscurity in the United States. The American Jazz colony in Copenhagen later included saxophonist Stan Getz, trumpeter Thad Jones and pianist Kenny Drew."

347   For a video of this performance, visit https://youtu.be/LO8AiRsEMLM (Part I) and https://youtu.be/xAMSk26ILwk (Part II with tap dancing McFadden Brothers).

brothers, who put on a tap dance performance worthy of Hollywood, all to thunderous applause.

Seeking to shore up his relationship with the music publisher, Horton and his then-girlfriend, Andrea take a trip to New York to meet with G. Schirmer.

To help document his efforts to complete his commission, Horton packs up and delivers copies of his three previous submissions, including the original handwritten score with the extracted dot matrix printed parts, samples of his re-handwritten score and the UNT students' computerized engraving. G. Schirmer executives and an attorney review them and instruct Horton to leave these files and papers with them so that they can be copied and returned.

One year later, in 1998, Horton returns to Schirmer's offices and meets with a senior representative at a nearby sidewalk cafe. The new executive looks over Horton's progress on the rewrite and discusses the added value that an archival recording might provide in converting Horton's skeptics. Horton reaches out to the new Executive Director of the ACO, Michael Geller, for an estimate to perform and record his orchestration under the terms of compulsory licensing.[348] Such a license would allow Horton to conduct a private performance that could eventually be recorded and potentially distributed to the public, provided the original upon which it is based has been previously distributed to the public, which of course the 1943 *Black, Brown and Beige* had been.

Around this time, Blue Note Recordings (later EMI) also expresses interest in distributing a future recording of the *Ellington-Horton Black, Brown and Beige*. And while Blue Note's interest is encouraging, the estimate from the ACO to make it all happen is anything but. Horton has

---

348  For a non-dramatic musical composition, a compulsory license allows a person to distribute a new sound recording of a musical work if the original that it is based off of has been previously distributed to the public. The copyright owner controls the public performance (or its transmission over radio) of the work or any derivative works, but if the original is well known, it, or a derivative work of it, can be licensed for public performance through ASCAP.

successfully raised funds for the two previous community performances of the *Ellington-Horton Black, Brown and Beige* and the 30-plus *Sacred Concerts* with little to no personal compensation. But the ACO's $87,000 estimate to perform and $82,000 to record the music are daunting funding targets.[349]

The letters of interest from the two organizations, however, are enough to buoy Horton spirits to keep him chipping away at the rewrite. But by now, fourteen years after the original commission (1987) and thirteen years after its premiere (1988), both parties have grown frustrated and disillusioned. Schirmer's replies to Horton's periodic updates grow increasingly contentious, necessitating repeated assurances by Horton of his commitment to the project. Their working relationship remains strained, yet intact, perhaps because of Schirmer's residual respect for Horton's acknowledged connections with Mercer Ellington, Ruth Ellington-Boatwright, the powerful Lou Levy and Kirke Mechem, or perhaps because of Horton's multiple performances of Ellington's *Sacred Music* for which the publisher receives royalties.

## The Second Performance of the *Ellington-Horton Black, Brown and Beige*

At the *Morton H. Meyerson Symphony Center*
concert in Dallas - 1999

An opportunity for a second (regional) premiere of the *Ellington-Horton Black, Brown and Beige* develops in Dallas on March 2, 1999 at the *Morton H. Meyerson Symphony Center*.[350] The first half of the program features Horton's concertizing of Ellington's *Sacred Music* followed after intermission by the *Ellington-Horton Black, Brown and*

---

349  The total estimated cost for the ACO to perform and record the music of $169,000 in 1999, would be the equivalent of $264,970 in 2020 dollars (assuming 2.16% annual inflation).

350  The Morton H. Meyerson Center is the home of the Dallas Symphony.

*Beige.* Maestro Anshel Brusilow,[351] former solo violinist and concertmaster for the Cleveland and Philadelphia Orchestras and the Director of Orchestral Studies for the University of North Texas, graciously authorizes Horton to conduct his 80-piece *University of North Texas Symphony* along with Horton's 17-piece gospel big band. The opportunity is particularly exhilarating for Horton as the UNT Jazz Studies program is one of the oldest and most prestigious university Jazz programs in the country, and remains a model for Jazz programs around the world.[352]

Several weeks before the concert, the *Fort Worth Weekly* newspaper features the upcoming concert in a seven-page article. In it, reporter Shannon Sutlief interviews Ruth Ellington-Boatwright asking her what she thinks about Randall Keith Horton. Ruth responds, "What I think about him is not important. Duke thought he was good or he wouldn't have hired him. Everything he's done with me has always been excellent."[353]

In a separate *Denton Record Chronicle* article just three weeks before the same concert, newspaper reporter Jen Graves also asks Ruth Ellington-Boatwright to elaborate on why she granted Horton permission to concertize and perform her brother's all-important *Sacred Music*, to which she replies, "because I think he's a very sincere young man, and I think he's sincere in his admiration of Duke and his Admiration of God."[354]

The UNT orchestra, Horton's 17-piece Gospel Big Band, a 120-member choir, two soloists, two tap dancers, six *praise* dancers and a

---

351  Anshel Brusilow returned to offer his support again in 2003, authoring Horton to conduct the UNT Symphony and chorus in the Dallas area premiere of the suite *Songs of the Slave* from the opera *John Brown* by Kirke Mechem. For additional information and photos, please see page 172 and visit http://www.randallkeithhorton.com/mechem.html.

352  David Joyner, "History of Jazz at North Texas," College of Music - Division of Jazz Studies, 1997, accessed January 7, 2019, https://Jazz.unt.edu/history.

353  Shannon Sutlief, "In Honor of the Duke, Randall Keith Horton Conducts Himself in the Manner Befitting a Jazz Legend", *Ft. Worth Weekly*, May 7-14, 1998, pp. 8-13.

354  Jen Graves, "UNT Student To Conduct Ellington Music," *Denton Record Chronicle*, January 10, 1999.

narrator are all under Horton's direction, necessitating several months of planning and rehearsals. Though recently appointed to the position of part-time Music/Worship Director at Vista Ridge Bible Fellowship, Horton is blessed with seed money that is graciously donated by congregants in order to reserve the venue and to pay the symphony and big band expenses. Horton approaches the university about possible compensation for his time coordinating, rehearsing, and conducting the staggering ensemble, but his request is turned down. Then a second blow is delivered. A few weeks before the performance, he is forewarned about mounting push-back over an African American conducting the UNT symphony. The President of the local Musician's Union calls Horton at home on a Sunday afternoon, telling him about a conversation he was party to during morning services at the First Methodist Church in Denton.

Horton is appreciative, although not surprised. He knows from his early Motown days that the Music industry is no place for the faint of heart. Still, the latest development immediately shifts his excitement for the performance to utter dismay.

Fearing just such a scenario and having preemptively established a rapport with one of the university's lawyers, he immediately makes a call to him. The attorney calls a meeting between Horton and the Music Department official. The Dean of the College of Music then re-affirms Horton's right to conduct the large-scale performance in a February1999 letter, and later documents and acknowledges "the endorsement and support that Maestro Anshel Brusilow [has] given [Horton], support which [includes] permission for [Horton] to conduct the UNT symphony orchestra during the upcoming Meyerson performance of Ellington's works."

The offending university official leaves the meeting chastised, but undeterred. The following week, he refuses Horton the use of the university's only rehearsal room large enough to accommodate the choir composed of area high school students and prospective UNT students from around the area. As a result, the Dean of Admissions steps in to straighten things out. The concert is ultimately performed in front of an audience of more than 2,000, who once again, show their enthusiasm for both works with a standing ovation.

"The quality of the production was enthusiastically acknowledged and very well received," says Horton. "I had raised enough money to pay the musicians and performers, but an outstanding balance remained for miscellaneous expenses."

Since Horton received no compensation for his rehearsing and conducting services, deducting these expenses from his own pay is not an option. But the brilliance of Ellington's music and Horton's efforts soon carry the day. Representatives of the *Meyerson Center* quickly approach Horton and tell him his debt is "paid in full" by the sheer quality and beauty of the concert.

A short time later, Horton receives a call from an editor for *Symphony Magazine*, asking if he knows of anyone who can write an article about Duke Ellington as a symphonic composer. Horton wants to wave his hands in the air and shout "*I can write it!*" But having no formal academic title, he refers the editor to his friend and long-time Ellington scholar, Mark Tucker, Ph.D.

"Tucker ended up writing about Ellington's *Black, Brown and Beige* (April 1999)," adds Horton, "and graciously mentioned the recent performances of my *concerto grosso* orchestration. Twice! Which meant a great deal to me."

In fact, Tucker's *No Strings Attached* article about Ellington's expanding symphonic repertoire does more than mention Horton's 1988 and 1999 performances of the *Ellington-Horton Black, Brown and Beige*. Tucker cites Horton, alongside Peress, Benjamin, Schuller, Gould/ Berger, Collier and Tyzik as the main figures involved in translating Ellington's big band pieces, concluding with, "Most everyone in this group has spent decades studying and performing Ellington's music, and they bring considerable expertise and well-honed skills to a formidable orchestration assignment."[355]

"The concert was a bittersweet moment of grace," says Horton. "It seemed each performance was destined to be accompanied by a roller-coaster of emotions, from encounters with flagrant racism and publishing delays to the joy of each performance. And they were redemptive performances despite the behind-the-scenes drama. I just had to keep repeating the mantra, *It's business. It's not personal. It's business.*[356] albeit, a very bone-wearying business."

"I was beaten," confesses Horton. "After the tensions at UNT, the multiple publishing rejections and Peress' superior assessment of his partial orchestration, I wanted to walk away from the burden of my orchestration for that was certainly what it had become."

Forty-five and fifty-six years separate the premiere of *Black, Brown and Beige* (1943) and the two performances of the *Ellington-Horton Black, Brown and Beige* (1988 and 1999) respectively. The passage of time allows Horton's audiences to feel more at ease with the music, but barriers and rejections continue. For a time, Horton detaches emotionally and loses hope of ever publishing, professionally performing, or recording the music.

But the tenacious voice of Horton's *callings* (1964-1973), keeps up a running and rather unwelcome dialogue with his conscience. And when the emotion and disappointment of his recent experiences dissipates, he realizes it is not about his frustrations or personal shortcomings, or the opinions of others, or the injustices, or a music publisher's expanding expectations. It is about maintaining his integrity, his loyalty and his personal commitment to Duke Ellington and the music itself. So, he picks himself up and begins crawling back through the labor-intensive rewrite,

---

355 *Ibid.*

356 Quote from the movie *The Godfather*, 1969.

hoping for its publication, or at least a private performance where a quality archival recording can be made.

Horton's expertise on Ellington's extended-length compositions continues to fly largely under the radar. He often refers to himself as the "obscure *Ellingtonian.*" Then in 1999 a glimmer of acknowledgement is received from the highest level. Wynton Marsalis, American trumpet player, composer and Artistic Director for *Jazz at Lincoln Center*, hires Horton to be his "Special Guest Consultant" on eight performances of *In His Solitude, The Sacred Music of Duke Ellington*, at *Jazz at Lincoln Center.*[357] These performances are held in celebration of the Ellington Centennial!

Horton works with Wynton Marsalis and Eric Reed, the Music Director at *Jazz At Lincoln Center* as they rehearse. According to Horton:

> With Duke Ellington's music there was, and always will be, questions about intent, technique, style, and approach. His composing and unique improvisational style present interpretive and conducting challenges. During a particularly difficult passage that was not gelling as Reed hoped, the director turned to me and asked, "Randall, can you please help us with this section?" I stepped up to the orchestra, gave the JALC musicians some stylistic instructions and a downbeat, and the music fell brilliantly into place. With Ellington's music, a little bit of nuance goes a long way. JALC valued my experiences with both Duke and Ruth as well as my religious and personal understanding of the music's intent and compensated me well for my services. It was an honor to interact with Reed, Marsalis and the JALC musicians on music that was so very personal and important to Maestro Ellington. Offering my

---

357 Wynton Marsalis is an American trumpeter, composer, teacher, artistic director of Jazz at Lincoln Center and one of today's most prominent and accomplished Jazz musicians.

expertise on those eight performances was a highly respectful, invigorating, and gratifying experience. And of course, it also meant a lot to me when Ruth Ellington-Boatwright called to congratulate me on the performance."

After swimming upstream against a steady current, the acknowledgement by Marsalis and JALC is restorative.

"It is human nature to move away from doubts and criticism," says Horton. "I eventually needed to temporarily step away from my Ellington work to focus on projects of my own making." Horton returns to Dallas as the Minister of Music for Eastridge Park Christian Church[358] where he establishes two community orchestras: *The Eastridge Park Chamber Orchestra* and *Symphonia Frisco*.[359]

In 2001, Horton receives a call from Billy Banks, the Director of Production and Touring Operations (1994 - 2001) for Wynton Marsalis and his *Jazz at Lincoln Center Orchestra* (JALC). He is the chief road manager who travels ahead of the band, solidifying contracts and logistics. Banks says he and the JALC staff have heard about Horton's performance of the *Ellington-Horton Black, Brown and Beige* at the *Morton H. Meyerson Center* in Dallas. He tells Horton he is coming to Texas and wants to meet with him to discuss an opening at JALC for a liaison between the Music Director and Marsalis. Banks is looking for someone to organize music, contracts, rehearsals and help direct the band in rehearsals. The two talk while Banks is on the move.

The two step into an elevator where Banks turns to Horton and inquires, "Well, Randall, are you ready to move to New York? If so, you'll have to talk with André Guess (Executive Director of JALC) about compensation when you get into town. We don't have the budget to help

---

358    First Christian Church-Disciples of Christ, Mesquite, TX.

359    Founded with the help of Maestro Brusilow, conductor and Music Director of the Richardson Symphony Orchestra (near Dallas).

with moving expenses, but there will be a job waiting for you when you get here."

"I was overwhelmed," recalls Horton, "and naïvely relied on our verbal agreement. "I reached out to Michael Geller, VP and Exec Dir at the ACO, sharing the exciting news of my possible move to New York City."

Geller restates the ACO's on-going efforts to concertize orchestral music of American Composers and suggests Horton also join their staff for a six-month period to conduct a *Sacred Concert* and raise funds for a future performance of his *Ellington-Horton Black, Brown and Beige*.[360]

"The votes of confidence from the JALC and the ACO were uplifting", Horton recalls, "as was the potential to mount a New York performance of my orchestration. It was everything I could have hoped for, all coming together at one time. But the move would require uprooting my wife Andréa from her family in Texas."

As the couple weighs the pros and cons of a move, they receive some good news. Conductor Anshel Brushilo has invited Horton to once again conduct his *University of North Texas Symphony Orchestra*, a 120-voice chorus and soloists in a Dallas-area premiere of the suite *Songs of the Slave* from composer Kirke Mechem's highly successful *John Brown* opera. It is beautifully received. Soon after, Horton is laid low by the devastating news of Ruth Ellington-Boatwright's diagnosis of advanced stages of lung cancer. It becomes the tipping point in the couple's decision to relocate to New York (2003), as the move will permit Horton to minister to Ruth in person. Once in New York, Horton sits down with the director of JALC André Guess.[361]

---

360 Horton had already secured written authorization from Skywalker Group and Skywalker Sound (1991 and 1996 respectively) to utilize the Skywalker Symphony Orchestra for a future performance of the "Ellington-Horton Black, Brown and Beige" (EHBBB). Horton interviewed with Sony Classical Records to record EHBBB. Capitol Records also provided a letter of interest for a distribution arrangement with Blue Note Records and/or EMI Classics (2002).

361 Andre (Kimo Stone) Guess, Vice President & Producer for Jazz At Lincoln Center (2002 - 2006) - Responsible to the Artistic Director and President and CEO for all programming and concert operations. Served as Executive Producer for all NYC concerts and national and international touring.

"He was a serious, but pleasant and respectful individual," says Horton. "Still, I was nervous and rather intimidated before I entered his office. He quietly asked me about my skills and background, then promised to get back with me with the final paperwork for my employment. We managed to secure an apartment, and Andrea continued her career in speech pathology. When I didn't hear from André Guess for a couple of days, I put a call into Billy Banks.

"I'm sorry," the receptionist says. "Mr. Banks no longer works here."

"Oh?" Horton replies, trying to regain his footing, "May I speak with the Executive Director?"

"I'm sorry," she replies apologetically. "He left to pursue other opportunities as well."

The news comes as a shock to Horton. When he collects himself, he places a call to Michael Geller, the VP/Executive Director at the ACO to confirm his proffered short-term fundraising position with its modest stipend and quickly secures a part-time position as the Musical Director for the First Baptist Church in East Elmhurst (Queens).

When the tumult eventually settles down, Horton hits the ground running in his new position with the ACO, assisting Geller with the organization's annual *Improvise! Festival*.[362] He helps raise funds to bring in the *Juilliard Jazz Orchestra* to perform Ellington's *Sacred Music* with the gracious cooperation of Ray Carmen, President of The Duke Ellington Society and Victor Goines, Artistic Director for the Juilliard Jazz Department. And he excitedly begins laying the groundwork for longer-range funding for a performance of his *Ellington-Horton Black, Brown and Beige*.

In his free time, Horton enrolls in evening Masters level classes at Brooklyn College TV Production and Media Management, incubating and refining his vision for his *American Music* educational television

---

362 The ACO's annual *Improvise! Festival* was dedicated to integrating Jazz and improvised music into the symphony.

series. He transfers its production to the college's TV department, gaining taping facilities and adding CUNY-TV (City University of New York's educational system) to the show's existing broadcast on PBS affiliate station KRCB-TV in the San Francisco Bay area.

One year later, in 2004, one of Horton's professors turns out to be none other than Jeffrey Taylor, the Jazz scholar who called Horton after his Dallas concert. In typical fashion, the amiable Horton introduces himself. Their conversations continue throughout the semester with Horton sharing more details of his Ellington experiences. The two discuss Horton's *American Music* educational television project.[363] Taylor is particularly impressed by H. Wiley Hitchcock's endorsement of the program and Horton's association with Ellington researcher/author, (the late) Mark Tucker and his wife Carol Oja, Ph.D., music scholars whom Taylor knows and respects. In fact, Oja is a former director of the H. Wiley Hitchcock Institute for Studies in American Music (HISAM). As the Director (currently Emeritus) of the same institute, Taylor continues HISAM's support of Horton's *American Music* educational TV program. He appears on a segment discussing Jazz pianist Earl "Fatha" Hines and announces his institute's formal partnership with the program in 2012.

"As Director of the *H. Wiley Hitchcock Institute for Studies in American Music*," writes Taylor in his letter to Horton, "I am excited about our shared *American Music* Educational Television Project. Dr. Hitchcock's vision for such a project is now a reality. I look forward to serving as a host for our *American Music* series and am happy that the Hitchcock Institute is now an official partner in this great initiative."[364]

It is a small world indeed.

"From our introductory phone call three years prior, Jeffrey Taylor

---

363 The *American Music* Educational TV Program: The only regularly-aired public television program that celebrates the creation, performance, scholarship and contribution of American music in full historical context. https://www.americanmusictv.org.

364 Jeffrey Taylor, Jeffrey Taylor Website Quote, 18 Sept. 2016.

did exactly what a professional music scholar is supposed to do," states Horton. "In my case, he sought to protect the accuracy and history of Duke's legacy, and I greatly respect him for that. He needed proof of my experiences and claims. I am grateful that I was able to provide it and earn his confidence and support in return."

Horton's *American Music* project is also supported by Sister Mary Dominic Ray's successor, Thomas L. Riis, (currently) Director Emeritus of the *American Music Research Center* (AMRC), who also writes a letter of endorsement in 2015:

> "I know that my predecessor, the AMRC's founding director Sister Mary Dominic Ray, who mentored [Randall Keith Horton] so many years ago in San Rafael, would be thrilled to learn that you took your ideas and made them into vivid reality through the American Music Educational Television Project and its series of programs *American Music*. These productions have undoubtedly impacted viewers in the best way across the country... By encompassing the astonishing diversity of American music styles, genres and historical contexts in *American Music*. You have done a yeoman's service. Your comprehensive approach is deeply meaningful at a time when our country seems more often divided than united by our rich shared cultural heritage."[365]

Dr. George Rodman, Chair of the TV Department at Brooklyn College, and Professor Stuart McClellan also helps guide and protect the project as do Stan Marvin and Nancy Dodd of PBS affiliate station KRCB-TV (Bay Area).

Sandwiched between his work with the ACO and his classes at the college, Horton visits Ruth Ellington-Boatwright in her home and later

---

365  Thomas L. Riis, "Thomas L. Riis Letter of Endorsement." Received by Randall Keith Horton
, Karen Barbera's Office, 14 Aug. 15AD, North Tustin, CA.

in her hospital room, singing her brother's *Sacred Music* at her bedside. Like her famous brother twenty years earlier, Ruth's in a short, intense struggle with cancer. When she succumbs on March 11, 2004, Horton experiences another intense wave of loss and a compulsion to honor her.

The perfect opportunity presents itself just two weeks later, when Horton conducts the Juilliard Jazz Orchestra, choirs, soloists, and others in *An Evening of Duke Ellington's Sacred Music* (ESC) in collaboration with the American Composers Orchestra and The Duke Ellington School (TDES). It is the featured performance of the ACO's 2004 *Improvise! Festival*, celebrating Duke Ellington's 105th birthday. As Horton steps up to welcome his audience, he dedicates the performance to his dear friend and mentor. How fitting that he is able to pay tribute to her through her brother's cherished *Sacred Music*.

In the audience that evening is Brooks Kerr,[366] the blind piano prodigy whom Horton has met years earlier at one of Ruth Ellington-Boatwright's Sunday soirées. Duke Ellington reportedly told a group to whom he was speaking, "If you have any questions about my music just ask Brooks Kerr."[367]

Horton recalls:

> It did not surprise me that Brooks Kerr was in the audience as I conducted Ellington's *Sacred Music* that evening. After the concert, I sought him out, re-introduced myself and thanked him for coming. He remembered our first meeting when he heard me play Duke's white baby grand piano at Ruth's. Then he surprised me by inviting me to his own home in the Lower East side. I called on him the following week, and we had a

---

366 Joe Bebco, "Brooks Kerr, Pianist And Duke Ellington Acolyte, Dies At 66." *The Syncopated Times*, 1 May 2018, syncopatedtimes.com/brooks-kerr-obituary/. Brooks Kerr (1950-2018) began playing the piano by age two and initially associated color with each note.

367 Sam Roberts, Brooks Kerr, a Prodigy On Piano and an Expert On Ellington, Dies at 66." *New York Times*, 11 May 2018, pp. 13–13.

friendly visit. He had an eidetic memory of Ellington's music, literally *seeing* and *sensing* the notes and sounds as colors. He shared a story about a time when Duke tried to stump him on his knowledge of his repertoire, asking him to play *Portrait of the Lion*. To which Kerr asked, "Which One? The 1939 *Portrait* or the 1955?" We had a good laugh over that and bonded over our love of Ellington and his music. He complimented me on my piano playing, telling me "I played with a sound that was inspired" and that he "loved the concept of my playing." That was the last time I saw him, but his compliment continues to inspire and sustain me to this day.

After the *"Improvise! Festival,"* Geller, the ACO's Executive Director, tracks Horton down, this time with different intentions.

"Congratulations on the performance, Randall!" He says as he enthusiastically shakes his hand. "We didn't know you could do *that*! We're (the ACO) impeding your progress."

It takes a few moments for Horton to realize that Geller is actually bringing his fundraising position with the ACO to an early close, and that there will likely be no future performance of the *Ellington-Horton Black, Brown and Beige*.

Horton's departure from the ACO marks the start of his semi-retirement at the age of sixty-two. But thanks to his time with the ACO, he is still able to attend the 2005 Essentials of Orchestra Management seminar sponsored by the *American Symphony Orchestra League of New York* where he interacts with some of the top US orchestral executive directors, including Peter Pastrich (formerly Executive Director of the San Francisco Symphony) and Deborah Borda (LA Philharmonic).

Says Horton:

> Sometimes, if you can't beat the system, you have to figure out a way to work around it. The Hitchcock Institute was

part of the Conservatory of Music at Brooklyn College, and I asked the Dean if I could focus the remainder of my academic work on, and in support of, my *American Music* educational television program. He agreed, and in 2006 I earned a B.S. (with honors) in Television Production from *Brooklyn College's Department of Television and Radio*. It was my first college degree! A treasured milestone, coming from a family and an era that emphasized the importance of an education. Fortunately, it didn't take long because of all the credits I transferred in with.

After graduating, Horton enrolls in the Master's program in media studies at Brooklyn College, with a focus on managing television in the not-for-profit business sector with a concentration in Jazz history studies with professors Jeffrey Taylor and Gary Giddins (CUNY Graduate Center). For the presentation of a written assignment, he augments his paper's content with a video of his interview with Ruth Ellington-Boatwright. It shocks his fellow graduate students, who demand to know why he hasn't advised them sooner of his association with Duke Ellington and his family.

"Sometimes you can stand up for yourself," Horton explains, "but I've also learned that I have to be circumspect." Not surprisingly, it seems that as long as Horton keeps a low profile and stays under the radar, things run more smoothly. His *Ellington-Horton Black, Brown and Beige* continues to languish in publishing purgatory, even though interest in performing it persists. The *Dance Theatre of Harlem* (DTH) commissions Horton to compose music for a ballet performance they present at the Guggenheim Museum and is favorably reviewed by *The New York Times*. During the collaboration, they express interest in mounting the *Ellington-Horton Black, Brown and Beige* as a ballet. It gets Horton thinking about the music's unpublished state as he continues his association with the DTH as a music faculty member and ballet-class pianist through 2008.

That same year, Horton and Kirk Mechem combine their respective talents for a third time at the world premiere of Mechem's *John Brown Opera* at the *Kansas City Lyric Opera House* with Ward Holmquist. A review in the *Kansas City Star* newspaper calls the performance "The sort of magical success that composers and musicians dream of... a natural from start to finish... could easily become an iconic American classic."

"It was another phenomenal experience," sighs Horton. "And it gave me the confidence, hope, and renewed energy to do whatever I had to do to drag my *Ellington-Horton Black, Brown and Beige* across the publishing finish line once and for all."

In early 2009, Horton makes a phone call to longtime Texas friend Roy Fletcher, the talented bassist who accompanied Horton at *Ellington's On The Square*. The two discuss Horton's recent successful performances of the *Ellington-Horton Black, Brown and Beige* (1988 and 1999), his attempted publishing submissions and his fear that the music may never be published. Horton asks Fletcher if he will help him create a computerized engraving of the score that can be used for a possible performance in New York, and a final submission attempt to G. Schirmer. The thought of the music continuing to languish sits uncomfortably with Fletcher. Several days later, the former singer, songwriter, and bassist for *The Killdares* calls Horton back to make a startling commitment.

"He told me he would help me jump the final hurdle standing in the way of the music being published," explains Horton. "He would use his musical and technical expertise to enter the conductor's score and parts into the latest *Notion* composing software."

It is an unanticipated moment of grace that leaves Horton momentarily stunned.

"Roy," replies a startled Horton, "I want to make sure you realize the scope of what you're agreeing to. It is a monumental undertaking.

There are over 340 pages of handwritten music in the score alone. I've been trying to re-copy it and the parts for more than *twenty-two years* (1987 - 2009)."

Fortunately, much like Horton, the orchestration resonates with Fletcher on a personal, spiritual and elemental level. He tells Horton he is committed to the undertaking if Horton will have him.

Fletcher recalls:

> By now the source materials were cumbersome for engraving purposes. There were Ellington's original big band parts, Horton's handwritten score with added notations and the dot matrix printed parts. But as a former Rock musician, composer and a current teacher for special needs children, I committed my entire summer to reverse engineer the materials into a complete and consistent computerized score. As Randall and I collaborated, we weren't just cramming the notes into a computer software program and proofing for accuracy. We were more like forensic musicologists profoundly committed to understanding and maintaining Ellington's overarching vision. Randall had already lived among the notes for many, many years. He already had the great *privilege* of stepping into the very mind of Duke Ellington, figuratively speaking, to touch and hear every note and nuance of Ellington's musical thought. But for me, sitting deeply among the music was like glimpsing the composer's soul laid bare. I was astounded at every measure by the music's complexity...its intricacies and the number of incongruous musical lines that seemed to defy logic, yet fitted perfectly together. The scope of what Duke Ellington accomplished with *Black, Brown and Beige*, was staggering to me on so many levels. Beyond the theme and length of the composition...or the venue chosen

for its premiere. Ellington composed the music using a continuous thread of the *Blues* to brilliantly convey the reality of the enslaved, African American experience, their joys, sorrows, ups and downs with an amazing sense of authenticity and intuitive knowledge of harmonies and the human spirit that only Ellington could have delivered. At the same time, he offered a parallel spiritual message of *hope* for a better life beyond peoples' earthly condition, and in so doing, captured the collective aspirations, dreams, and souls of not just African Americans, but of all humanity.[368]

When Daniel Kingman petitioned Mercer Ellington for Randall Keith Horton to write the full-length orchestration, he either knowingly or instinctively recognized that Horton was one of the only people who possessed a wide enough band width of intelligence, skills, knowledge and experiences to understand and faithfully manage the Jazz legend's complex vision. And by that I mean, Horton was *chosen* by Ellington. He sat in with *The Ellington Orchestra* and understood Jazz, Classical, Blues, Negro Spirituals, the Bible, religious hymns and African American music history. And as a result, his orchestration was a fulsome treatment of the original composition, not a partial one, or a two-dimensional version. He took painstaking steps to make sure that the orchestration of *Black, Brown and Beige* re-emerged as Ellington envisioned. He cradled every line of musical thought and lovingly created a custom fitted symphonic accompaniment.[369]

And so, for the next *eleven years* (2009 - 2020), Fletcher and Horton continue the exhausting yet exhilarating process of discussing and keying

---

368   Karen Barbera, "Roy Fletcher interview", September 2019.
369   *Ibid.*

in every single musical note and notation. They shoehorn hundreds of hours of work in between jobs and family commitments. The engraving and proofing of the music by two relatively unknown individuals may seem perplexing to some, but their efforts eventually create the most complete and authentic full-length *concerto grosso* orchestration of Duke Ellington's *magnum opus* the world is ever likely to hear.

In 2009, Horton sends sample pages of the newly engraved to the music publisher and includes a recap of his submission attempts to date. This marks his sixth attempt. A few weeks later, G. Schirmer's production department returns the sample pages to Horton by mail with edits marked in red ink. He is instructed to make the noted corrections and complete the computerized engraving of the score *and now, all parts.*

When Horton returns to Schirmer's Manhattan offices to discuss the edits in person, he is met by a sea of new faces and ushered into the office of the corporate attorney where he is told that legal action could result if he does not make the corrections and live up to the terms of his contract. The meeting concludes with Horton's exasperated declaration that he has spent the last twenty-two years attempting to do just that, further stating, "I am here in service to Maestro Ellington!"

The relationship between Horton and the music publisher reaches an all-time low. G. Schirmer's lawyers initiate no legal action, and the commission remains surprisingly in play. Roy Fletcher makes the requested corrections and begins engraving the individual parts. And Horton, now 67, moves ahead with plans to mount a performance of his orchestration in New York to create an archival recording per G. Schirmer's previously approved directive. For the recording, Horton needs to reserve a venue, put out an open call for talented musicians (big band, symphony, and soloists), publicize the event, pay G. Schirmer's sheet music royalties, conduct auditions and rehearsals, promote the concert and attract a paying audience to cover all of the aforementioned costs. It is a formidable gamble that quickly becomes a personal financial commitment when Horton writes a check from his own retirement funds and signs the rental contract for the *Rose Theater at Lincoln Center.*

"I thought, if the record company executives could hear the orchestration — if there was audible *proof* of its quality, beauty and the manifestation of Ellington's symphonic intentions, it might soften the executives and hasten their acceptance and publication of the music," explains Horton.

To help raise awareness and funds, Horton performs a piano concert of Ellington's *Sacred Music* for the members of his Riverside Church on October 18, 2009. Word of Horton's fundraising challenges reach Phoebe Jacobs,[370] the tenacious publicist for some of Jazz's most iconic legends (Louis Armstrong, Ella Fitzgerald, Duke Ellington, Benny Goodman, Sarah Vaughan, and Peggy Lee). Jacobs has enjoyed a sprawling behind-the-scenes career in Jazz and is particularly astute in harnessing the power of publicity and show business for her clients' benefit.

Hoping to help Horton, she introduces him to a high-profile manager and producer in the music industry who is a successful concert and tour promoter.

"[The promoter] maintained an office in the Chrysler Building," recalls Horton, "but Phoebe arranged a meeting in her home office on East 74th street. She was sitting at her desk when I walked in. The promoter was already present, sitting on her couch. She welcomed me and introduced the two of us, telling the promoter, 'This is the next guy you need to promote.'"

Jacobs goes on to discuss what the promoter has the power to do

---

370   Phoebe Jacobs was an American promoter of Jazz musicians particularly associated with Louis Armstrong. She helped establish the Louis Armstrong Educational Foundation and co-founded the Jazz Foundation of America, a nonprofit organization that provided support to musicians in need. She was also an avid supporter of the Louis Armstrong Center for Music and Medicine at Beth Israel Hospital. In an interesting testament to her power, tenacity and thoughtfulness, she once arranged a surprise birthday party for Ella Fitzgerald, whom she discovered, had never had a birthday party, in less than 24 hours with a guest list that included Duke Ellington, Benny Goodman and Stan Kenton as well as Mickey Mantle and Vice President Richard M. Nixon. Nate Chinemay, "Phoebe Jacobs, Publicist for Jazz Greats, Dies at 93," *The New York Times*, May 4, 2012.

if he decides to take on Horton as a client. He has promoted artists and concerts all over the world and hints that when Horton has something of an international scale, he might be interested in representing him, but he does not offer promotional or funding assistance for Horton's upcoming concert.

A few days later, as Horton prepares to leave for a rehearsal for his concert, he receives a call from a man accusing him of lying about his connections to Ellington. Horton asks with whom he is speaking, but the stranger simply continues,

"You were never with Ellington. You're lying! Take it off of your website. Every word of it!"

Horton tells the stranger he would be happy to show him proof of his credentials during a break in his rehearsal.

When the two meet at the church where Horton is rehearsing, he gives his accuser physical evidence of his connection to Ellington but is told by the man that *he* will take over performing the Duke's music.

"All I could think of at that moment was, *Who is this guy?*" says Horton. "*How credible are his threats?* That's when I decided I was *way* out of my league," says Horton, "and I don't mind telling you. genuinely frightened."

Based on the response from his two previous performances, Horton feels confident that ticket sales for his upcoming concert will cover the musicians' salaries and the balance of the rental fee for *Lincoln Center*, but what if "*obstacles*" to the performance develop? In the morning, he calls his musicians and his contacts at *Lincoln Center* and pulls the plug on the entire performance. It is a humiliating and financially devastating decision.

About six months later (April/May 2009), Horton receives a call from the same concert promoter with whom he met in Phoebe Jacobs' office.

"Hello Randall. How are things going?" He asks.

"Oh, okay," Horton replies half-heartedly. The caller listens as

Horton tells him of the confrontation in the church and his resulting decision to cancel his performance of the *Ellington-Horton Black, Brown and Beige*. The promoter surprisingly informs Horton that he recently had dinner with two individuals, one of whom seems to fit the description of the man who confronted Horton. He tells Horton of their request to finance a play with tap dancers Gregory and Maurice Hines.

"Do you need me to produce it or something?"

"He asked if I knew who you were," the promoter continues. "I didn't let on that I did. He asked if I could help him finance and produce a concert tour of Ellington's music, including a symphonic version of *Black, Brown and Beige*."

The news hits Horton like a punch in the gut.

"Don't worry about him," the man advises Horton, sensing his shock. "I told them I wouldn't be able to help either one of them."

"Then the promoter repeated his interest in signing and promoting me in a tour of Ellington's music," says Horton. "He told me he was going to 'make me famous.' He obviously felt there was money to be made, or he wouldn't have wasted his time with me. The confrontation, the cancelling of my concert, and all the behind-the-scenes maneuvering were precisely the reasons I left the commercial music industry in the mid '70s. I had no desire to return to it. I thanked him and said, 'When I am ready to mount the *Ellington-Horton Black, Brown and Beige* again, I will let you know.'"

"I may not have taken him up on his offer, but I was still thankful. He did two important things for me for which I will always be grateful. He removed my fear of the person who confronted me, and he encouraged me to get a copy of my contract from G. Schirmer for my own protection, and I'm sure, his too, if we ever did business together."

Horton calls G. Schirmer the next day to request a copy of his contract. After being placed on hold for an extended period of time, the records employee returns and asks, "Are you sure you have a contract with us?" To which Horton replies with decades of pent-up frustration, "*Of course I have a contract with you!*" But in 2009, G. Schirmer is unable to produce a copy.

Horton retires from his full-time directorship of church music in 2005 at the age of 65, but continues to take on piano students to augment his social security income. In 2013, he and Fletcher dedicate themselves to four additional months of rigorous work of engraving and proofing, but the score is still not finished. Horton is growing older. Decades of naysayers and accumulated friction have depleted the last of his reserves. The irony being that he never solicited either of the Ellington-related commissions. He even humbly vocalized his doubts about his own qualifications. Through the years, at each point of adversity, he stiffened his resolve by following the advice of the late Reverend Dr. Martin Luther King, Jr. who said, "If you can't fly then run, if you can't run then walk, if you can't walk then crawl, but whatever you do, you have to keep moving forward."

Horton crawls for decades over barriers and racism, past ridicule and rebuke, around egos, greed and his own shortcomings and away from threats and violence. And throughout the difficult journey, he feels the presence and pressure of Duke Ellington holding him personally accountable, denying him a moment's rest until his orchestration of *Black, Brown and Beige* is completed.

"The spirit of Duke Ellington has been an unrelenting, and sometimes unwelcome, taskmaster!" Confesses Horton good-naturedly. "I heard him whispering in my ear every morning, '*Get up, Randall!*'" Horton says, intoning Ellington's elegant, and distinctive cadence…

'Get moving!'

'Finish your work!'

'What's taking you so long?'

"And every time an obstacle threatened to slow or halt my forward progress, someone or some*thing* saw fit to illuminate a new path *over, under, around* or *through* me. So when my crawling came to an exhausted standstill in 2013, I wasn't entirely surprised when a random stranger sat down across from me in the breakfast car of an Amtrak train and helped me get moving again. I doubt Karen Barbera or her daughter Cameron heard the echo of Ellington's voice that morning, but I did."

*'I want to hear my music, Randall!'*

*'The world needs to hear my music!'*

*'I've been waiting a long time!'*

"I'm telling you!" Horton repeats, eyes wide with conviction; "A taskmaster! Not a moment of peace!"

# HISTORICAL CONTEXT
## 2000's

General Colin Powell becomes the first African American Secretary of State in January 2001. Nine months later, the United States suffers its gravest foreign attack on home soil since Pearl Harbor with the terrorist attacks on 9/11 that claim 2,996 lives.[371]

The iPod and advancements in computer/music technology (auto-tune and quantizing) widen the pool of people creating and interacting with new genres of music (Techno[372] and Dubstep[373]), thereby weakening the music industry's stranglehold on music production and profits. Innovative music festivals also emerge (*Coachella*,[374] *Burning Man* and *Lollapalooza*) which bring large, diverse audiences together for an expanding variety of musical genres and choices.

In 2002, the Oscars are hosted by Whoopi Goldberg. Halle Berry becomes the first African American woman to win an Oscar for Best Actress, Denzel Washington is the second African American man to win an Oscar for Best Actor (Sidney Poitier being the first in 1964) and Sidney Poitier receives the Academy Honorary Award. Disney releases its first animated movie featuring a black princess (*The Princess and the Frog*, 2009), and President Barack Obama is elected to a second term (2012).

Racism is threaded through many decisions, policies, and behaviors in the United States, but some trying to change the warp and weft of America's cultural fabric begin to make progress. At the beginning of the second decade of the new millennium, 17-year-old Trayvon Martin

---

371  2,977 victims and 19 hijackers.

372  Techno is an electronic dance music that began in the United States in the 1980's and became globally popular in the 1990's with glacial synthesizer melodies and brisk machine rhythms. It was a product of the fascination of middle-class African American youths in Detroit, Michigan for European electronic dance music.

373  Dubstep is a form of dance music, typically instrumental, characterized by a sparse, syncopated rhythm and a strong bass line.

374  The Coachella Festival originated by Pearl Jam in 1993, when the band performed for almost 25,000 fans at the Empire Polo Club in Indio, California as part of a protest over Ticketmaster's service charges on ticket purchases in Los Angeles.

dies due to violent action by a so-called neighborhood watchman, and dozens of other people of color suffered similar fates at the hands of law enforcement officers. The absence of retribution for the few officers who are charged and found guilty ignites the Black Lives Matter movement. Slayings persist throughout the 2000's, placing a flawed American justice system on full display through the lenses of police body cameras, security cameras, and cell phone footage. The year 2016 is marked by sharp contrasts in rhetoric and behavior, as well as growing divisions over the perception of racism. NFL football star Colin Kaepernick begins a movement among professional athletes by kneeling during the National Anthem in protest of systemic police brutality against African Americans and other people of color. Donald Trump, elected president in 2016, responds to the peaceful protest by saying, "Wouldn't you love to see one of those NFL owners, when someone disrespects our flag to say, 'Get that son of a bitch off the field right now. Out. He's fired.'" Two years later, Americans debate the racial implications of flying the Confederate flag and celebrating Southern war heroes. Three years after that, the United States government decides it is right and proper to rename 14 military bases currently bearing the name of Confederate heroes.

A disconnect emerges between the treatment of African Americans and the country's burgeoning demand for African American culture, fashion, entertainment, and music. Jazz maintains a dedicated fan base. Hip Hop achieves mainstream status and Contemporary R&B dominates the charts with songs by Usher, Beyoncé, and Rihanna.[375]

---

[375]  In 2004 alone, 15 of the 25 Billboard Year-End Hot 100 singles were listed as Contemporary R&B.

## CHAPTER 12

# I'M BEGINNING TO SEE THE LIGHT

---

*"My attitude is to never be satisfied,*
*never enough, never."*
- Duke Ellington

The day I meet Randall Keith Horton in the dining car of our Amtrak train in 2013, I do not hear the ephemeral voice of Duke Ellington urging him to complete his orchestration, but I do sense the power of our mutually attuned intentions drawing us together. Our backgrounds complement one another's like two perfectly fitted puzzle pieces; Horton with his fascinating story, and me with my background in writing and pitching newsworthy stories to the media. I get excited about big inspirational projects. I like the challenges they present. I like strategizing. And I enjoy the satisfaction that comes from getting stories of real value out into the world. Ellington's and Horton's intertwined odysseys not only tag each of these bases, they hit a home run. As we continue our telephone conversations, I try to tamp down my growing interest, to remain cautiously uninvolved, but I can't escape the gravitational pull of his story. So when Boston University taps Horton to perform selections of Ellington's *Sacred Music* for their 2017 Martin Luther King celebration, I volunteer my media pitching services.

Associate Provost and Dean of Students, Kenneth Elmore, and Professor of Music and Chair, Musicology and Ethnomusicology, Victor Coelho, Ph.D., stumble upon Randall Keith Horton and his obscure connection to Duke Ellington after reading his 2013 application for a PhD fellowship in musicology at *Boston University's College of Fine Arts*. He applies based upon his research on the life and music of Gustav Mahler. Horton tops their wait list, but is, regrettably, not accepted as a doctoral fellow. In consolation, three years later he is invited to lunch with Elmore and Coelho, whose conversations circle concentrically around Jazz's golden years and Ellington's contributions.

"I was shocked and confused by some of their assertions," states Horton. "They were not accurate, and against my better judgement, I plucked up the courage to correct the two distinguished academics."

Elmore and Coelho can't be more pleased. It turns out their casual lunch is part of a final vetting process of Horton and his nexus to Ellington. He passes, and the two academics ask if he will conduct the *Boston University Big Band, Inner Strength Gospel Choir*, soloists, and dancers in four selections of Ellington's *Sacred Music* at the university's MLK celebration *Hope, Despair and The Blues* just four months away. The event, co-sponsored by the university's *Howard Thurman Center for Common Ground*,[376] features VIP speakers and several other musical performances. It is a collaboration that will bring Horton full circle to his

---

376 The Howard Thurman Center for Common Ground acting on Howard Thurman's belief that "...meaningful and creative shared experiences between people can be more compelling than all of the faiths, fears, concepts and ideologies that separate them. And, if these experiences can be multiplied and sustained over a sufficient duration of time, then any barrier that separates one person from another can be undermined and eliminated."

childhood in Boston and the BU campus where he briefly studied and his father and sister both earned advanced degrees. Interestingly, it is also the same campus where the late Howard Thurman,[377] the reverend and moral compass of the university's Marsh Chapel, mentored Martin Luther King, Jr. while the civil rights leader completed his doctoral degree in systematic theology in 1955.

I assume the role as Horton's publicist and fly to Boston to help promote his involvement with the Boston news media. The concert is inspiring and well attended. It is the first time I personally see Horton rehearse and conduct the student musicians and speak in public. He lives up to all expectations. He is eloquent, elegant, and engaging and delivers a swinging, worshipful performance to an audience of 1,700 who convey their appreciation with a standing ovation.

Coverage by the Boston media is strong, surpassing the university's expectations.[378] It seems everyone is keenly interested in this little-known aspect of Duke Ellington's musical legacy and Horton's intertwined contributions. In fact, there are even discussions about a future academic conference at BU to study the impact of *faith* on Ellington's music, the teachings of Howard Thurman and the impassioned civil rights statements of reverend Dr. Martin Luther King, Jr. Of particular excitement, at least to Horton and me, is the university's idea of *bookending* the proposed conference with performances of Ellington's *Sacred Music* and the *Ellington-Horton Black, Brown and Beige*. We ride the bow wave of

---

377  Howard Washington Thurman (1899–1981) was an African-American author, philosopher, theologian, educator, and civil rights leader whose theology of radical nonviolence influenced and shaped a generation of civil rights activists, including Martin Luther King, Jr. He advised, "Don't ask what the world needs. Ask what makes you come alive, and go do it. Because what the world needs is people who have come alive."

378  Marilyn Schairer, "Duke Ellington's Sacred Music Elevates BU's 45th Martin Luther King Day Observance," WGBH News, *WGBH*, January 15, 2017, https://www.wgbh.org/news/2017/01/15/local-news/duke-ellingtons-sacred-music-elevates-bus-45th-martin-luther-king-day; Jon Garelick, "At BU, A Reverent Rendering of Ellington's Sacred Music"; Bologna and Mosley, "Remembering Duke Ellington's Sacred Music"; additional media interest included WHDH-TV, WNTN Radio, WGBH-TV (PBS), WERS Radio and WCVB-TV (CBS).

Horton's successful collaboration with university to re-establish contact with the music publisher to finalize and publish his orchestration.

"It has been more than thirty years!" Exclaims G. Schirmer's Director of Publishing Administration when I telephone him to arrange a meeting. "We have shut the door on this contract," he states.

I acknowledge the gentleman's frustration and assure him of our commitment to seeing this project through to completion by the first quarter of 2019. We talk about the (now) fully engraved score, our recent partnership with Boston University and their interest in showcasing the music as part of an academic conference. After much cajoling, the director agrees to meet with us on April 7, 2018, to view and assess Fletcher and Horton's engraving.

We are greeted at the publisher's Madison Avenue offices in New York one week later with a cool handshake and a brief introduction to the newest Director of Production. The Director of Publishing Administration dismisses G. Schirmer's interest in Randall's orchestration because of the "numerous other exemplary arrangements of *Black, Brown and Beige* already in the company's catalogue." He singles out the alternative 1970 arrangement with particular pride. Thankfully, Randall has armed me well with historical facts to set the record straight.

I tell him we are aware of Mr, Peress' 17:00 minute arrangement, noting the fleeting look of amazement on the Director's face, and continue with the unfortunate fact that Mr. Peress' arrangement is only a partial treatment of Ellington's 48:15-minute *Black, Brown and Beige*. I make him aware that Mr. Horton's is the only full-length orchestration in existence, the only full-length arrangement commissioned through the Ellington family and the only arrangement that interpolates Ellington's 1958 *Come Sunday* and *23rd Psalm* into the third movement as the composer intended, but never accomplished before his death in 1974.

Noting the Director's somewhat chagrined expression, I press on, informing him that Mr. Peress' setting was written and premiered by the Chicago Symphony in 1970[379] and later received a blistering review from renowned Jazz critic Gary Giddins which led conductor Daniel Kingman to approach Horton, Duke Ellington's son Mercer and G. Schirmer Publishing to commission Mr. Horton as the optimal person to write what Mr. Giddins' review demands.

I make my point, but it is as if someone or something prods me to place an exclamation point at my statement. The next thing I know, I hear myself say, "If you hold Maurice Peress' partial treatment up as the definitive orchestration of Duke Ellington's *Black, Brown and Beige*, people will laugh at you."

An uncomfortable silence blankets the room. I blink but keep my gaze steady as I silently wonder what forced me to verbalize such an uncharacteristically harsh rebuke. The Director keeps his eyes downcast, meticulously squaring the sheets of Horton's conductor's score on the table in front of him, before dismissing my final comment out of hand, saying, "Well, that is *one* opinion."

After the ripples in the ether quiet, the four of us are finally able to get down to business. We show the two publishing representatives Horton's letter of endorsement from Ruth Ellington-Boatwright and Mercer Ellington's handwritten authorization. We talk about the interest by a number of individuals and institutions in the historically significant orchestration as part of Duke Ellington's pioneering subtextual legacy. But what captures their interest most is the 1999 video of Horton conducting *The University of North Texas Symphony* and his big band in a performance of the music at the *Morton H. Meyerson Symphony Center* in Dallas. They witness for the first time the fullness of Horton's arrangement and his interpolation of Ellington's 1958 *Come Sunday* (with lyrics)

---

379  Sean Colonna, "Celebrating the Maurice Peress Archive," *American Music Review* XLVIII no. 2 (Spring 2019), http://www.brooklyn.cuny.edu/web/academics/centers/hitchcock/publications/amr/v48-2/colonna.php.

and *Twenty-third Psalm* (new music) into Ellington's third movement. After the video, there is a small but perceptible shift in their assessment of Horton, but the Director of Publishing Administration still cannot help himself from nitpicking stylistic minutiae in Fletcher's engraving: The score should have been printed on eleven by seventeen-inch paper. There should be more measures on each line. Each page needs to conclude on one or more measures of rest to allow for page turns.

Despite his comments, the Director acknowledges that, "...the score in its current engraved form completes the arranging portion of Horton's original contract and that no corrections to the score are needed at this time"; however, holding up yet another hoop for Horton to jump through, he asks to see a complete Violin I part, adhering to the exact specifications of G. Schirmer's (engraving) *Style Book*, before he can render a final decision on whether G. Schirmer will publish the music. It is the first time that a publishing *Style Book* has ever been mentioned. The Director takes further umbrage with Horton and Fletcher's choice of *Notion* composing software, citing G. Schirmer's preference for *Finale* or *Sebelius*. When I ask how much it might cost to *re-engrave* the music using their preferred software, the Director of Production graciously secures an in-house estimate of $46,000 *nearly seven times Horton's original compensation to write the orchestration*. Since a fully engraved score, *and now parts*, were never part of Horton's original understanding of his Work-for-Hire contract, I ask if G. Schirmer will at least consider sharing the re-engraving expenses if it becomes necessary.

The Director of Publishing Administration denies the request for additional compensation. Nonetheless, we hold tightly to the director's earlier statements that "the score completes the arranging portion of Horton's contract" and that "no corrections (to the score) are needed at this time." We make a second request for a copy of Horton's original contract and emerge from our meeting with our main objective intact: the re-establishment of the withered relationship and the confirmation of the publisher's willingness to reconsider publishing the music. And we are hopeful that the engraved *Violin I* part will be the final hoop we will have to navigate. We content ourselves with G. Schirmer's terms for the time being and submit the *Violin I* part a few weeks later. The Director of Production approves it in a thoughtful email with minor corrections and gives Horton the green light to engrave the remaining 143 parts in similar fashion.

Horton and Fletcher, establish a rigorous schedule for the next eleven months to revise their work according to the publisher's *Style Book* with a targeted completion date of March 29, 2019. Fletcher once again commits himself to the project, building upon the *nine years* of engraving work he has already invested.

As Horton and Fletcher engrave and proof, I search for ways to improve our power dynamic with the publisher with a carrot and stick approach.

We secure the interest of a book publisher and two documentary producers. We also reach out to four of the top US symphonies, who each express interest in reviewing the score prior to its publication. To determine the audience reach and value of the publicity that can be generated by a national premiere of the music, I extrapolate the actual media coverage Horton enjoyed in Boston across the sixteen major US media markets. I arrive at a conservative estimate of reaching 80 million people for a total of $40 million in publication relations and news value.[380]

We also retain the services of a Madison Avenue entertainment attorney who is also a distinguished professor for the NYU Steinhardt School's master's degree program, covering "cornerstone" deals in the music business, including publishing. Together, we become an effective team of four: Fletcher, engraving; Horton, proofing; Barbera,

---

380  The "Publicity/News Value" is calculated based upon how much it would cost to purchase the same amount of advertising exposure commensurate with the print/radio/TV/social media coverage it would garnered as a news story, times a multiple for the added credibility of a news story versus a paid advertisement of equal size/duration.

strategizing/publicizing; and a seasoned attorney negotiating, who represents Horton's interests.

Horton and Fletcher comb meticulously through the engraving to make sure it conforms to G. Schirmer's *Style Book*. In the process, they more than *triple* the original volume of work from 50 to 144 individual parts, from 340 to 1056 total pages (score and parts) and from $46,000[381] to $142,871[382] in engraving services, a significant financial value to Schirmer and loss to Horton and Fletcher. The entertainment attorney directs Horton to hold off submitting the complete electronic music files until Schirmer produces a copy of Horton's original contract, to ensure that his commission and arranging credits can be concluded legally and bindingly.

Samples of the engraved conductor's score and parts are sent to the company with the understanding that the complete electronic music files will be made available upon receipt of Horton's original contract. This elicits no immediate response from the publisher.

As we wait, I try to discuss supporting marketing initiatives for the music's ultimate premiere and to make a fifth request for a copy of Horton's contract. The following reply arrives a short time later.

> "As I understand it, Mr. Horton has yet to complete the project, which began 10 years ago.[383] Before we would be in a position to embark on any type of promotion or marketing plan with orchestras, we would need to have the final score approved, edited, and proofed.[384]

However, the Schirmer executive is interested in discussing the

---

381  Engraving cost based upon Schirmer's own in-house estimate for 340 pages of music and 50 parts.

382  Engraving value based upon Schirmer's own estimate of $46,000 multiplied by 310% for the increase in actual pages engraved (1056) and parts (144).

383  The date referred to in this letter is in error. Horton's commission actually began thirty years ago in 1987.

384  Robert Thompson, Publicity for the *Ellington-Horton Black, Brown and Beige*, 2018.

names of the US symphonies who have expressed interest in the music. "You mention there is interest from several top symphony orchestras," his email continues. "Can you tell me which ones? We work with all the major North American orchestras, and it would be helpful for us to know."[385]

His email makes no mention of Horton's contract. While we wait for Schirmer to produce a copy of it, we receive an email on March 11, 2019, from the *New York Philharmonic* requesting a face-to-face meeting the following morning to review the pre-published conductor's score and parts. I take a red eye from California, joining Horton at a diner in Manhattan for a quick cup of coffee before our 10:00 a.m. meeting with the symphony's Artistic Director, Director of Education and Community Outreach and Assistant Artistic Director.

They review a hard copy of Horton's engraved score, read the newspaper review of its 1988 Sacramento premiere, watch the video of Horton's 1999 Dallas performance and express considerable interest in the music throughout our ninety-minute meeting. The Artistic Director asks about the supporting marketing initiatives as well as the news and publicity values that might attract potential sponsors. She asks what other symphonies we have spoken with and requests that we discontinue further discussions with them until she can get back to us with a definitive commitment. This we cannot promise, but she assures us that she will be in touch in less than one week's time.

"And if you don't hear from me by Wednesday, March 20th," she emphasizes, "please, pick up the phone and call *me!*"

It seems too good to be true. One of the finest symphonies in the world, and a partner that could deliver a high-quality performance and recording of the music as well as the necessary credibility, prestige, and contacts to accelerate the existing momentum for the documentary, book, concert series and national media tour. With a strange sense of

---

385  *Ibid.*

foreboding, Horton and I travel to Madison Avenue to discuss strategy with our attorney and decide we can safely provide G. Schirmer with the names of the interested symphonies they requested. In an email, listing the symphonies we have contacted, we also include a *sixth* request for Horton's missing contract. Two days later, we receive a reply from the publisher, quoting what appears to be terms from Horton's contract.

> "The 1987 agreement states that 'Mr. Horton must provide G. Schirmer with clear, legible full score masters of the arrangement, including all corrections and revisions made in preparation for and subsequent to the premiere performance.'[386] … While I appreciate the (March 13, 2019) excerpts you sent, Schirmer can only consider moving forward in earnest with publishing this arrangement upon receipt and approval by our editorial department of a complete and corrected master score and set of parts, as per the 1987 contract."[387]

The email doesn't add up. If they can quote directly from Horton's contract, why don't they attach a copy? By now, a week has also passed without a call from the *New York Philharmonic*, so I place a call to them as instructed.

The Artistic Director picks up on the first ring only to inform me that they are not interested in premiering the music at this time. Our call concludes with her saying it was really great to meet Randall and me and wishing us the best of luck reaching out to other symphonies. I slump back into my chair, staring blankly at my computer screen. *What in the world could have caused such a dramatic shift?* But the twists and turns continue.

---

386 Stephen Culbertson, "G. Schirmer Contract with Camellia Symphony Orchestra ." Received by Daniel Kingman, Karen Barbera's Office/G. Schirmer's Office, 16 Oct. 1987, North Tustin/New York, CA/NY.

387 Robert Thompson, Citing of Camellia Symphony Contract for the *Ellington-Horton Black, Brown and Beige*, Premiere, 2018.

As proof of Horton's *contract*, Schirmer provides copies of Mercer Ellington's handwritten approval for Randall Horton to execute the full-length orchestration of *Black, Brown and Beige.*

"This is the okay for *Randle* [sic] *Horton Black, Brown & Beige.* I give agreement."[388]... and their contract with the Camellia Symphony Orchestra, signed by conductor Daniel Kingman and Randall Horton authorizing the premiere of Horton's orchestration upon its completion, with a curious final sentence.

"4.) Upon approval by Mercer Ellington, G. Schirmer will engage Randall Horton to arrange this work for a flat fee. Mr. Horton must provide G. Schirmer with clear, legible full score masters of the arrangement, including all corrections and revisions made in preparation for and subsequent to the premiere performance. Mr. Horton and G. Schirmer will sign a separate agreement for this arrangement."[389]

Horton recalls:

I learned for the first time in *thirty-one years* that, although there is written proof of my commission, there is no existing contract. The revelation made me realize my own naivety and better understand the inherent difficulties in trying to fulfill the publisher's terms. In years past, I certainly didn't have the benefit of an engraver like Roy Fletcher (1999-present), a publicist like Karen Barbera (2013-present), or a knowledgeable

---

388  Mercer Ellington, "Mercer Ellington's Approval for Randall Horton's Orchestration of Black, Brown and Beige." Received by Stephen Culbertson, Karen Barbera's Office/G. Schirmer's Office, 11 Nov. 1987, North Tustin/New York, CA/NY.

389  Stephen Culbertson, "G. Schirmer Contract with Camellia Symphony Orchestra ." Received by Daniel Kingman, Karen Barbera's Office/G. Schirmer's Office, 16 Oct. 1987, North Tustin/New York, CA/NY. Mercer Ellington, "Mercer Ellington's Approval for Randall Horton's Orchestration of Black, Brown and Beige." Received by Stephen Culbertson, Karen Barbera's Office/G. Schirmer's Office, 11 Nov. 1987, North Tustin/New York, CA/NY.

attorney (2019-2021). Duke knew better than anyone when he said to me in 1973 that the music industry was "…too much for one person" and that "It takes a team." After all these years, I finally had a *team*, and it gave me confidence that I was in a more informed position to get my orchestration published, but more personally important to me to fulfill my *calling* and personal obligation to Duke Ellington.

We find ourselves at an unexpected impasse. According to our attorney, in the absence of the original contract, or any contract, neither party has the legal right to do anything with the music. A new contract must be drawn up and signed by both parties. Schirmer agrees, extending the following olive branch:

> If Mr. Horton is still, after thirty-one (31) years, interested in concluding the terms of the 1987 commission agreement, Schirmer must first receive a corrected and complete set of masters to review, per section 4. If and when Schirmer's editorial department approves the quality of those materials, then Schirmer will issue Mr. Horton a work-for-hire agreement that incorporates the [amount omitted] flat fee paid to Mr. Horton at the time of the commission agreement, and the work will then be published and available to orchestras.[390]

We submit the requested electronic files for all 1056 pages of the engraved conductor's score and 144 parts in good faith with our attorney's following appeal, "Mr. Horton has dedicated the last thirty years of his life to this music. Please don't deny him his moment of deserved glory," to which [the Schirmer executive] assures us that he will do his best to comply "if it can be done and is not too financially onerous."

---

390   Robert Thompson, *EHBBB Contract*, 23 Mar. 2019.

Randall continues: "For the first time in a very long time, there seemed to be a light at the end of the tunnel."

One month later, we receive an email from G. Schirmer "respectfully declining to publish 'the work'," but leaving the window cracked in the email's final paragraph, stating, "If Mr. Horton receives an offer to make his arrangement available via a third-party print publisher, G. Schirmer will enter into good faith negotiations with said publisher to approve a third-party print license to administer the arrangement."[391]

Horton is not the first, nor will he be the last to experience these types of difficulties. Even the great Duke Ellington endured challenging publishing terms in the dog-eat-dog music industry. His agent Irvin Mills opened many doors for him, but he also demanded 45 percent[392] of his gross earnings, leaving his client to pay the band's travel expenses and salaries from his own 45 percent share before realizing any personal revenue himself. This led Ellington's fellow musicians and historians to claim that the long red carpet that ran from one end of Mills' residence to the other was dyed with Ellington's blood.[393]

Schirmer offers the official reasons for its decision, but we may never know the underlying currents that may have also held sway. *Black, Brown and Beige* challenged the classical world's perceptions of race and musical genres in 1943, yet even today, minority composers, conductors and their music remain under-represented in the classical music world.

Schirmer's rejection leaves a bitter taste in my mouth, but it rolls off Horton like water off a duck's back. I have to remind myself that he is a seasoned processor of rejection. There were undoubtedly frustrations for both Schirmer and Horton through the years, as well as actions that in

---

391  Robert Thompson, Schirmer's Decision Not to Publish the EHBBB, 25 Apr. 2019.

392  Query sheet for the Duke Ellington Itinerary Database, Joe Igo, Gordon Ewing and Art Pilkington, October 1926 column F-7 entry, http://tdwaw.ellingtonweb.ca/IgoDukeElliingtonItinerary.html.

393  Karen Barbera and Randall Keith Horton . "Irvin Mills." Feb. 2019.

hindsight could have been handled differently by both parties. But if for no other reason than the beauty, weight, and historical significance of the music, I hoped that all parties could have ignored the distracting "chaff" to conclude, at the very least, a sound business transaction, and at best a tangible and profound gesture toward the inclusion of more American music and greater racial parity within the modern Classical music realm.

## Categories

Biases of all kinds may have diminished in America, but they still exist. And instead of the undisguised, unchecked expressions of the past, they have become subtle; rarely overt enough to be blatantly called out, yet pervasive enough to intimidate, delay or prevent advancement, cause talented individuals to question the value of their work, or worse, their own self-worth. And many times, the very people who perpetuate such practices do so not fully understanding their own role in it.

My thoughts flicker back to 2018 when Randall and his wife Andrea are guests in our home in Southern California for a week of documenting and videotaping Horton's oral history. On the final evening before their departure, my husband and I take them to our favorite restaurant, one with excellent food and a cozy atmosphere. I call ahead and receive a verbal reservation for our party of four with an estimated wait of one hour. *Perfect*, I think. *We can enjoy a celebratory round of drinks while we await our table.* Our one hour wait grows to ninety minutes, then to two hours. Restaurant staff keep assuring us that our party will be seated next, but I watch as walk-ins are seated ahead of us. I scan the restaurant. There are no other African Americans. After two hours, and yet another "delay," we walk out and are seated immediately at a nearby restaurant, but as a host, I am mortified…and furious.

And this is just an evening out. It isn't a denied college admission, job application, deserved promotion, or a refusal to publish a musical arrangement. And it certainly isn't an overtly racist gesture like a flat-out refusal to serve or lodge us, or a cross burning in our front yard, or bystanders crowding around a hanged corpse to smile for a newspaper photographer, or the modern-day equivalent of individuals and police officers not being charged for the killings of unarmed African Americans. Society's inaction or unwillingness to sanction such behaviors tacitly condones and encourages more of the same; *Categories*—what Ellington and his musicians decried through their genius, skills, behavior, and the sheer beauty of their music. Yet the deep-seated embers of bias are once again being fanned in America's increasingly divisive social climate.

Duke Ellington and his orchestra personify American's foundational ideals and our on-going hope for their genuine realization. His notes shimmer in red, white and blue. His musicians trumpeted the ideals of freedom, democracy, and equality. His music absorbed the elements of America's history, her evolution and the contributions of every hyphenated-American who has come to her shores. He resisted having his music pigeon-holed as Jazz or any other classification. As a composer, conductor and purveyor of social consciousness, all things to Ellington were either good, or they weren't. He was not to be drawn out on matters of categories or mechanics.[394]

"I don't believe in categories of any kind," Ellington said, "and when you speak of problems between blacks and whites in the U.S.A, you are referring to categories again." Ken Rattenbury, author of the 1990 *Duke Ellington, Jazz Composer* comments, "Before anyone else in Jazz, Duke Ellington accomplished a genuine methodical integration of Black folk-music practices with white urban ones. Through his own dedicated personal effort and acute powers of aural observation — through the acts of writing and presenting his own works — he chronicled the development of Jazz to a crucial stage. To follow the progress of this remarkable musician's career is to document musically the evolution of Jazz through several stages, the

---

394  Ken Rattenbury, *Duke Ellington, Jazz Composer*, Yale University Press, 1990, IX.

last of which corresponds to the stable, recognizable form that the music assumes today."[395]

---

395  Andrew Homzy. <i>Notes</i> 48, no. 4 (1992): 1241-246. Accessed September 5, 2021. doi:10.2307/942115.

## CHAPTER 13

# ONE MORE TIME FOR THE PEOPLE

---

*"Create and be true to yourself and*
*depend only on your own good taste."*
- Duke Ellington

If Horton's orchestration is ever to be published, we need to stay focused on the immediate baby steps that might move us in that direction. I begin with the one thing we have control over, verifying and writing the story behind Ellington's music and Horton's efforts to champion it. Over the next several years, I research, document and write the Ellington-Horton story while trying to secure a third-party publisher for Horton's orchestration. I also reach out to the Principal Librarian of the *New York Philharmonic* for his expert opinion on the quality and "playability" of the (*Notion*) engraved score and parts, reasoning there is little sense in trying to interest a third-party print publisher if the engraving is not "acceptable" as Schirmer's correspondence suggests. Forty-three days later, we receive his emailed response.

> Karen – I did have a look at several pages of score. I haven't the time to page through the entire score or set of parts. What I saw looked just fine, and if you followed G. Schirmer's style book, you should be just fine.[396]

This opens the door for discussions with several "third party" publishers who all acknowledge the worthiness of the arrangement and the importance of publishing it. EJazzLines is the first to step forward to "publish the music 'as is,'" only to send the following email three months later.

> … while this project is very important, it is not something that we can take on at this point. The amount of time necessary to prepare it will far outweigh the commercial viability for us. I do, however, encourage Mr. Horton to pursue publishing the work on his own. Ultimately, that may be much more rewarding for him. We do really appreciate your interest in working with us."[397]

We explore the possibility of Horton self-publishing under Randall's 501-(c)-3, ASCAP-licensed publishing company Rakeiho Publishing Company,[398] but are advised by an industry insider that G. Schirmer will likely require a more "established" third-party music publisher, so we move this plan to the back burner. Several calls and referrals

396 Lawrence Tarlow NY Philharmonic Librarian's Review of EHBBB Notion Engraving, September 13, 2019.

397 Robert DuBoff, EJazzLine Publishing Declines To Publish The EHBBB, 17 Oct. 2019.

398 Part of RAKEIHO Musical Offerings Inc. (is a not for profit, 501 (c)(3) educational corporation that produces the American Music educational television project (a Public Television forum for scholars, musical artists and storytellers that airs on PBS affiliate stations KRCB-TV (San Francisco Bay Area) and CUNY-TV (New York) and the Kate Wolf tribute CD Unfinished Life: Dreams, Friendships and Farewells.

later, I contact Subito Music Corporation[399] and speak with its founder and president. In fact, he is surprisingly knowledgeable about the music and rather shocked that Schirmer has released Horton from "any and all contractual obligations" pertaining to the orchestration. He asks what condition the music is in and states that after verifying the quality of the engraving, he will also likely publish the music "as is." He says he will need to see written confirmation of Schirmer's "release" and that a simple phone call to Schirmer will likely be enough to secure the necessary print licensing.

It is only after I share the encouraging news with Randall Horton that he helps me connect the dots that I have overlooked in my excitement. The print publisher is the very same Director of Rental and Performance at G. Schirmer in 1987 when Horton's commission began and whose signature appeared on the 1987 contract for the Camellia Symphony Orchestra's 1988 premiere. After thirty-four years, our musical odyssey has come full circle.

Roy Fletcher and Randall Keith Horton complete a final polish of the engraved files before submitting them to Subito Music Company on Sunday, February 9, 2020. As we wait for Subito to contact G. Schirmer to negotiate a print license, Horton and I lay the foundation for a fallback plan in the event that Subito's interest also wanes. We contact a *third* established publisher (Second Floor Publishing).

Two months later, we are turned away by Subito Music in an email that states, "Hope you are well. I have not made contact with [G. Schirmer]. I have to say this is a pretty low priority on my list, and I would guess [theirs], too. I'll get to it when I can, but if you want to make other arrangements, please feel free to do so."[400]

---

399 Subito Music Corporation (SMC) is a leader in the concert music publishing industry with a reputation for publishing, producing, and distributing the finest quality music with state-of-the-art service. SMC provides a wide range of production and distribution services for both composers and publishers, including engraving, printing, rental, sales, and copyright administration.

400 Stephen Culbertson, Subito Music Declines to Publish EHBBB, 24 Mar. 2020.

We take Subito Music up on its suggestion, initiate our own licensing requests for each of the sampled songs and reach out to G. Schirmer for a letter officially "re-authorizing" the orchestration[401] with all new copyright ownership percentages spelled out. Schirmer's parent company Music Sales' Manager of Digital and Mechanical Licensing[402] promptly replies and acknowledges the difficulties African American composers historically face, garnering recognition and publication of their music. He assures us of Wise Music's/G. Schirmer/'s commitment to making the next steps toward publication as easy as possible.

In early June, Wise Music officially re-authorizes Mr. Randall Keith Horton to write a full-length, *concerto grosso* orchestration, featuring Duke Ellington's 1943 underlying work *Black, Brown and Beige* (for which G. Schirmer holds all copyrights except for five sampled songs) as a musical *sampling*. Copyright ownership of this new orchestration for all future revenue streams to be as follows: G. Schirmer - 94.75 percent."[403]

Horton sends two letters: One to G. Schirmer's New York office, thanking them for keeping the door open for third-party publication of EHBBB. A second one to Wise Music in Los Angeles, acknowledging receipt of their "reauthorization letter" for EHBBB and proffering his own Rakeiho Music Publishing as the proposed third-party music publisher.

There is no mention of remuneration for Horton's licensing or

---

401  A *derivative work* is a new arrangement, orchestration or treatment of an existing piece of published music; a composer/musician must first obtain permission from the copyright holder of the underlying work (in this case *Black, Brown and Beige*) and pay a copyright royalty for its use. If this new arrangement, orchestration or treatment "adds to," "modifies," or "expands" the underlying work by more than 30 percent, as a rule of thumb, it is then considered a *derivative work*, (basically a new composition that includes a "sampling" of the underlying work). A royalty must still be paid for the underlying "sampling," but the new work must also be copyrighted and ownership percentages determined and split between both parties, the owner of the "sampled music" and the composer of the new derivative piece.

402  Kevin McGee, Manager, Digital & Mechanical Licensing for Music Sales Corporation (a subsidiary of Wise Music and sister company of G. Schirmer, Inc.) and the same person who first signaled (5/4/2018) G. Schirmer's lack of a physical contract for Randall Keith Horton's *Ellington-Horton Black, Brown and Beige* commission.

403  Kevin McGee. Wise Music's Reauthorization of EHBBB, 10 June 2020.

engraving costs. And without knowing these final licensing percentages demanded by the owners of the five songs sampled in the new EHBBB, total licensing percentages could add up to more than 100 percent. The result? No room for copyright ownership/revenue for Horton, or worse, creating a situation where Horton could actually *owe* money every time his orchestration is performed.

I forward Wise's email to Horton and a tug-of-war discussion ensues. At 78 years of age, Horton simply wants his music published and performed during his lifetime.

Knowing we may need more industry specific advice to review a final contract, I make a call to the only person I know in the entertainment industry, an Oscar Award-winning screenplay writer to whom I was introduced by a mutual friend two years earlier. The story resonates with her. She thinks it will make a fascinating screenplay and encourages me to write it, even offering to help. But she cautions me about the more cynical aspects of the entertainment industry and urges me, in no uncertain terms, to "find a brilliant, entertainment attorney before signing ANY documents." She tells me that after years of getting ripped-off due to horribly-written contracts, she and her writing partner finally found an exceptional attorney who made all the difference in the world.

"In fact, I'm going to reach out to him," she graciously offers. "If he can't work with you, he'll know someone amazing who can."

As it turns out, her attorney can't work with us due to a potential future conflict of interest if we work on the screenplay together, but he recommends a renowned entertainment and media attorney who is in the midst of transitioning from a shareholder of the global law firm to his own private practice.

The attorney acknowledges the merits of the *Ellington-Horton Black, Brown and Beige* story and offers to work with us on a *pro bono* basis. Schirmer's contract gets put on the back burner as he helps us identify tangible opportunities for the music. He introduces us to a former entertainment lawyer, Motown producer and the current founder and president of *Hidden Beach Recordings* (1998) in Santa Monica. He, in turn, introduces us to one of the founding members of *Princeton Entertainment Group*, a respected producer of live entertainment for cross-generational audiences. All three have worked together before.

"You have an incredible concept," the entertainment expert tells us. "I love Ellington, and the messages behind this music are incredibly timely for the world we find ourselves in today. The *Ellington-Horton Black, Brown and Beige* could be a great fit for a project we're currently working on, the grand opening celebration of Steinmetz Hall at the Dr. Phillips Center For The Performing Arts in Orlando. We're bringing in the London Royal Philharmonic Orchestra for a month's residency... maybe the timing is finally right for the professional premiere of the music. Send me all the information you have."[404]

It feels like the wild ride may finally be coming to an end. I blanket the gentleman from Princeton Entertainment Group with a trove of supporting materials which he immediately forwards to his partner for a proper vetting. Mark McCoy, a PhD in Music, the former President of DePauw University and Dean of its School of Music and, miraculously, a jazz musician who toured Europe in 1999, playing Ellington's library from his original arrangements.

A few weeks later, Mark McCoy calls us:

> I just finished reviewing all the materials and reading your manuscript. I think you're really on to something. The score appears to be beautifully engraved. There's no doubt there will be push-back from purists who will question the briefness of Randall's time with Ellington and whether he had the right to insert and interpolate "new" material, even if the "new" material was music later written and recorded by Ellington.
>
> It was helpful to listen to the MP-3 recording from Dallas

---

404   Karen Barbera and T. "Princeton Entertainment Group." Jan. 2020.

in 1999, to hear Randall's conducting and interpretation of the music. Between that and the supporting material in your book, I can see that Randall is not a charlatan. He had direct contact with Ellington, albeit briefly…and he wrote a quality orchestration, although he took some liberties in doing so. Purists like Gunther Schuller, for example, would likely find these or any additions by any orchestrator problematic… though he would have also celebrated the effort to make *Black, Brown and Beige* accessible to symphonies and their traditionally classical repertoire. [405]

I've reached out to a friend who is the Distinguished Professor of Jazz Bass and Director of Jazz Studies at Michigan State University. He is very familiar with Ellington musically and was, serendipitously, a member of the *Jazz At Lincoln Center* (JALC) band when Randall was the special consultant to Wynton Marsalis for the band's *Sacred Concert* performances in 1999. He was impressed by Randall.[406]

The score is sent to Rodney Whitaker who reviews it with a knowledgeable and meticulous eye and, according to McCoy, has "no problem with Horton's interpolations" and sees the orchestration as a welcome addition to a genre "in dire need of good music."

The *Ellington-Horton Black, Brown and Beige* is now vetted by several professionals which propels Horton's orchestration toward yet another daunting hurdle, clearing the licensing for each of the five sampled songs. It requires two years of work, the expertise of a rights recapture expert and a personal email from our entertainment attorney to his friend Jon Platt, CEO and Chairman of the Board of SONY/ATV Music Publishing.

---

405   Karen Barbera and Mark McCoy, "Princeton Entertainment Group." Feb. 2021.
406   *Ibid.*

## CHAPTER 14

# T.G.T.T.
## (TOO GOOD TO TITLE)

*"A goal is a dream with a finish line."*
- Duke Ellington

### The Happy Ending For Which We All Hope

More than a century after the notes of American Jazz resonated from Duke Ellington's very first big band in 1918,[407] the purity of his egalitarian beliefs, musical genius, charm and composure in the face of adversity continue to inspire. It has been eight years since the meeting of two strangers in the dining car of an Amtrak train, who have since done what they can to create awareness, generated interest and lay a solid foundation for the ultimate publication of the *Ellington-Horton Black,*

---

407  In 1918, at the age of 19, Ellington formed his first band *Duke's* Serenaders.

*Brown and Beige,* and the celebration of one of the most iconic, prolific and pioneering composer of any musical genre.

We remain hopeful that the *Ellington-Horton Black, Brown and Beige* will be published, premiered with its accompanying backstory or documentary, recorded and streamed, performed in all 50 states, championed by a generous corporate sponsor and be shared with international audiences.

"To me personally," concludes Randall Keith Horton, "an archival recording and permanent (audio and/or video) educational recording of the symphonic version of orchestration of *Black, Brown and Beige* that Duke Ellington envisioned for his *magnum opus* would represent the ascendancy and fulfillment of my fifty-eight-year-old *calling (1964 - 2022)*; what I have come to accept as my musical and spiritual connection with…and very humble service to…the most extraordinary and prolific composer in Jazz history and one of the most famous American composers of any genre, Edward Kennedy "Duke" Ellington.

## CHAPTER 15

# "DON'T PUSH IT. LET IT FALL."

---

*"Jazz is a good barometer of freedom… In its beginnings, the United States of America spawned certain ideals of freedom and independence through which, eventually, Jazz was evolved, and the music is so free that many people say it is the only unhampered, unhindered expression of complete freedom yet produced in this country."*
- Duke Ellington

As with so many GOAT's (Greatest Of All Time), Ellington simply raised the bar for everyone and everything around him. He shattered racial barriers and stereotypes, bridged cultural divides, helped audiences feel their shared humanity, and dared people to imagine, even if only for one evening, a world without *Categories*.

Along the way, Ellington believed it possible – imperative – to elevate Jazz music and American composers on par with their European counterparts. He challenged the Eurocentric, values-based approach of judging one style or folk origin of music as "better" than another. And he used his musical notes and charisma to pick the locks to concert halls and places of worship to broaden the audience for American music and expand social consciousness.

Like a true pioneer, Duke Ellington took risks to provide music that people *needed* to hear, and in doing so, set lofty expectations for a country (a world) that was, unfortunately, ill-prepared to live up to them during his lifetime. But as he understood, sometimes all one can do is plant and nurture the seeds of thought and possibility. For more than fifty years, he woke up each day, monitored the temperament of people's thoughts and moods and altered the tone of his music and messages accordingly. *How are my musicians feeling? What is the mood of my audience...our country...the world? What do they want to hear? What do they need to hear?* Life was never static for Ellington, nor was his approach to composing and performing. Music scholar Mark Tucker perfectly illustrated this point, citing *Black, Brown and Beige* specifically.

> Ellington did not view the piece as an inviolable, finished masterpiece in the Western European art-music tradition. Rather, he displayed a practical attitude toward the work, adapting and transforming it as the situation warranted-whether this meant cutting its length, focusing on different sections, using portions to highlight soloists, or incorporating material in other works (*My People*, his *Sacred Concerts*). In this way *Black, Brown and Beige* resembled a tune or Jazz standard, providing raw material for reworking and revisiting on different occasions.[408]

Duke Ellington embraced change. He was thrilled when a young Billy Strayhorn demonstrated how differently he would have arranged

---

408   Mark Tucker, 1991. *Ellington: The early years*, Urbana: University of Illinois Press, 1993. Letter to the author, August 3.

one of Ellington's standards. And he would have been riveted by Randall Keith Horton's ability to divine and develop a symphonic accompaniment perfectly fitted to, and in support of, his longest and most ambitious work.

In 1973, Jazz scholar Andres Homzy made a prophetic appeal, writing:

> I would be happy to hope that *Black, Brown and Beige* will come out of its sleep and reappear one day in extenso and not in bits, because it seems to me that the time has come for a rightful appreciation of this grandiose musical fresco... .A day will come when *Black, Brown and Beige* will be played by orchestras other than Ellington's. Young black musicians will form them and sound, to the four corners of America, this suite that tells the story of a people coming out of submission, which is their own history.[409]

We are on the very cusp of the day for which Homzy calls. Maestro Ellington has been kept waiting long enough. The *Ellington-Horton Black Brown and Beige* stands ready for publication, performance and recording. It awaits the opportunity to reawaken the hearts and minds of a more progressive world with the notes and messages that the world may finally be ready to *HEAR*.

And now we wait...

---

409 Andrew Homzy, "Black, Brown and Beige in Duke Ellington's Repertoire, 1943-1973."

## EPILOGUE
# BY RANDALL KEITH HORTON

---

*"This Is Randall Keith Horton.*
*He Is A Great Artist!"*
- Duke Ellington (1973)

Thank you for reading this book. I appreciate Ms. Karen S. Barbera's keen interest in telling this story and have enjoyed our years of correspondence. My first point in writing this Epilogue is that I have authorized Karen to write this book because of her background as an author and investigative journalist, her proven sincerity and her determination to conduct research, especially as related to the essence of this story: my direct experiences with Maestro Duke Ellington, his orchestra, his music and his family.

Karen's perception has intuitively overridden my reluctance to create an autobiography or memoir, one which would have claimed that I had crossed paths with "The Maestro" at all. I have resisted that impetus for decades. Once I passed the tests of her original inquiries into my background, (!) she pursued references, extracted their commentaries, read reference letters, programs and newspaper reviews related to my Ellington experiences, cross-checking as she moved ahead, and wondered why I am what I yet deem myself to be: "The Obscure *Ellingtonian*." She frequently asked that question. It was not always easy to provide accurate answers, but it was important to do so.

If you don't mind my answering that question with a touch of disbelief, because I myself still don't understand the totality of the experience, I will identify this whole biography, from the 1964 "calling" (that is, the "Light" that led me to Mr. Ellington), to the time of this writing (Summer, 2021), as one of blessings, grace (unmerited favor), divine guidance and, most importantly, preparation for entering and sustaining the next level of this journey: presenting the *Ellington-Horton Black, Brown and Beige*, and its genesis, to you and to the public.

So, first, I submit this appreciation to Ms. Barbera, to her family, and to the professionals from the world of literature, media, business and the legal profession, whom she has consistently referenced, and at times engaged. She has with complete fervor pursued her mission to inform the world of this heretofore unknown story. I am indeed greatly honored that the "stranger on a train" (Amtrak!) has persevered through the years it took to complete this task.

The public would not hear this music if it were not for the decades of support from my dear friend, Mr. Roy Fletcher, whose participation as the engraver of this music is outlined in this book. Every time I have thanked him for his brilliant work, for which he has consistently refused financial compensation directly from me, he has responded by telling me that God told him to do so. I am eternally indebted to Roy.

From my vantage point of still being nearly-invisibly-privileged, I wrap up an important dimension of this story by clarifying a term Mr. Ellington created, one which I associate directly to my years of experience with his music; indeed, one which, to me, engenders an atmosphere of strangeness, secrecy and mystery: "*Skillapooping*," as defined by Duke is interpreted as "*the art of making what you're doing better than what you're supposed to be doing.*"

Taken in two parts, "what you're *doing*" and "what you're *supposed* to be doing," the meaning should be obvious: The latter relates, in most scenarios, to others' present expectations, resulting from what they have experienced from the artist in the past. If the public or the gate-keepers in the music industry expect Mr. Ellington to continue what they had become accustomed to in his music (playing his popular hits in performances), then they will demand that "what he's *supposed* to be doing is practical music performance: earning an income for his orchestra." Of course! That's what he's *supposed* to be doing! That's what they *expect* from him!

But regarding the former: behind-the-scenes, or out-of-the-view of those who hold such expectations, what he is *doing*, according to Mr. Ellington's definition, is *better*! Note that he identifies this process as an *art*. It's as if he is secretive about it. Some artistic creativity is achieved away from the purview of those who would hold rigid opinions about what the artist is *supposed* to be doing, as if he/she shouldn't be doing *anything else*. (!) Duke's idea of *better* is secured by the creative freedom entailed in *accomplishing* whatever the artist is *doing* – away from the critics, the naysayers and judgmental authorities who would prevent the exercise of cherished artistic liberty. Gate-keepers could require that the artist is not *supposed* to change: "Play the music we're familiar with! Stick to the good stuff!" This is a challenge that is, in the field of music, common to the artistic process. Is it, however, not *better* to satisfy one's artistic muse than it is to attempt to please the masses? (My frequent italicizations are intentional.)

When Mr. Ellington chose and appointed me in 1973, he was not *supposed* to be developing *Black, Brown and Beige* into its next-level of form and existence – of course not! It was yet fifteen years prior to the world-premiere of my commissioned orchestration. But that is exactly what he *was* doing, even if he could not have verbally articulated it at that time. What he was, in fact, *doing*, concurrently above the audience's reception of my conducting my music in performance with his orchestra in that moment of time, was *better* than the performance of my music: He was *simultaneously creating a new musical/spiritual relationship. A new musical seed was being planted.*

So, by definition, what he was *doing* was opening the new musical-spiritual realm that was needed for our future artistic communications, which are effective to this very day. He was exercising the *art* defined in his mysterious concept. Thinking retrospectively, and respectively, both the creation and performances of my orchestration of *Black, Brown and Beige,* and of my leadership of his *Sacred Music,* as decades have passed, have only required (as is cited in this book) that I remain mindful of the fact that he *chose* me. His "*Skillapooping*" concept defines that reality as it applies to my life and musical experiences with Duke, his music and his family.

A seed was planted. With the guidance of Ruth and Mercer Ellington and other mentors, that seed has borne musical fruit, and was manifest, and remains, in the future. That spiritual preparation, what Duke was *doing*, was, by his own definition, *better* than what was actually happening aurally on that stage at *Disneyland* in the moment: He was *supposed* to be continuing to play his familiar music for the purpose of keeping his orchestra employed. I was his surrogate as I conducted my music in that performance; but he was "performing" on both levels at the same time. He was auditioning me and sowing seeds. I am the beneficiary.

The entire foundation was established. I have, since that time at *Disneyland* in 1973, remained obscure, nearly invisible but very-highly-privileged within the music industry, serving primarily in church and synagogue music. It has taken decades for what he was *doing* (when he chose me) to become known beyond what he was *supposed* to be doing: auditioning a young guest conductor leading his own musical composition. I was devastated when he passed away the next year.

But the years since have shown that this great mystery has power far beyond my understanding. Indeed, what he was *doing* at the time was *far better* than what he was *supposed* to be doing. I remain in awe.

My motivations and reasons for perseverance will, I am sure, be of interest to those who inquire about the genesis of the *Ellington-Horton Black, Brown and Beige* orchestration. Given the experience of the "calling", about which I have frequently testified, I have, however, weighed the doubts of detractors who have scoffed at my account. I do understand such skepticism: without the publication of this book, my unique path-in-life, as it now enters the historical record of American music, would certainly have been implausible. Now, as an invigorated "late bloomer," at this empowered point in my life, there is no justification for credence or plausibility for such doubts. There was – is – only one Duke Ellington, and one recipient of the experiences seen and discussed herein. It is, therefore, my profound responsibility to document those life-stories. It is also incumbent upon me to serve as the third-party publisher, consultant and conductor for concert performances of my *concerto grosso* orchestration of *Black, Brown and Beige*, and I will continue to work with G. Schirmer, Inc. / Music Sales Corporation to concertize Mr. Ellington's *Sacred Music.*

A stalwart contrast to skepticisms and doubts (even my own), the text of a prayer, written for me by my mentor, Mr. Wynn Westover (1928 – 2013), is seen below. Composed two years (1966) after the "Light" had visited me (1964) in my tiny Cambridge MA studio apartment, "The Westover Prayer" has served as a personal guide and empowerment in myriad life circumstances – too many to itemize. Thus, it's included as a supplement to this story.

In 1964, I had no idea where the command was leading, other than to "Go to San Francisco and study music." I know now where it led. Mr. Westover knew nothing of the "Light." I lacked the understanding needed to relay that experience to him. His prayer was composed in support of my musical future.

### The Westover Prayer

Dear Lord,

We are gathered to ask Thy blessing for the musical life and teaching of Thy servant, Randall.

We pray that Thou will guide his every step, bless his progress with increasing strength, clarify his vision at every crossroads, that his message of Thee may develop in perfection.

Fill him with Thy inspiration in teaching, that he may reach the hearts of the people and direct their minds and souls to Thy Great Message.

And we pray that Thou will keep him safe, in his work and in his life, through all dangers and deceptions, that his music may stir Thy people for generations to come.

And finally, we pray thanks for Thy Divine Guidance, that prepared and brought him to this place of work among the people, and for the voice and purpose which Thou hast endowed him.

Amen.

*Wynn Westover, Sausalito, California, 1966*

As previously noted, Mr. Westover's unique approach to music-theory-through-sight-singing and ear training, utilizing his specialized, chromatically identified numerical approach, that is, with *numbers,* enabled me to hear full symphonic music scores simply by looking at them, and opened the door to hearing and writing/composing music without the use of a piano. (I must insert an anecdote here: As a result of this inculcated aural training, my band members affectionately nicknamed me "Elephant-Ears"!)

His influence led to my meeting Dr. Paul Freeman, guest conducting the *San Francisco Conservatory of Music Symphony Orchestra*, serving as assistant conductor of the *Westover Chamber Orchestra* and substitute-teaching his method of music theory at the University of California at Berkeley, Evening Division. From those beginnings, the story of my "calling" is chronicled by Ms. Barbera.

Today, my love for serving humanity is manifest beyond church and synagogue music ministry. Prior to retirement, I was privileged to serve congregations as a licensed minister, to conduct choirs and orchestras, to direct Black-Gospel-Music and even "Southern Gospel" (religious Country-and-Western music) in addition to presenting the *Sacred Music* of Maestro Ellington.

In that service, I learned that my greatest joy emanates from the privilege of bringing people together and/or helping them to realize whatever music lies within them, no matter how basic or advanced that potential is, and whatever the social context of that music – provided that it is purposed for the betterment of humankind. Certainly, publishing and concertizing the *Ellington-Horton Black, Brown and Beige* serves that purpose. But beyond even that, assisting artists from disparate backgrounds and serving in cooperation with like-minded print and music publishers is an extension of that joy. Projects such as these are exciting!

Ms. Karen S. Barbera has afforded needed space for this Epilogue. I greatly appreciate her flexibility in allowing me to "speak in my own voice."

To conclude, the commissioning publisher(s)/administrator(s) of my *concerto grosso* orchestration, G. Schirmer, Inc., and Wise Music, Inc., have shown remarkable grace. After previous years of sometimes arduous negotiations with the former, the generosity of its current president recently restored the project's original potential.

## "SKILLAPOOPING.

The art of making what you're doing...
better than what you're supposed to be doing."

## - Duke Ellington

"This Is Randall Keith Horton. He Is A Great Artist!"
**Duke Ellington (1973)**

"We know Randall to be a friend and an outstanding conductor. My brother Edward Kennedy (Duke) Ellington invited Randall to conduct the Ellington Orchestra, directing his own music, in a concert in 1973. At my request, Randall has directed some of the Duke Ellington *Sacred Concerts* (since 1984) and was very successful in composing and conducting his own *concerto grosso* symphonic orchestration of my brother's *Black, Brown and Beige*. Randall Keith Horton is certainly an asset to the Ellington musical legacy." (1998)

"What I think about him is not important. Duke thought he was good or he wouldn't have hired him. Everything he's done with me has always been excellent." (1999)
**Ruth Ellington-Boatwright**
**Duke Ellington's sister and longtime business manager**

"This is the 'OK' for Randle (sic) Keith Horton [to orchestrate] *Black, Brown and Beige*."

**Mercer Ellington - Musician, Composer and Duke Ellington's Son (1987)**

"I am greatly impressed by Randall Keith Horton and his performance experience with Duke Ellington and his orchestra, as well as his unflagging efforts to "complete" Ellington's *Black, Brown & Beige* in a full-length *concerto grosso* format, and to concertize Ellington's *Sacred Concerts*."

**Gary Giddins, Jazz critic and author *Visions of Jazz* and *Bing Crosby: Swinging On A Star* (2017)**

"In 1991, Randall conducted the Sacramento Symphony, chorus and soloists (at my request) in a preview of my suite "Songs of the Slave" from my opera *John Brown*. ... The Sacramento Bee called the concert "an outstanding success".... In 2003, he conducted the same suite at the University of North Texas Symphony, a large choir and soloists. I have been happy with these performances."

**Kirke Mechem, American Composer (2014)**

"Mr. Randall Keith Horton audited rehearsals of the [San Francisco Symphony] Orchestra on a regular basis. During the course of his continued attendance at these rehearsals, Mr. Horton had an opportunity to be present during the preparation of a wide range of repertoire, including classical, romantic and contemporary works."

**Josef Kripps, Former Conductor and Music Director - San Francisco Symphony Orchestra (1970)**

"During his formative years, Mr. Horton was a fellow in my orchestral conducting seminar. Through that seminar, he conducted the San Francisco Conservatory Orchestra in a public concert.
His performance was outstanding."
**Dr. Paul Freeman, Former Conductor, Composer, and Founder - The Chicago Sinfonietta (1974)**

"I remember you [Randall Keith Horton] from one of Ruth's Sunday gatherings where you played Duke's piano. You played with a sound that was inspired, and I loved the concept of it."
**Brooks Kerr, Jazz Pianist, Band Leader, Noted expert on Duke Ellington's Music (1997)**

"I am deeply impressed by [Randall Keith Horton's] vision for the [American Music educational Television Series], adding up to a comprehensive portrayal of the history of our nation's musical development."
**H. Wiley Hitchcock, Founder/Director - Institute for Studies In American Music**

"By encouraging the astonishing diversity of American music styles, genres and historical contexts in American Music, [Randall Keith Horton has] done a yeoman's service. [His] comprehensive approach is deeply meaningful at a time when our country seems, more often, divided than united by our rich shared cultural heritage."
**Thomas L. Riis, Director - American Music Research Center (2015)**

"…[Horton]…has spent decades studying and performing Ellington's music, and [he] bring[s] considerable expertise and well-honed skills to a formidable orchestration assignment."
**Mark Tucker, Ellington Scholar and Author *Ellington: The Early Years* and *The Duke Ellington Reader* (1999)**

## ACKNOWLEDGMENTS
# FROM KAREN BARBERA

The power of music and *intention* are themes that run throughout this book with good reason. Of the hundreds of people I spoke with during the last nine years, *all* were fascinated by this story, and *many* graciously stepped forward to offer information, guidance, encouragement and significant help. But like the messages woven throughout Duke Ellington's music, their contributions would remain little-known without the following acknowledgements and our deepest gratitude...

For Those who stayed in the trenches with me throughout the research, writing and the endless (annoying) discussion about this project: Randall Keith Horton for patiently sharing his life story and vast musical knowledge, his wife Andrea Horton for her research, input and support and Randall's sister, Jann Horton's careful review; faithful music engraver and story contributor Roy Fletcher; great friends and business minds Lauren Hagan and LWS Literary Service founder Lynn Wiese-Sneyd; sounding board and part time editor, Evan Doseck; East Coast entertainment attorney and level headed advisor extraordinaire

George Stein; Oscar-award-winning screenplay writer and amazing mentor Diana Ossana; publisher and founder of Armin Lear Press Maryann Karinch and her team who saw the merit of this story and went above and beyond to deliver a book worthy of one of America's greatest composers and civil rights advocates, and the brilliantly talented cover artist Gale Fulton-Ross who believes artists are the humanistic conscience of a materialistic society and graciously allowed the use of her watercolor portrait of Duke Ellington.

For the early believers who created a foundation of hopeful confidence that supported us throughout the long journey toward publication for both the book and the music: Composer and Horton mentor, Kirk Mechem; renowned Jazz critic Gary Giddins; mentor and Sr. VP Animation & Mixed Media for The Jim Henson Company, Sydney Clifton and Boston University's: Victor Coelho, Kenneth Elmore, Aaron Goldberg, Herbert Jones and Katherine Kennedy.

With special thanks to the President, Schirmer Theatrical, G. Schirmer, Node Records, AMP (part of Wise Music Group) and current President, Music Publishers Association of the USA, Robert Thompson and the sampled song owners/administrators.

And to my family: My husband of 37 years Randal L. Barbera, who believed in this project… who was always there when I need his strategic, financial, and always-honorable business acumen or a good pep talk. To my adult children, Audrey, Calvin, Cameron, Abigail, Avery and Chandler, who supported me and graciously listened to every new twist and turn. And to my mother Angie and late father Richard E. Schreder who showed me that dreaming big and focusing on *what* and *who* you love makes for a very happy and fulfilling life.

# FROM RANDALL KEITH HORTON

Karen S. Barbera's acknowledgments need no redundant statements of appreciation on my behalf: Those individuals and the institutions whom she has thanked were indispensable as participants in the collective support system I cite, below.

Families are very important to the success of this book. I add my dear sister Jann's husband Keith as a friend and sounding board whose wisdom has been a motivation to persevere in completing this project. My twin sister, Joyce, has long been an important help in witnessing the power needed to survive life's difficulties. While my cousins, from both sides of my family, are too numerous to thank individually here, two, who have passed away, must be thanked as erstwhile elders: Ms. Eloise B. Allen and her husband, the Reverend Preston Allen, Jr., whose love brought me through challenging personal times as I was preparing to lead Mr. Ellington's Sacred Music concert at the Gem Theatre, in Kansas City, MO, are remembered with heartfelt appreciation. All elders who went before them helped to raise and nurture me, and to prepare me for this journey. My first Cousin, Elaine Sutherland, now in her '90s, consulted for Ms. Barbera about my parents as preparations were made for the 2017 Ellington Sacred Music concert at Boston University. My recently deceased brother, Lloyd Trevor Horton, Jr. whose musical talent exceeded my own, is dearly missed. Without him, there is a deep void in my daily life.

Mentors who provided orchestral conducting training and experience through the years are indispensable to these acknowledgements. In addition to Dr. Paul Freeman, who provided my initial rigorous training and rich conducting opportunities, I offer deep appreciation to Dr. Denis De Coteau, Music Director of the San Francisco Ballet Orchestra. As African American conductors of international standing, they taught me appreciation of our African American predecessors, the challenges I faced in the American classical-music field, and encouraged me, nevertheless, to persevere. Other world class conductors provided invaluable training and experience: Maestros Josef Krips, San Francisco Symphony Music Director; Anshel Brusilow, Cleveland Orchestra and Philadelphia Orchestra Concert Master and Director of Orchestral Studies at the University of North Texas; and Harold Farberman, Founder of the Conductors Institute at Bard College (NY), are each indispensable to these acknowledgements.

As unlikely as it may seem, some of my most profound mentored influences came from Roman Catholic nuns, priests, pastors in various Protestant denominations, and from rabbis: the experiences and guidance I received as I developed as a conductor were nurtured as I led orchestras and/or choral groups in the colleges, churches, a cathedral, and synagogues in which I served as music director under their leadership. The spirituality ingrained in their respective professional positions consistently enriched my approach to my craft as a conductor.

My wife, Andrea B. Horton and her family of origin hold a very special place of appreciation in my thoughts. Andrea's constant love and support have made the completion of my contribution to this book possible. Our frequent talks about the Ellington experience, and her life experiences with me in managing that challenge have been life-enriching. She brings several years of international choral singing experience with the Texas Girls' Choir to her wide appreciation of music and has shown great compassion in helping me to fight the good fight.

Finally, my profound appreciation for Ms. Karen S. Barbera has the highest position in the years it took for her to write this book. Her thorough approach, patience and inspired perspective in responding to the "stranger on the train," when we first met in the dining car of the California Zephyr Amtrak train, have not only opened a great sense of hope in this experience, but have afforded Andrea and myself to meet her husband Randal and to learn about their wonderful family.

The towering presence of Maestro Edward Kennedy Ellington and his wonderful family are the missing link in my heartfelt statement of appreciation. Duke, Ruth, Mercer, Mercedes, Paul and Michael and Stephen James are the family members with whom I have worked. "Thank you" for your consistent endorsements of my Ellington experiences. Although Karen did not meet any of Duke's family members, I thank her again, and all whom she cited in her acknowledgements! I appreciate you also!

# AUTHOR BIOGRAPHIES

**Karen S. Barbera** is a Public Relations professional who has worked with of some of the top consumer product companies, including Wendy's, Kraft Foods, Procter & Gamble, Avon Products, The Campbell Soup Company, Dial, Abbott Laboratories, Junior Achievement and The Ford Motor Company. She is the author of four biographical books on historically significant individuals and a contributing writer to several magazines. She has also conducted investigative journalism for *The Wall Street Journal*, KVOA-TV (NBC), Ohio's Bureau of Criminal Investigation (BCI), and the Arizona Attorney General. She and her husband Randy reside in Southern California and enjoy spending time with their six grown children and their expanding families.

**Randall Keith Horton** identifies himself as a "quintessential late bloomer." His life is traced in these pages from his infancy in Boston, MA (born in 1942) to his presently self-defined identity as an "obscure Ellingtonian." Between those two identities the reader will engage in the slowly blossoming trajectory toward his self-perceived future. Beyond his superbly outlined Ellington experiences covered in this book, two fledgling projects remain: Horton's American Music Educational Television Project, which, in partnership with the Society for American Music, has presented artists, scholars and story tellers for PBS member station KRCB-TV in Northern California and for CUNY TV of the City University of New York; and his work as a published scholar researching the music and life of composer Gustav Mahler.

In Spring, 1964, Horton received his calling in Cambridge, MA: A light, similar to a laser beam, to which he ascribes the power leading him through all of his Ellington experiences, descended from above him, commanding him, literally, to "Go to San Francisco and study music." The resulting high point occurred in 1973, when Mr. Ellington invited Horton to compose and conduct original music for his orchestra at a concert at Disneyland. Ellington subsequently appointed Horton to serve as his composing and conducting assistant. His leadership of Duke's *Sacred Music* is unparalleled, including consultation for Jazz at Lincoln Center. His unique *concerto grosso* orchestration of Ellington's full-length *Black, Brown and Beige*, commissioned in 1987 by G. Schirmer, Inc. through Mercer Ellington, fulfilled Duke Ellington's vision for that composition and received standing ovations at each of its performances. He credits the late Ruth Ellington as having closely mentored his Ellington experiences.

Randall holds graduate degrees in media studies and in music theory. Horton's participation in writing this book is dedicated to his parents and siblings, also seen herein, and to his son, Kevin Drew Horton. He resides with his wife, Andrea, in Queens, New York.